Common Land, Open Country

Defining a future for the countryside

of England and Wales

Steve Byrne

D1477645

JON CARPENTER

Our books may be ordered from bookshops or (post free) from
Jon Carpenter Publishing, Alder House, Market Street, Charlbury, OX7 3PH

Please send for our free catalogue

Credit card orders should be phoned or faxed to 01689 870437
or 01608 811969

First published in 2003 by
Jon Carpenter Publishing
Alder House, Market Street, Charlbury, OX7 3PH
☎ 01608 811969

ISBN 1 897766 81 5

Printed in England by Antony Rowe Ltd, Eastbourne

To May

Contents

List of maps and tables

Acknowledgements

The author would like to acknowledge the support he has received from the Joseph Rowntree Reform Trust Ltd for the research, the writing and the production of this book. Without the support of the Trust the book would not exist. He would also like to express his gratitude to the staff of the (then) Countryside Commission. Thanks go, in particular, to Paul Johnson, for his help and advice; to Chris Moos; and to the staff of the Commission's library at Cheltenham. Many thanks also to the staff of the central libraries at Blackburn and Burnley; to Lancashire Library, for the valued public service it provides; and to those local authority officers who made available facilities for the writer to study the registers of common land for Northern England and who answered related enquiries. Thanks, finally, to Andrew Dalby for an early critique; to Richard Harland, for describing to the author his involvement in the registration process under the 1965 Act as the representative of the Ramblers' Association for a substantial part of the northern uplands; and to Jon at Jon Carpenter Publishing, for his patience, understanding and insight.

Table 5 is adapted from an existing table. It is reproduced, together with Maps 1 and 2 and Table 3, by permission of the Countryside Agency. The figures for Table 4 are taken from an article by Olivia J and Geoff A Wilson. They are included here with the kind consent of the authors; as are the quotations in Chapter 9 from Marion Shoard's *A Right to Roam*.

1

Introduction

It is a popular misconception that common land is "owned" by everyone. This is not the case. The term "common land" derives from the fact that certain people held rights of common over the land. The different types of rights of common signified different entitlements to the product of the soil of the common, e.g. to the pasture, to sand and gravel, to peat, etc. Around 80% of common land is privately owned and subject to the interests of any commoners, owners enjoy essentially the same rights as the owners of other land.

DEFRA Website. *Wildlife & Countryside.*[1]

Almost by convention, a book about common land should begin with a caveat like the one above. Not only are such 'misconceptions' claimed to be widespread amongst members of the public. As with the present case, it seems to follow invariably that the truth lies in the recognition that common land is private land. If land is 'a common', then, this does not mean that it is public land, or that it 'belongs' to 'everyone'. Nor is there any implication that such land is ownerless, or incapable of ownership in some sense, and therefore 'common' to all. (And by 'land', it should be noted here, is meant not only the land surface, with the areas above and beneath it, and any buildings; but also the natural vegetation it produces, and the wild creatures that live in and upon it. In law, common land is 'essentially' the same as any other kind of land in all these respects. It is private property).[2]

In the same way, it is suggested, common rights – to graze animals, say, or to fish, or to take turf, bracken or peat – must be conceived of as property rights belonging to private individuals. In many cases, they will be 'attached' to a farm or a dwelling next, or near, to the common – a feature reflecting their origin in the shared use of the land as a communal resource. And where shared use persists, the attachment of rights in this way, and the regulation of their use by representative bodies of rights-holders, obviously has a continuing significance. In more recent years, however, institutions and practices such as these have been increasingly undermined by the progressive 'privatisation' of the commons. So that common rights, nowadays, may as often be seen by their owners as tradable assets, or as private assets whose exploitation is determined solely by individual profit.

This may also be true, to a greater or lesser extent, of those 'rights of taking' which – though not strictly rights of common – are held 'in common' under a trust. On the one hand, the land itself may be jointly owned by the rights holders – the right of use being proportionate to the share that is owned. Subject to the terms of the trust, the rights may well be dealt with as private property. A trust for common use, however, will more usually be found to involve the vesting of ownership in a public body such as a local authority. In a number of respects, the case is similar to that of town or village greens – though the rights connected with the latter are of a rather different kind (rights to do, rather than to take, something). A green, in fact, may also be subject to common rights. Though, again, if there are rights of piscary in the stream that crosses it, this does not mean that 'anyone' – be they local or visitor – may come there to fish.

The land: misconceptions and meanings

There is room enough here for popular 'misconceptions'. But a broader perspective only confirms this impression. Many areas of common land are in fact ownerless. And a good deal of land that is common, or that was historically common, is owned or held in trust by public or quasi-public bodies. In this case, there are rights that are clearly 'public' rights which may often be exercised by 'anyone'. In other cases – with village greens, for example, but with many commons as well – though the legal rights involved are strictly those of local people, *de facto* public rights of access will almost invariably be recognised. Such *de facto* rights will also be found to apply more generally over the extensive commons of the uplands and over a similar area of open hill country that is unenclosed and largely unimproved. All of these areas are private land in the legal sense. The question is whether they are 'essentially' private. Or, if this is admitted to be the case, of how the public rights described here, or the more general public interest in respect of the valued characteristics of 'the land' – related to access, preservation, protection and land or conservation management – are to be expressed. In truth, the matter is less one of public misconceptions than of a conceptual *vacuum*, related specifically to the law and to the legal status of public rights. It is the aim of the present book to account for this state of affairs; to describe its effects; and to show how public rights in the land may, and must, be secured for the future.

Clearly, a common is different from a village green, but they are also similar in a number of ways – and either may be subject to rights of common. At the same time, each defines a category of land the members of which exhibit a range of differences. Commons, in particular, differ greatly in their size; in their natural characteristics; in the geographical distribution of certain distinctive types of land; and in the rights, the practices and the traditions which may attach to them. If the commons registers are examined, an even greater variety is revealed. Included here are quarries; upland peat allotments; highways allotments for road materials; recreation grounds; places where animals may be watered, or people may drink; stretches of foreshore; intertidal mud flats; landing places for boats; pinfolds; areas of woodland. It may well be that the land is mis-registered in many of these cases. But this diversity is also an indication of the kinds of land that have been considered to be 'common' and not automatically rejected as such by the authorities – usually, it should be noted, because they are dedicated to the public in some sense, or to public use.

Again, the status of these 'commons-like' areas and features, and the rights which may attach to them, are manifold. Moreover, their origins may be obscure and difficult to establish, deriving as they do from any number of parliamentary acts related, most often, to the Inclosures of the eighteenth and nineteenth centuries. The general case of what would more usually be recognised as common land is somewhat similar. The law of commons comprises a large number of local and general acts of parliament. It also includes the case law of court judgements stretching back to the Middle Ages, which may in turn be based upon customs going back even further. By virtue of its long lineage common land is often referred to as our oldest surviving institution. But it is for all of these reasons – legal, historical, social, ecological, geographical – that the land which has survived as common to this day is so varied and the subject of common land may appear so complex.

If the subject itself is complex, however, and in some cases obscure, it seems, at least in the conventional view, that there is one simple truth that is clear enough. No matter what else it may be, common land is private land. And common rights are private rights. They may be shared by groups of people (the 'commoners') which, in the past at least, would have constituted a distinct community of some kind. Nevertheless, both the land and the rights belong to particular individuals, and each is 'essentially' private. On this interpretation, 'a common' may be defined, in a strictly legal sense, as the relationship that subsists between the rights-holder and the landowner. The relevant contrast here, then, is not with some kind of *individual* right (for this is what common rights are), but with 'sole' rights. The latter are rights of taking of a similar kind – and may, in fact, be registered as rights of common under the 1965 Commons Registration Act. In this case, however, the owner of the land possesses no residual right to the produce involved. Sole rights are exclusive rights. In contrast, holders of common rights are entitled only to a limited amount – usually, what is sufficient (or was sufficient in the past) to a household or a land-holding. Whatever is left belongs to the owner of the soil. It is this limited right of taking, then, shared with the landowner by private individuals, that is 'a common' under the law. In this strict legal sense, the word would seem to carry with it few, or none, of the connotations described above as misconceptions.

The trouble with this kind of legalistic approach is that it tells only half of the story, and even less of the history – though this is surely what is intended. It is hardly an accident that a whole dimension of meaning related to legitimate public concerns and interests is declared to be 'inessential'. What is presented as a legal principle ('all land is private land') is in fact both a tautology and an equivocation ('business is business'). As a principle, moreover, it is ultimately incompatible with the subject matter it claims to describe. For if common land is private land, it is also something more. Where common rights exist any right of use is necessarily shared. But in many cases the use itself is of such a kind that, even today, control of the land may be effectively severed from its ownership – which is the opposite of the more usual case of 'exclusive' private property rights.

Historically, what is 'essential' about common land and common rights is their communality. In their origin, and for much of their history, they were the basis of a collective subsistence economy which relied in large part on the natural produce of the land. Common rights provided, amongst other things, grazing for livestock and poultry, bedding for animals, and materials for building, fencing, tools and equipment. Common land was an important source of food for the household, including game – a right of taking that was widely exercised outwith the hunting preserves of the Crown and the nobility prior to the imposition of the eighteenth-century Game Laws.[3] Whilst a common of estovers ('firebote' for wood) or of turbary (peat) might often be the only source of fuel.

It was the Inclosures of the eighteenth and nineteenth centuries which finally swept away this form of life, replacing it with a market economy. But the expansion of the market, the Inclosure Acts which facilitated its growth and the Game Laws that so blatantly asserted the privileges of private property and its private 'enjoyment' in the face of the needs of the poor, were in turn based upon a political revolution that had immediately preceded them, a revolution which redefined the nature of land and of land rights.[4] In this light, what are represented above as public misconceptions may equally be seen as echoes of this change and of the collective values it displaced, not least because the earlier notion of shared rights in the land was revived by the reformers of the mid-nineteenth century in their attempts to define the modern idea of a legitimate *public* interest in the countryside and rural land. Less an echo, then, than a continuing resonance; and also perhaps the basis for a further re-awakening and re-assertion of shared public values.

There is an alternative view of the commons, then, that has far deeper political and historical roots than the accepted legalistic view. In its present form it dates from the reaction, and the surge of popular opinion in the mid-nineteenth century, against the Inclosures. If the values that took shape at this time are considered, a very different explanation may be offered of the kinds of 'misconception' referred to above – an explanation which affords full recognition to the actual truth they represent. It is this account, of the commons and their history and of the wider implications of the commons debate for countryside and rural policy, that is the central theme of the following chapters. From this point of view, popular opinions and aspirations reflect an alternative discourse of public rights that has been progressively marginalised by mainstream developments since the late nineteenth century. Over against this are placed the forces that have determined these developments in respect of the countryside and rural land: the power and the political influence of landed property interests. It is the continuing predominance of these interests, in political, legal and ideological terms, that has dictated the development of law and of policy – not least, in the adoption as a defining principle of 'exclusive' private property rights in land. But the same interests have also shaped the discourse of the countryside and of rural policy as a whole. They have defined, that is, the way issues are conceived of and discussed, the way they are resolved and, perhaps most importantly, whether or not they are considered to be issues at all.

Common land: geography versus ideology

In terms of their extent (see Map 2), the surviving commons of England and Wales are concentrated in the uplands of the north and the west. Thus, Northern England includes approximately 70% by area of the English commons.[5] Of this area, it is the larger hill commons that comprise the overwhelming part. It is these upland commons of the north that are the starting point of the present book and that provide material throughout the text, including case studies, that is taken to be representative. It will, perhaps, come as no surprise that it is the opposite claim – that the northern commons (and the other 'heather commons' of the uplands) are unique and atypical – that has largely determined the course of the recent commons debate and the continued failure of reform. But it is for this very reason that they are of crucial importance. As may already be evident from the preceding discussion of private and public interest claims, the key issues of the countryside debate are necessarily, and essentially, political. It is *because* of this that the northern commons may be taken to be representative.

In one sense, it is true, the commons of the uplands may be considered to be a special case, simply by virtue of their size. There are over 7000 separate 'units' of land that are registered as common in England. But a mere 220 of these make up about 75% of the total area. Only ten of these larger units (>1000 acres) are lowland commons. Furthermore:

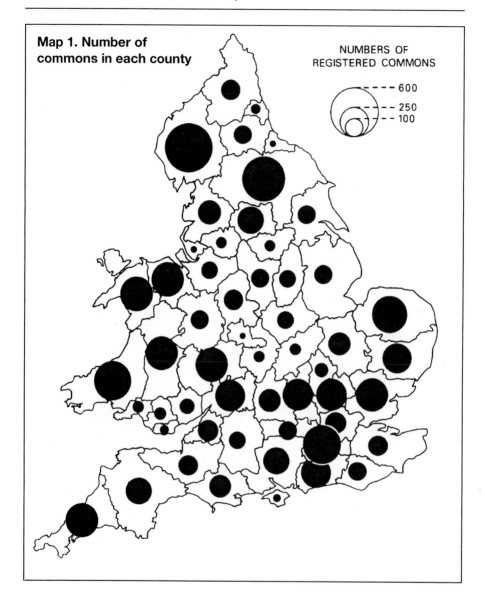

Map 1. Number of commons in each county

NUMBERS OF
REGISTERED COMMONS

- - - - 600
- - 250
- - 100

Of these ten only four were over 5000 acres [20 sq kms] and these were all forest commons: the New Forest, Epping Forest, Ashdown Forest and the Forest of Dean. The overall picture in England seems to be one of a large number of small commons, mostly of the village green type and size, with the majority of the commons of significant acreage mostly confined to the uplands of the north and west of the country, excepting, of course, the old Royal Forests.[6]

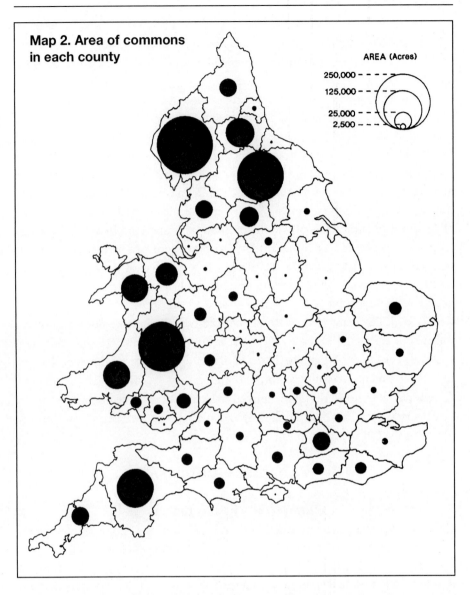

Map 2. Area of commons in each county

AREA (Acres)
250,000
125,000
25,000
2,500

In terms of their number, then, rather than their geographical extent, it is the smaller commons of lowland areas that may be said to be the more typical (cf Maps 1 and 2). Northern England itself includes many small lowland commons and village greens similar, or of a related kind, to those that are to be found in the south and east of the country. Thus, 60% of the northern commons are less than 10 acres in extent and about 80% are less than 100 acres. The corresponding figures for England are 68% and 88%. Those for the south of the country are virtually the same as for the nation as a whole; whilst for the Midlands and Eastern England – the areas, that is, most affected by the inclosures of the eighteenth and the nineteenth centuries – they are 73% and 95%.[7] In these terms, then, it is the smaller commons of the lowlands that are 'typical' – though a great many of them, including the various 'commons-like' areas described above, are very small indeed.

It was the Common Land Forum, in devising management schemes as part of its proposals for commons reform, that drew a formal distinction between the 'grazing' commons of the uplands and the 'amenity' commons of the lowlands.[8] What was intended, however, as a functional definition was recast as an ideological boundary. It has come to mark out a divide whose purpose is to exclude any claims of substance on behalf of the public in respect of the greater part of the land that is common land. What is in question is the legitimacy of such claims. Yet the uplands – of which common land and land like it (most often land that was historically common) form so characteristic a part – have in many respects become a test-bed for the future of agriculture, of the rural economy and of countryside policy. It is for reasons such as these that the commons debate is so important, and that it is argued in this book to be paradigmatic. Crucially, it has generated statements of the case for both public and private rights of a clarity and a coherence that are notable elsewhere only for their absence. The effect of this is to lift a veil of misrepresentations that has plagued the development of countryside law and policy. Again, it is the upland commons of the north that have proved to be a fertile source of controversy in this respect. How this has happened, and the reasons for it, are examined at length in the following chapters.

Chapter Outline

Chapter 2. The Commons

Chapter 2 offers a basic introduction to the subject of the commons. Common land and common rights are defined, and their relationships with a number of other types of land in shared use are examined in the context of their historical development. The effects of the commons legislation of the modern period are then discussed, together with the role of the Commons Preservation Society and its members in securing the protection of the commons through court action and legislative reform. However, despite the relative success of the reformers, and the stop imposed on statutory inclosure, an area of common land almost equal to that which has survived has been lost in the period since 1870, about two-thirds of it from the upland areas of the north and the west of England and Wales. The causes of this are suggested, and the case of the uplands of Northern England is examined more closely.

Chapter 3. The Royal Commission on Common Land

The work of the Royal Commission (1955–58) is central to the present book. It derives from a tradition that had its origins in the mid-nineteenth century. It is by virtue of this that the Commission's proposals embody a coherent, principled and radical (re)definition of 'the public interest'. Public access rights are seen as fundamental to this definition. But they are also conceived of – in opposition to the conventional view of access as destructive or anarchic – as complementary to the principles of preservation, protection and conservation. Chapter 3 examines the historical development of this alternative tradition, relating it in particular to popular concerns in the nineteenth century and to the later appearance of an organised working class. The values of the tradition were crystallised by the Royal Commission in its proposals for commons reform.

Chapter 4. The Commons Registration Act

The 1965 Act is invariably described as a 'first stage' implementation of the Royal Commission's proposals. This is not so. The Act gave no legal force to the proposals of the Commission. Nor did it mention or anticipate any 'second stage' reform. As a result, the process of registration achieved the opposite of what the Royal Commission had intended. Chapter 4 explores the actual consequences of the Act through a number of case studies. In the absence of any legal recognition of the public interest it was, inevitably, the rights of private property owners which prevailed – in the process of registration, in the intentions and actions of the registration authorities, in court judgements on appeal and in the hearings of the Commons Commissioners.

Chapter 5. A Changing Context: The Common Land Forum

Given the failure of reform, the management and status of common land was increasingly undermined in the years after 1965, largely by structural changes in agriculture. Drawing, again, on examples from Northern England, and from Wales and the Welsh Borders, Chapter 5 discusses the new threat of deregistration, and the progressive 'privatisation' of commons management in the face of upland change. It is in this context that the work of the Common Land Forum (1984–6) is considered. Once again, proposals for reform – reflecting those of the Royal Commission, though in a diluted form – were opposed. And once more, they were shelved. This time, however, the opposition was forced out into the open. The response of the Moorland Association (representing the owners of the 'heather commons' of Northern England) is examined at length in Chapter 6 – as stating a case for private rights diametrically opposed to that of the Royal Commission. What is argued, however, is much more than this: that the principles (now openly) elucidated by the Moorland Association have, in fact, defined the overall development of countryside law and policy.

Chapter 6. The Moorland Association

The Royal Commission on Common Land is perhaps the only official body that has attempted a coherent definition of the public interest in respect of the countryside – albeit one applying to a specific category of land. It was this vision, rather than the somewhat diluted proposals of the Forum, that unearthed the counter-arguments of the Moorland Association. What is truly remarkable, however, and equally enlightening, is the way the Moorland Association's principled statement of private rights was misrepresented in the wider debate as simply, and only, an opposition to public *access*. The reasons for this are examined in Chapter 7. Chapter 6 looks more closely at the arguments advanced by the Association. What is clear from this analysis is that its opposition was to *any* recognition in law of the public interest – in effect, there exist only private (property) rights. Thus, common land is not only 'like any other sort of private land' – it is also like 'any other sort of private *property*'. But if the Moorland Association overstated its case, it certainly did not overstate the effects of the case. It is clear that countryside policy is deeply rooted in history and tradition. But the strands of the tradition that have determined the development and implementation of law and policy go back, not to 1949, or to 1865. They extend much further back than this – to a definition of the exclusive rights of property that came to prevail in the seventeenth century.

Chapter 7. Public Rights and Private Interests

Taking as its starting point the public and private interest claims examined in the preceding chapters, Chapter 7 develops a general analysis of law and policy, drawing on insights afforded by the discussion of commons reform. The countryside legislation and rural policies of the post-war period are considered in this light, together with the more recent elaboration of market mechanisms for access and conservation. The determining influence of private property interests is clear. Opposed to this is a discourse of public rights that has its origins in the commons debate. Though it has in fact defined the stated objectives of law and policy, this alternative discourse has played little part in determining their form or implementation. It is proposed here as a means of remaking the law and policy of the countryside in a way that would incorporate legitimate public interests and concerns. The possibility, and indeed the necessity, of such change is suggested by the scale of projected reforms in the Common Agricultural Policy. But if CAP reform is to embody public interest claims, it will require political, legal and institutional change of a kind that is sufficient to engage with the pervasive influence of private property interests.

Chapter 8. Common Land and Open Country

The analysis developed in Chapter 7 is applied here to the legislation and proposals for reform of the present government. The recent consultation over commons reform, and DEFRA's subsequent *Common Land Policy Statement*, are examined first. Though it proposes a number of significant changes, the Policy Statement is seen to lack any basis in principle and any coherent intention. The crucial importance of public involvement in the management of the commons is ignored, as are the implications of the so-called right to roam legislated for in the Countryside and Rights of Way Act. The latter is seen to define not a right but a permitted use hedged round with regulations, conditions and exceptions which reflect the mainstream conception of access as inherently destructive and disruptive. An alternative view of the reforms is suggested that offers a coherent definition of the public interest, and thus a means of resolving the contradictions in the government's proposals. Here, access is conceived of not as an illegitimate desire that is destructive of its object but as the fundamental vehicle of public concerns. The reforms of the current government lack any principled framework of this kind. The attempt to re-define proposals of radical intent within parameters determined by the mainstream discourse is seen to be fatally flawed, since the latter recognises the legitimacy only of private property interests.

Chapter 9. Conclusion

Chapter 9 returns to the question of access as a pivotal issue of the countryside debate. Marion Shoard's critique of a 'partial' right to roam is introduced and is compared with ideas drawn from the current debate over land reform in Scotland. The latter is acknowledged, even in official circles, as a conscious attempt to re-define the relationship between 'the people and the land'. As such, it has many similarities with the discourse of the commons. It is because of these wider implications that common land is important not only for its intrinsic value but as a representative case. The discourse born of the commons debate embodies a transformation and a re-expression of traditional rights of the locality – in terms that articulate a coherent definition of *public* rights in a modern context. In contrast to the mainstream discourse, which retains and is grounded in an archaic notion of exclusive private property rights, it defines a conception of the shared control – and, by extension, the shared ownership – of the land. The book has argued for this wider case – and that principles such as these, stated most clearly by the Royal Commission on Common Land, should determine the future development of countryside law and policy. They offer, at a time of critical change, a means of remaking the public interest in respect of the countryside in a way that is not, as in the past, simply a veiled projection of private interests.

NOTES

1   DEFRA website, Wildlife & Countryside/Countryside Issues/Common Land, Town And Village Greens/Background at: www.defra.gov.uk/wildlife-country-side/issues/common/index.htm (as at Jan 2003).

2   Strictly, wild creatures – since they are in law *res nullius* – must be 'reduced to' ownership by trapping or killing them; whilst certain species of plant, animal, insect or bird, specific sites, and individual earth-features may be protected by statute to some extent. That the definition suggested here needs to be qualified in this way, however, deprives it of none of its force. It is this conception of 'the land' (i.e. as explicitly comprising, or including, these naturally-occurring things) that best defines the subject matter of common rights and other 'rights of taking'. Importantly, it is also the definition employed by wilderness writers in their attempts to articulate a land ethic. It therefore both encompasses and underlines the nature and extent of the conflicting rights claims whose legitimacy is the central theme of the present book.

3   Tim Bonyhady, *The Law of the Countryside: the Rights of the Public,* Professional Books, 1987, Ch I.

4   For an accessible account of these changes see Marion Shoard, *This Land is Our Land,* Gaia Books, 2nd ed, 1998, Ch 2, pp 38ff.

5   Throughout the book, the northern commons are taken to include those of the present counties of Northumberland, Durham, Cumbria, North Yorkshire and Lancashire; the former metropolitan counties of Tyne and Wear, Cleveland, West Yorkshire and South Yorkshire; and the more recent 'unitary' authorities included in these areas. A listing of the larger commons of Northern England is to be found in the Appendix below.

6   G D Gadsden, *The Law of Commons,* Sweet & Maxwell, 1988, p 10, [1.21]. In writing this, Gadsden was drawing on the *Report* of the Royal Commission on Common Land, which was produced in 1958. But the figures, at least in this respect, have changed little since that time.

7   The figures given here are taken from: *Common Knowledge...?,* Countryside Commission, CCP 281, 1989.

8   Common Land Forum, *Common Land Forum Report,* Countryside Commission, 1986.

2

The Commons

The apparent complexity, and the occasional obscurity, of the subject of common land is a reflection of the long history of the commons as an institution, and of the range of different types of land to which the institution has been applied. But it is the law of common land that is perhaps most often referred to as obscure. In this respect, a helpful point of departure is suggested by G D Gadsden in his book *The Law of Commons*. Firstly, it should be recognised that 'the common lands are not one particular type of land but a series of interrelated classes with discreet rules applicable to each class'.[1] Common land is defined as 'land subject to rights of common'. 'The common lands' make up a wider grouping. This includes common land (as already defined); but also a number of other types of land in shared use, the legal basis of which is derived in a different way. The apparent obscurity of the subject, then, is often the result of a failure to distinguish these classes, and a consequent confusion and misapplication of the different sets of rules which apply to them.

The types of land described by Gadsden largely coincide with those listed as 'land subject to be inclosed' under the General Inclosure Act of 1845. Broadly, they include:

- Land subject to rights of common
- Land subject to sole rights
- Land in joint ownership held as (i) divided or (ii) undivided shares, and subject to common use that is derived from the ownership

The list distinguishes the different types of land in legal terms. For a fuller picture, a further (historical) dimension needs to be introduced.

Common land and common rights

Common land pre-existed the manorial system of the medieval period.[2] But it was the judicial interpretation of local customs of the manor in the King's Courts that laid the basis for the Common Law. As part of this process of standardisation, the lowland English manor – with its arable system of agriculture – was

Table 1: Distribution of common land in Northern England

COMMON LAND

LAND AREA	(sk)	Area (sk)	% Land area	% Total area northern commons
Northumberland	5032	96.29	1.9	3.8
Cumbria	6810	1129.1	16.58	44.7
Durham	2434	287.85	11.83	11.4
North Yorkshire	8312	786.9	9.47	31.2
Lancashire	3066	96.39	3.15	3.8
West Yorkshire	2036	116.84	5.74	4.6
South Yorkshire	1561	13.79	0.88	0.55
Northern England	29,250	2527.2	8.64	100
Northumberland NP	1050	1.5	0.14	0.06
Lake District NP	2292	656	28.6	26.0
North Pennines AONB	1998	554.3	27.7	21.9
Yorkshire Dales NP	1770	473	26.7	18.7
Forest of Bowland AONB	802	56	7.0	2.2
Nidderdale AONB	603	59.9	9.93	2.4
North York Moors NP	1436	235	16.3	9.3
NPs/AONBs	9951	2035.7	20.46	80.6
Northern England	29,250	2527.2	8.64	100
England	129,724	3689.3	2.84	–
Wales	20,635	1853.3	8.98	–
England & Wales	150,359	5542.6	3.69	–

adopted as a representative type, or model.[3] The medieval manor was held directly from the King, or through one of his vassals or sub-vassals. The lord of the manor would retain a part of this as his *demesne* (for his own use), and might also grant land to his free tenants (his own vassals). His copyhold tenants (whose customary rights were recorded as 'copies' of the court rolls of the manorial court) held arable land as strips in the open fields in return for services on the lord's *demesne*. There were two or three such open fields in each manor, which were farmed in rotation and left fallow every second or third year, the strips in the field(s) currently under cultivation being reallocated annually amongst the tenants. Other areas under collective use included the common meadows, which like the open arable fields might be held in separate lots until the hay crop was taken; the common pastures; and the 'waste land' of the manor.

Much of the land of the manor was subject to common rights of one kind or another. Thus, after the hay crop, the meadows would be thrown open for common grazing. Similar grazing rights would apply to the open arable fields after the harvesting of the strips, or when the land was laid fallow. The common pastures and the waste, in contrast, might be grazed throughout the year, though their use as a shared resource would also be regulated ('stinted') in a number of ways. In addition to grazing, the waste of the manor was subject to a range of other common rights. These might include, for example, rights of estovers (for wood, furze, bracken); of turbary (for peat or turf); rights to take wild creatures for food; or to take clay, earth or stone for building work or repairs. The waste land, that is, provided access to natural resources that were essential to a subsistence economy.

It was this model of the manor that was adopted as a standard, and it therefore offers a means of understanding the nature of common land and common rights. It is subject to a number of exceptions (e.g. the common rights that were quite often held by town corporations), and it is limited in its direct applicability to areas with a pastoral economy. But, above all, it needs to be understood in the context of a system of land holding and land use which, almost from its beginning, was affected by historical change and development. Thus, land was taken out of the system by grants of various kinds, or by the progressive, piecemeal inclosure of the open fields. Waste land of the manor, in particular, was constantly subject to 'illegal' encroachment, or settlement by squatters – which, since they could quite clearly not be prevented in historical periods when the demand for land was high, were typically confirmed by fines in the manorial courts (and thus brought into the local custom). By the seventeenth century, more systematic, larger-scale inclosures were being carried through by agreement. And inclosure by Act of Parliament followed in the eighteenth and nineteenth centuries. So that, from this later period, for the land that survived in common use, a further layer of statutory rules was imposed upon local customary practices and the provisions of the Common Law.

It is against this background, then, that 'the common lands' should be understood. Historically, land subject to rights of common may be seen as the basic type. The nature of common rights – in particular the way in which they are quantified with reference to the needs of individual holdings or households – reflects their intrinsic relationship to the kind of subsistence economy sketched out above. Though they are similar, as land in shared use, the other types that make up the common lands are in this sense derivative – the rights are defined, not by their relationship to subsistence needs (though they might still be intended to serve such needs) but by the nature of the resource itself. The effects of the Inclosure Acts are particularly important in this respect. In many cases, the common lands that survived the Inclosures were the result of grants in lieu of previous rights of common. They might still be of vital importance, as a source of income or a means of subsistence, to the grantees. But, in essence, they are recognisable as a form of artificial (legal) instrument. In all of these cases, the management of the land, since it is based upon shared use, is often very similar. But use 'in common' does not necessarily imply a right 'of' common in legal terms.

Though the Inclosures of the eighteenth and nineteenth centuries were especially important in this respect, land in shared use (other than common land) might equally have been the subject of a grant in an earlier historical period. In addition to rights of common, for example, the lord of the manor, whilst retaining the ownership of the soil, might at some time have granted (perhaps out of the waste) **sole rights** over a given area of land. This would usually involve some kind of right to graze animals (*sole pasture*), though the right also to cut the grass (*sole herbage*), or to take in addition the 'underwood' of any trees (the right to all these three would amount to *sole vesture*), might also be included. The grant might be to one person or to a group of people, usually the latter. The use, in other words, is a 'sole' use in the sense that it is exclusive, either to a specific person or group of people. In the case of sole vesture it might be, in effect, a right to all the natural produce of the land – thought the lord might retain, for instance, mineral or sporting rights. The use in this case is obviously very similar to customary rights of common in the waste. Sole rights, however, are invariably held as **rights in gross**. In legal terms, what this means is that they are not 'attached to' a property (a household, or a piece of land). The ownership is a personal possession and the individual owner may freely dispose of it. In practical terms, the rights are defined, not by reference to some kind of external need (which might be adversely affected by their sale), but simply as a proportion of what the land in question is capable of producing.

A similar kind of grant, at least in practical terms, would be that of a **regulated pasture**. In this case, however, it is the land itself that is shared by the grantees. The management of the land might be much the same as under a regime of sole use. But here, the rights derive from, and are proportionate to, the share of the land that is owned. Typically, a regulated pasture would be of more recent origin. It might, for example, have formed part of an Inclosure Act. Or it could have been one element of the kind of agreed inclosure that took place in the period immediately prior to the parliamentary inclosures of the eighteenth and nineteenth centuries (and, as a consequence, might also have been confirmed, or redefined in some way, by a subsequent Inclosure Act). Parliamentary inclosure, however, would probably be the most usual instance. Here, as in the other cases mentioned, areas of land were allotted in return for the extinguishment of common rights. Where these areas were too small to form viable economic units, they might be consolidated as a regulated pasture for the joint benefit of the grantees. Each of the joint-owners would then hold grazing rights proportionate to his share of the whole.[4]

The rights in this case, then, though they are exercised in common, are not rights of common at law – the latter are rights over another person's land, whereas these are rights of shared use over land that is part-owned by the rights-holder, the share of the use being proportionate to the share of the ownership. **The effects of inclosure upon open fields** or **common meadows** might have a similar outcome. In this case, the usual result of inclosure would be for the land that was formerly held as strips to be combined into separate units.[5] These would then be divided and fenced as freehold. An alternative, however, in the case of open fields, was for the land to continue to be cultivated as a single unit, or as a number of unfenced units, with the owners 'inter-commoning' their cattle or sheep after taking the crop (or when the land was left to lie fallow). A similar arrangement might apply to common meadows.[6] Again, the rights of inter-commoning (subsequent to inclosure) would be shares in the use of the land which derived from part-ownership of the whole. Though, in a further complication, the land in both these cases (and also in the case of a regulated pasture) might occasionally continue to be subject to rights of common (on the part of non-owners) that had survived the conversion of the land to freehold. And these rights of common would usually be exercised, of course, at the same times of year as the owners' rights of 'inter-commoning'.

Another kind of land which, though it is not, is very similar to common land, exists where the rights over it (e.g. for grazing, turbary, estovers) are **subject to a trust**.[7] Again, this would usually be the result of an inclosure, as a grant in lieu (or a reallocation) of common rights extinguished by the inclosure award. A typical example would be where a town corporation, or a parish body, held land in trust for the benefit of a group of freeholders or householders. Historically, the rights would usually derive from rights of common. However, as in other cases, the original rights (now exercised by a specified group of people, though often 'attached to' qualifying properties) might not fit easily into the manorial model. Again, the assignment under statute has the effect of redefining pre-existing rights.

Registration and leased rights

The modern period, then, has seen the imposition of an additional layer of statute law upon rights that ultimately have their origin in pre-medieval times. The most recent example of this is the Commons Registration Act of 1965, which required common land to be registered if it was to continue to be recognised as such. Section 22(1) of the Act defines common land as (a) **land subject to rights of common**, or (b) **waste land of the manor not subject to rights of common**. An obvious problem applies to part (a) of the definition. If 'land subject to rights of common' is a fair enough (legal) definition of common land, the question arises of how all the other types of land described above as part of 'the common lands' are to be treated. Are they, or are they not, to be considered to be common land? Part (b) presents an equal difficulty. 'Waste land not subject to rights of common' – apart from its statutory definition here – could, in fact, only be considered to be common land in an historical sense. Given the absence, or the fragmentary nature, of the historical record on this score, there is room enough here for disagreement. However, much of the land that might have been registered under this part of the definition was also subject to 'leased' rights. Not only were such rights explicitly excluded from registration under Section 22(1)(a) of the Act, but at the same time any land that was subject to leased rights was considered to be 'occupied'. Land that was occupied could not, by definition, be waste of the manor.[8] It could not, therefore, be registered under Section 22(1)(b).

In legal terms, rights of common are necessarily freehold rights. They are of equal status, in this sense, with the freehold ownership of land. The ownership of common land is therefore conditional, in that it depends upon the exercise of any rights of common which apply to it. The subject matter of **leased rights**[9] (the most important nowadays are grazing rights) might be precisely the same as that of common rights. But though usually exercised *in* common, they are not rights *of* common. Leased rights are considered, at least in law, to be little more than a permitted use, or a licence, on the part of the landowner.[10] This is in itself a major anomaly, given that the exercise of leased rights of grazing may be essential to the viability of a hill farm, and that such rights apply to an area of the uplands comparable in extent to that which is registered as common land.[11] But if the aim of the 1965 Act was indeed to register land that was historically common (and this is the only coherent interpretation of Section 22(b)), to disqualify land subject to leased rights from registration on these strictly legal grounds was to exclude the very areas that were the subject of the provision. The question of leased rights is considered further below. But it is clear that most of the land that is now subject to leased rights, at any rate in the north of England, is historically common land; and that much of it was 'bought out' in the late nineteenth and early twentieth centuries.

The Act itself offered a part-solution to registration under Section 22(1)(a). 'Sole' rights were defined as rights of common for the purposes of registration. And rights exercisable only for some part of the year are also registrable. However, though the definition of common land in the Act is open ended (the wording is inclusive rather than exclusive), it is doubtful that any of the other kinds of land described above as part of 'the common lands' (regulated pastures, rights held under a trust, former open fields subject to inter-commoning) qualify for registration – unless, that is, they are *in addition* subject to rights of common. In spite of this, many such areas were in fact registered, as were areas subject to leased rights – and it was most usually those with a legal interest in the land who registered them. In contrast, a strict legal definition was adopted in most of the disputed cases, with the result that much land was excluded that to all intents and purposes was no different from land that was finally registered. As will become evident in Chapter 4, the motivating sentiment surrounding the Act was that it should protect land that was recognisably common land, and that the related types defined above (the common lands) should also be included. This intention, at least, might be claimed if the Act were seen to derive – as it generally was – from the original proposals for legislative reform of the Royal Commission on Common Land in 1958. No such intention is evident from a reading of the Act itself, however; nor was it interpreted in this way by the courts when they were called upon to decide appeals against the rulings of the Commons Commissioners. And it was the decisions of the courts which largely determined the course of the registration process.

Leased rights or lost rights?

The Inclosure Movement and the agricultural revolution of the eighteenth century were necessary conditions of the urbanisation and industrialisation of British society. And up until the mid-nineteenth century, the process of inclosure was driven by the demand for agricultural land, for mineral resources and for urban development. But by the 1860s, popular opposition to the loss of common land had gained the support of an increasingly powerful urban middle class. It was the metropolitan commons (i.e. those in the Greater London area) that benefited first from this alliance, initially through the support given by members of the Commons Preservation Society[12] to individual commoners in bringing group-actions in the courts on behalf of rights holders.[13] The Society's members, however, also included a small but influential group of parliamentarians, whose subsequent efforts secured a series of Metropolitan Commons Acts (1866–98), the principles of which were then applied universally in the Commons Acts of 1876 and 1899. In addition, the parliamentary representatives of the Society successfully opposed the permanent dedication of common land to military use by the extinguishment of common rights. Similarly, they attempted (under the 'Birmingham Clauses',[14] or provisions like them) to preserve common rights, and to establish permanent public rights of access, in the many cases where common land was acquired for water catchment purposes in the late nineteenth century through acts of parliament.

The acknowledged motive of these actions was to preserve land as common on behalf of the public. And there was an increasing recognition (even though, strictly, they might only confer rights on local people) that this should be the sole function of the Commons Acts. But despite the growing recognition that it should be regulated for the public benefit rather than inclosed for private profit, the figures show a continued loss of common land. After the mid-1870s, very little of this was due to statutory inclosure, which had virtually ceased by the early years of the twentieth century. About 575 square kilometres (sq kms) of common was inclosed in this way.[15] But this is only 11% of an area of more than 5000 sq kms of common land in England and Wales that has disappeared since 1870. The question is, how is this loss – of an amount almost equal in extent to the common land that has survived – to be accounted for?[16]

The landowners opposed by the Commons Preservation Society in the metropolitan area had attempted to revive ancient legal provisions and customary rights as a means of circumventing the more recent legislation. The most important of these was the right of approvement, whereby (under thirteenth century statute law) the lord of the manor might inclose common land if sufficient was left for the rights of freeholders to be exercised. An alternative was customary inclosure. But this depended on an agreement with the tenants of the manor that was seldom forthcoming in the metropolitan cases and might be difficult to obtain elsewhere. In practice, whilst these ancient rights were pursued in the courts, owners in the metropolitan area had resorted to the expedient of buying out surviving rights of common. If all the rights could be extinguished in this way the land would simply cease to be common land.

Since the right of approvement was effectively abolished in 1893 by the need for ministerial approval under the Law of Commons Amendment Act,[17] the buying out of common rights is quite clearly the only means by which such a large amount of common land could have disappeared from the record in the period since 1870. Commons in rural areas, and especially in remoter areas of the country such as the uplands of the north and the west, would be particularly vulnerable to such action. In these cases there would be little external support for any local opposition. And such opposition, where it existed, would be likely to be weak in the face of an agricultural depression that lasted from the 1870s until the 1930s. The provisions of the Law of Property Act introduced obstacles of a kind. And it was probably in the period prior to 1925 that much of the loss of common land occurred. But rural areas were largely exempt from Section 193 of the 1925 Act. And the obstacles posed by Section 194 might be largely irrelevant if, for example, the intention was not the physical enclosure and improvement of the land, but a closer control of its management and use.[18]

One of the reasons behind the wider acceptance of the principle of the preservation of common land – as opposed to its inclosure and improvement – was that, after 1846, the growing national demand for agricultural produce was provided for by free trade. Free trade also undermined the profitability of agriculture and was a major cause of the depression in the industry in the late nineteenth century. Owners, therefore, including owners of large estates, were seeking alternative uses for their land. In Scotland, but also in England and to a lesser extent in Wales, one such alternative use was sporting. So that, at precisely the time that the preservation and protection of the commons were afforded statutory recognition and growing public support, the sporting potential of common land was also recognised by its private owners. In many cases, sporting use was a commercial proposition which, from the beginning, was at least part-financed by paying guests. In these cases in particular, it might involve a new use of existing estate lands. But it was also a socially exclusive activity, which might as frequently be subsidised by the new flows of income (urban rents, mineral rights) that some landowners (and especially large landowners) enjoyed as a direct result of the Industrial Revolution. The sporting estate, dedicated solely to this socially exclusive use, would most often be financed in this way. Commons closer to urban centres might be better protected by the recognition of their value as part of a shared heritage. Those of the remoter uplands, however, were for the most part turned over to the uses of the rich and privileged. By the time of the Commons Registration Act of 1965 this most recent theft of the commons was a fact of history. And the thieves, or their descendants, held deeds to prove their entitlement.

To this day, large estates, including sporting estates, are a predominant feature of extensive areas of Northern England. Many of them have existed, in one form or another, for centuries. But from the 1860s, the areas of the north previously devoted to the medieval chase were subject to a wave of re-colonisation by new sporting owners. In the Forest of Bowland, for example, the Earl of Bective was one of the first to establish a sporting estate, at Barnacre. Here, in 1876, he built a hunting lodge that was served by the opening of a new railway station at Catterall, near Garstang, for the exclusive use of the Earl and his guests.[19] Ten years later, in 1886, the Earl of Sefton acquired the Abbeystead Estate, together with the title of Master Forester of Wyresdale,[20] from William Garnett – a wealthy merchant who had invested extravagantly in the improvement of the former 'royal forests' of the western part of the present AONB. The Earl of Sefton's new shooting lodge took the form of an imposing mansion at Abbeystead. Improvements were also carried out to provide kennels, and 'cottages for the keepers and foresters'.[21] The Garnetts, meanwhile, maintained a presence at Bleasdale Tower on the edge of the former Forest of Bleasdale, for which game books are in evidence for the period 1830–1920.[22] In North

Bowland, the Fosters – a manufacturing family whose wealth had been acquired through their ownership of the Black Dyke Mills in Yorkshire[23] – purchased the 12,500 acre Hornby Estate in 1861. Just next door was the Farrars' Ingleborough Estate, whose 15,000 acres included extensive areas of heather moorland.

The Bowland area is typical in this respect. The same process of re-colonisation was occurring in the North York Moors and in the Yorkshire Dales (in Barbondale, Swaledale, and Arkengarthdale, for example). The North Riding of Yorkshire also included the Strathmore Estate, which was to become famous for the visits of royalty to its grouse moors at Lunesdale and Holwick. Just across the river, in Teesdale, was the Raby Estate (recognisable today by its white-painted farmhouses – a provision, it is said, of the owner for his sporting visitors, who should have land-marks in the mist). Further north, in Northumberland, were the extensive holdings of Lord Allendale and the Duke of Northumberland. In Cumberland and Westmorland, sporting owners included large landowners such as the Earl of Lonsdale and the Earl of Egremont. But here, as elsewhere, there were also many smaller estates – including those of the Howards, the Bagots, the Penningtons and the Cavendishes – whose heather moors were devoted to grouse shooting.

Some indication of how these changes affected the commons may be gleaned from the registration process under the 1965 Act. In the north of England, all of the larger areas that were claimed as common, but failed to be finally registered as such, were in the ownership of large estates. In the cases that were subject to a hearing, and where evidence was required to be produced, the registrations were declared to be void on the grounds that the rights that existed were leased rights and not rights of common. This, in turn, is confirmed for the cases that did not reach a hearing by the surveys previously undertaken on behalf of the Royal Commission on Common Land. The surveys had shown that all of these areas were subject to shared rights of grazing of one kind or another. The land, then, was either common land or land grazed 'in common'. The extent of the areas involved will become evident in Chapter 4, where the workings of the 1965 Act are examined more closely. But in the North York Moors, for example, the land that was claimed to be common, but failed to be finally registered under the Act, covered an area (about 250 sq kms) equal to that which was. This general impression, which is clear enough in itself, is further confirmed by Geoffrey Sinclair's study of the uplands for the Countryside Commission, published in 1983.[24] Sinclair describes an area of land under 'common grazings' that is almost equal in extent to that covered by what he refers to as 'true' common. Roughly 5500 sq kms of land is at present registered as common under the 1965 Act. And, at a minimum, about 4550 sq kms of common land has been lost since 1870 that is unaccounted for. For the land that was lost, all the available figures point to the conclusion that these commons were bought out and that, in upland areas where the farming system depended on a regime of shared grazing, the rights were reassigned as leased rights that could be more closely regulated by the landowner.

Some of the common land that has been lost since 1870 may have been taken by public bodies, for example for military use or for water catchment land; though land acquired for such purposes under an act of parliament would at least have been subject to some kind of public scrutiny. But the activities of the Forestry Commission after 1919 were perhaps less closely supervised. And common land that had originally been bought out by private interests might well have been sold on for uses such as these. This was the case, perhaps, with those parts of the North York Moors that were planted for forestry in the early twentieth century; and with the extensive areas of upland sold to the Forestry Commission by the Duke of Northumberland at about the same time.

In England and Wales, at least 4550 sq kms of common land have been lost since 1870 that are unaccounted for by the figures for statutory inclosure. Two-thirds of this loss was from the upland areas of the north and the west. The figure for Northern England (with a total estimated loss, including statutory inclosure, of 1666 sq kms) is about 1500 sq kms – though, given that the Parliamentary Returns of 1873 (from which these figures are derived) were a gross underestimate, as much as 2000 sq kms of common may have been bought out in the north of England, much of it for sporting use. It is difficult, as things stand, to give hard figures, though the studies that exist and the figures they have produced confirm what is argued here. The fact of the loss is clear enough, as is its scale. But the fact of what happened is perhaps less remarkable than its subsequent legitimisation by the 1965 Commons Registration Act.[25]

NOTES

1   G D Gadsden, *The Law of Commons*, Sweet & Maxwell, 1988, Preface.
2   On the historical development of common land and common rights, see W G Hoskins and L Dudley-Stamp, *The Common Lands of England and Wales*, Collins, 1963, Part I.
3   Gadsden, op cit, 1.05ff.
4   The shares in a regulated pasture are described as (so many) *beastgates* or *cattlegates*. And an area of land subject to sole rights of pasture is a *stinted pasture* – with the rights referred to as *stints*. Most rights of common grazing, in contrast, would be defined as *sans nombre* (unquantified), or as for beasts *levant and couchant* – i.e. with reference to the needs of the holding to which they are attached. However, in quite a few cases common grazing rights have at some point in their history been subject to quantification for one reason or another, and may subsequently have come to be referred to as stints, or even as cattlegates or beastgates. Furthermore, *all* rights of grazing registered under the 1965 Commons Registration Act as rights of common were required to be quantified – though not with the intention, recently confirmed as law by the House of Lords in the case of Bettison v Langdon, that they should be capable of being sold away from the holding to which they are attached (with the

implication that *any* kind of quantification has the effect of creating a right 'in gross'). Gadsden's emphasis upon different classes of land, with specific sets of rules, is of obvious relevance here. And not only with reference to the possible confusion of common rights with these other, similar rights. Land that is defined above as a regulated pasture is referred to as a stinted pasture in some parts of the country. The confusion, in cases such as this, may be simply a matter of local usage.

5   Inclosure refers to a legal process involving the extinguishment of common rights. *Enclosure*, on the other hand, though it might be required as part of an Inclosure Act, is a reference simply to the fencing, or walling round, of an open area of land.

6   Sometimes referred to as 'lammas lands'.

7   In strict legal terms, a regulated pasture is also 'land subject to a trust'. Although the 'beneficial' ownership rests with the 'share holders', the legal ownership is usually vested in the Public Trustee. In the present case, it is the town or parish body which owns the land, subject to the rights which may be exercised over it.

8   In order to be registrable under Sect 22(1)(b), 'waste land' must be 'parcel of' a manor and it must also be 'unenclosed, unimproved and unoccupied'.

9   Rights that are leased from year to year, or for a number of years, from the owner of the land.

10   Gadsden, op cit, 3.11ff.

11   Geoffrey Sinclair, (ed), *The Upland Landscapes Study,* Environment Information Services, 1983.

12   Renamed in 1899, when it incorporated the National Footpaths Society, the organisation finally adopted the title 'The Commons, Open Spaces and Footpaths Preservation Society' in 1929. It is now known informally as The Open Spaces Society.

13   Lord Eversley (J G Shaw-Lefevre), *Commons, Forests and Footpaths*, Cassell, 1910.

14   ibid, pp 266–273.

15   For the figures on inclosure, see Gadsden, op cit, p 6. Those for the overall loss of common land are derived from the 1873 *Parliamentary Returns*. Though acknowledged to be inaccurate, they are also quite obviously an underestimate. On these, see W G Hoskins and L Dudley-Stamp, *The Common Lands of England and Wales,* Collins, 1963, Ch 8.

16   Virtually all areas of England and Wales were affected by this process, including the lowlands – which in some cases suffered a greater loss than upland areas. However, the uplands of the north and the west (including the Southern Pennines, the Welsh Borders and the south-west of England) account for about 65% of the area lost that is unaccounted for by statutory inclosure. The northern uplands are taken to be representative because of their subsequent history and because of their role as a focus of the more recent commons debate. That they are representative in an even wider sense is argued at length in the later chapters of this book

17   Customary inclosure was subject to a similar provision, under the Copyhold Acts of 1887 and 1894.

18   On the provisions of the 1925 Act, see Chapter 3 below.

19   J M Robinson, *The English Country Estate,* Century, 1988, p 128.

20   A Hewitson, *Northward,* SR Publishers Ltd, 1969, pp 106–7.

21   Robinson, op cit.

22   Lancashire Record Office, Ref (DDQ), Garnett of Quernmore.

23   J K Walton, *Lancashire: a Social History. 1558–1939,* Manchester University Press, 1996.

24   Sinclair, op cit.

25   On the effects of the 1965 Commons Registration Act, see Chapter 4 below.

3

The Royal Commission on Common Land

The Royal Commission on Common Land met from 1955 to 1958. It produced, in its *Report*,[1] proposals encompassing the preservation and protection of the commons, their management for conservation ends, and a public right of access. The proposals, then, covered a range of public concerns in relation to the countryside. But of equal importance was the way the Commission saw these concerns to be related to each other. The commons that had survived into the middle of the twentieth century represented an irreplaceable 'national reserve' of land.[2] They ought, therefore, as a matter of public interest, to be preserved and protected, and to be managed so as to retain their existing characteristics. The best way of assuring this, however, would be through the granting of a 'universal right of public access'.[3] Such a right, indeed, should be considered to be 'a prerequisite of [the Commission's] other recommendations'.[4] The right of access, then, was seen to be fundamental. It defined a primary 'guardianship' role for the public itself. This would in turn be augmented by more formal powers and duties assigned to the local authorities. Together, these provisions would establish a basis not only for the preservation of common land but also for its right management and conservation.

The objectives of the Commission

This last point requires some amplification, given the Commission's original terms of reference. These stated that it was to recommend '…changes in the law relating to common land in order to promote the benefit of those holding manorial and common rights, the enjoyment of the public, or, where at present little or no use is made of such land, its use for some other desirable purpose'.[5] There are several important considerations here. First, the Royal Commission proposed that the private interests of owners and rights-holders should be secured, but that this would be through the proper management of common land in the public interest. The latter would exclude any possibility of permanent inclosure. Nor should any 'improvement' detract from the value of the land as a 'national reserve'. The projected management schemes, including any proposed 'use for some other desirable purpose', would in all cases be subject to close scrutiny and to review in the light of public concerns. Commons might be improved for grazing, then, or subject to temporary cultivation in order to increase their productivity, but not in such a way as permanently to erase access rights or the basic conservation value of the land. It was suggested, for example, that any plantation for forestry should have characteristics not dissimilar to present-day 'community forests' – though, unlike the latter, such a 'parish wood or forest' would be managed under a local advisory committee in its initial stages, and should finally be placed in the hands of 'the appropriate local authority'.[6]

It is important to stress the Commission's objectives in this respect, since its terms of reference – and in particular the reference to 'some other desirable purpose' – have sometimes been taken to imply an original intention (perhaps with the suggestion that the Commission ignored this) to release areas of common for agricultural or forestry development. Thus, certain commons had been appropriated for agricultural use or for military training during World War II. The former had, in one or two cases, proved quite productive.[7] And the matter of their restoration to previous owners remained unresolved at the time the Royal Commission sat. This did not, however, constitute a defining issue for the Commission. The Report describes a much broader historical context for its work, which determined both the nature and the scope of its proposals and their continuity with a tradition of public aspirations and values stretching back to the mid-nineteenth century. The overriding objective was to assure the preservation of common land and its right management within a coherent framework of law. Indeed, it was the collapse of the traditional management structures of many commons, and the consequent neglect and deterioration of the land, that was seen by the Commission to be of most immediate importance.[8] Any references to 'improvement', therefore, should be understood in this context.

Common land, whilst constituting a national reserve of land valued for its intrinsic characteristics, was also 'a wasting asset'.[9] Its deterioration was largely the result of a long-term economic depression in agriculture that had lasted up until the recent war. This had, in turn, been exacerbated by the abolition of copyhold tenure under the 1925 Law of Property Act and by the consequent lapse of the manorial courts through which ownership rights and rights of common had been enforced. In these circumstances, it might become impractical, with the passage of time, to provide for continued management or to initiate any improvement, simply because of the difficulty of identifying the interests or the areas of land that were involved. Where this was the case, it would also be impossible to assure the benefits of any joint action. Thus, whilst the 1925 Act had been effective in preserving common land it had also contributed to its neglect. It had provided in some part for public access through Section 193. And it had provided, in Section 194, for ministerial oversight of any inclosure for purposes of improvement. But the latter provision might constitute a further obstacle to justifiable management schemes in circumstances where these were already almost impossible to effect.[10]

The existing law of common land, then, was serving neither public nor private interests. A central aim of the Commission, therefore, was to provide a legislative framework for the proper management (i.e. the 'improvement', in the sense of a restoration to their former productive state) of the commons. The means it proposed of achieving this end, however, far from entailing a release of the land for development, were of a kind that would enhance public benefit through an increased public involvement. Sections 193 and 194 of the 1925 Law of Property Act, which now largely defined the general public interest in respect of the commons, were to be abolished and replaced by new provisions. The intention here was to go behind the 1925 Act and to revive its original objectives. The latter had implied a much closer relationship between public rights of access and public concerns for preservation and conservation than was finally provided for. If this could be provided for now, it would bring to a logical conclusion the process initiated in the nineteenth century acts of parliament that had afforded increasing recognition to the public interest in the commons.

Though the Commission looked back to this earlier tradition, it did so with a full awareness of the changed circumstances of the post-war period. By the mid-1950s, the national economy had entered a period of sustained growth. The agricultural industry, with continuing government support, was also undergoing a radical renewal. This, and other forms of development, represented a potential threat to the surviving areas of common. At the same time, there existed a growing public interest in the countryside which reflected the increasing affluence, leisure and mobility now being experienced by many of the population. There was, then, a new sense of urgency about the need to achieve a resolution of the problems surrounding the question of common land and to secure for the future the heritage it embodied.

It was these factors which defined the work of the Royal Commission. Before introducing its proposals for reform, however, it will be useful to take a brief look at the tradition of public values on which the Commission drew. It will also be necessary to examine the aims that originally lay behind the 1925 Act. These were to be revived by the Royal Commission in circumstances that presented a renewed threat of exactly the kind they had been intended to anticipate.

The commons: an alternative tradition

In his book *Freedom to Roam*,[11] Howard Hill identified two distinctive strands, or traditions, in the development of the access movement. The first had its origins in the working class and grew from a base in the northern industrial cities, where it emerged as an organised force in the 1920s and 1930s. The other tradition is that of the middle-class reformers who founded such national organisations as the Commons Preservation Society as part of the struggle to preserve the metropolitan commons. The former represented a much more radical commitment to public rights, including a 'right to roam' over 'open country'. The latter, in contrast, has sought gradual change through progressive legislative reform within the framework of the existing law of property.

This distinction, though crucial, is more obviously relevant to the twentieth than to the nineteenth century, depending as it does on the emergence of national organisations representing a broader spectrum of political values, including those of the organised working class. However, the perception of a need for radical change in the law related to property rights had already emerged in the late nineteenth century in the movement for land reform.[12] The demand for a right to roam had also found expression in conflicts over access to the Scottish Highlands. Here, the deliberate exclusion of the public from the ever-greater areas covered by grouse moor and deer forest presented a challenge that was more obviously political, set as it was against the historical background of the Highland Clearances. It provoked in response, in 1884, the first of a long series of Access to the Mountains Bills. Though these made little progress in a parliament dominated by the landowning interest, the demand for a public right to roam over upland areas was to be taken up by the emerging working-class movement in its struggle for access to the Peak in the 1930s.

As Hill points out, the changes brought about in the nineteenth century by middle-class reformers relied for their success on the wider popular support they could command. Thus, many inclosures had already encountered organised opposition, including direct action, from commoners who stood to lose the rights on which their livelihoods depended.[13] The early activities of the Commons Preservation Society, which involved the defence of the commons through legal intervention on behalf of rights-holders, also relied on such action on the ground. As Hill suggests, whilst acknowledging the role of individual middle-class reformers 'it is well to remember that the more important part was played by the nameless thousands of people who took direct action to halt the inclosures'.[14] The importance of action of this kind, and of the popular feeling from which it sprang, cannot be over-stressed. In essence, its significance lies in the expression of a developing sense of public rights in the face of inclosure through the assertion of a fundamental right of access. This may, in turn, be seen to derive from the common law remedy of 'abatement', whereby the holder of a right of common is entitled to take direct, physical action against encroachments such as illegal fencing. It also underlines the practical significance of such customs as 'beating the bounds'.

The Commons Preservation Society, founded in 1865, had initiated its first actions through the courts, opposing the further inclosure and development of common land by supporting the rights of individual commoners. But its greater achievement lay in a series of legislative reforms that reflected the widespread popular reaction against the inclosure movement. Applying initially to commons in the metropolitan area – where the movement in favour of public rights and the countervailing pressures for development were each particularly strong – the reforms were further extended to cover common land as a whole. They incorporated three basic changes. First, the power to inclose was limited in a number of ways, recognising to a greater or lesser extent a public interest in the preservation of common land. Secondly, provision for the positive management of existing commons came to be seen increasingly as of greater benefit than that which might be obtained by inclosure and improvement. Finally, the public interest was embodied in the recognition of the importance of rights of access and of a legitimate role for the local authorities in the management of commons for the public good.

These changes lie at the root of subsequent developments in countryside law and policy and of attempts to articulate a clear definition of the legitimacy of the public interest claims in respect of rural land. They are to be found, as they applied to the Greater London area, in the Metropolitan Commons Acts (1866–98). The Commons Acts of 1876 and 1899 express them in a more general form. The former specifies 'the benefit of the neighbourhood' as of equal importance with that of private interests in the decision as to whether or not inclosure should be permitted. It also makes provision for the management of common land through Boards of Conservators, and for the establishment of limited access rights on the basis of the same criterion of 'local benefit'. Any measures under the 1876 Act, however, depended on a cumbersome procedure involving the confirmation of a Provisional Order by an Act of Parliament. The 1899 Act provided a much-simplified administrative machinery, whereby local authorities might be involved in the drawing up of 'schemes of management'. Again, any benefit was limited to 'the neighbourhood', though access could now be granted to all parts of a common. In practice, given the difficulty of policing such provisions, both Acts implied a *de facto* right of access for the general public. 'The neighbourhood' was, in any case, defined quite broadly, so as to include neighbouring towns and cities. Furthermore, a number of Provisional Orders made under the 1876 Act by the Inclosure Commissioners, and subsequently confirmed by Parliament, actually specified a general public right. Though strictly outside the terms of the Act, these continue to carry independent statutory force by virtue of their confirmation.[15]

The role of the local authorities was consolidated and extended by the 1906 Open Spaces Act. This gave them new powers to acquire and manage land, including common land, as public open space. A related (quasi-public) role for the National Trust, founded in 1895 as an offshoot of the Commons Preservation Society, was defined by the National Trust Act of 1907. The acquisition of land by the local authorities or the Trust obviously has implications for the whole range of public concerns, including preservation, protection, conservation management and access. Each of these elements, however, is already evident, in a way that does not imply the necessity of public *ownership*, in the Commons Acts of 1876 and 1899, and in the Metropolitan Commons Acts. Though in many respects more limited in scope, these Acts represent a progressive re-evaluation of the perceived role and status of common land and a corresponding legitimisation of the public interest claims related to it. But it was the Law of Property Act (1925) that finally gave such claims a more general, though still imperfect, legal expression, and which remains in force to the present day.

The 1925 Law of Property Act

As was indicated above, a major concern of the Royal Commission was the deterioration of common land following the lapse of management structures. Where this had occurred, it was largely the result of the 1925 Law of Property Act. The Act had abolished copyhold tenure, redefining the rights attached to such holdings in terms of the law of freehold. Rights of common – which had, in the majority of cases, been attached to copyholdings – were therefore newly assigned under this 're-enfranchisement'. Consequently, the manorial courts, through which common rights had for centuries been validated and enforced and which had acted as regulatory and management bodies for the commons, were made largely redundant. In most instances, they simply ceased to exist. So that, unless some other management provision had been made – under a Local Act, for example, or under the 1876 or the 1899 Commons Acts – there was now no formal mechanism to control the management and use of the land. The passage of time could only make this situation worse – through, for example, the loss or consolidation of holdings; through the unrecorded transfer of rights; or simply through the general neglect of common land as a consequence of the depression in agriculture. Factors such as these could only increase the number of obstacles to positive management. Hence the parlous state of the commons identified by the Royal Commission.

The 1925 Law of Property Act, then, had profound consequences for the management of common land. It is more often noted, however, for the legal changes instituted by Sections 193 and 194. The former established a public right of access to 'urban' commons. These included '...any land which is a metropolitan common within the meaning of the Metropolitan Commons Acts, 1866 to 1899, or manorial waste, or a common, which is wholly or partly situated within a ...borough or urban district...'. To these areas the public was granted 'rights of access for air and exercise'. The access was subject to existing statutory provisions. It might also be made conditional upon an Order of Limitations on the consent of the Minister to applications from the owner or from rights-holders. 'Limitations' intended to protect specifically private interests could be quite far-reaching. One example, offered by Hill as representative,[16] is the case of Rombalds Moor in West Yorkshire. Rombalds includes both Burley and Ilkley Moors, which are urban commons under the Act. Here, the unilateral attempts of the owner to close the moor for five months each year, during the grouse-nesting and -shooting seasons, led to a public inquiry in 1934. As a result of this, the period of closure was reduced by one month under an Order of Limitations confirmed by the Minister.

Perhaps as great a limitation on the effects of the Act, though, was the failure to record, or map, the areas covered by Section 193. This, together with a lack of clarity (at least in legal terms) of the definition of 'common land', meant that owners could in many cases contest the applicability of the Act to specific areas of land. By way of contrast, a further, more positive provision meant that the right of access might be extended to non-urban commons under a Deed of Declaration made by the owner. Since the Deed might also be subject to an Order of Limitations it could be seen as offering some advantages as a means of regulating *de facto* access over rural commons. Only a few such deeds were executed, however, the most significant covering 68,000 acres of Crown commons, mostly in Wales – over 50% of the total area of 120,000 acres covered by this provision.[17]

Section 194 of the 1925 Act applies to all land subject to rights of common on January 1st 1926. The first thing to note is that the definition of common land adopted here is much narrower than that applied in Section 193. The latter, it seems, must be taken to include any land 'subject to be inclosed' under the 1845 Inclosure Act.[18] This in itself is a very broad definition of 'common land'. But Section 193 applies also to 'manorial waste' – again, a quite loose definition, encompassing any waste land that is (or was) *historically* part of a manor.[19] There is clearly a lack of fit, then, in the definitions adopted in Sections 193 and 194. This absence of clarity has already been referred to above in considering the difficulties encountered in enforcing access rights over urban commons. But it also reflects, and embodies, the contention surrounding the insertion of Sections 193 and 194 into the 1925 Act that is described below.

With these qualifications, Section 194 imposes a strict control on the erection of any 'building or fence...or other work' that would constitute an obstruction to access. Any work or inclosure of this kind is subject to the consent of the Minister, who must consider 'the benefit of the neighbourhood', as defined in the 1876 Commons Act, in coming to a decision. For such an inclosure to take place, then, it must first be agreed between the owner and the rights-holders and must then pass the test of ministerial scrutiny. As the Royal Commission was to suggest, it was the difficulty, in the absence of formal management structures, of taking the first step in this process which made positive improvements (which might well be for 'the benefit of the neighbourhood') so hard to implement. But by the same reasoning, the protection afforded by Section 194 against encroachment might in many cases be less effective.

Sections 193 and 194, then, gave a broader, though somewhat flawed, recognition to earlier aspirations concerning preservation, protection and public rights of access – though the 1925 Act itself failed to provide for, and indeed contributed to the decline of, the positive management of the commons. The most evident fault in the Act, however, lies in the failure to define a clear relationship between Sections 193 and 194. In particular, it is unclear how the reference to 'access' in Section 194 should be interpreted. If the two sections are related in an obvious way, then it must refer, on the face of it, to public access – though this would bring into question its applicability to rural commons. However, it is clearly stated (in sub-section 194[3]) that Section 194 'applies to any land which at the commencement of this Act is subject to rights of common'. As Clayden suggests, since the intended reference is to *all* such commons, the word 'access' must be taken to include the access necessary to commoners in the exercise of their rights.[20] The Act, nevertheless, has not always been interpreted in this way. Moreover, in the case of rural commons with few rights, or where the commoners agreed to the action in question (and where, in the absence of a public right of access, there might in practice appear to be no need to apply for ministerial consent), there exists no firm guarantee that an inclosure would come to light. Objections, that is, would be far more likely as a general case where any obstruction was to *public* access – where it might also be expected that they would be more vigorously pursued. In fact, there exists a simple explanation for these inconsistencies. The original intention behind the present provisions of the 1925 Act was that there should be a public right of access to *all* common land.

The intentions behind the 1925 Act

The Law of Property Act (1925) was one of the seven major Acts of that year which brought into force the very large, and equally significant, Law of Property Act (1922). The basic aim of all this legislation was to make conveyancing (i.e.

the buying and selling of land) easier through a simplification of the definition, the recording and the administration of property rights, and thus 'to revive the depressed market in land'.[21] Copyhold tenure was therefore an obvious target, with its reliance on the records (the court rolls) of local manorial courts.

The lapse of the manorial courts had the consequences described above for the management of common land. Changes such as these had been anticipated, at least in their legal aspect, in the debate over the original Law of Property Bill (1920). It was realised, for example, that since 'it would become more difficult to ascertain the rights of commoners...inclosure would become easier'.[22] It was therefore proposed, by the Joint Select Committee which examined the Bill, that members of the public should be granted rights of access 'in respect of the surface of all commons and commonable land not enclosed at the commencement of this Act'[23] in order 'to secure that commons, particularly those near large towns, shall not be inclosed to the prejudice of the public'.[24]

That such a proposal should be entertained was '...the result of prolonged and intense pressure from the Commons, Open Spaces and Footpaths Preservation Society from the 1880s onward'.[25] It was however immediately rejected by landowning interests and met with concerted opposition in the House of Lords. The final outcome of the ensuing debate was the compromise that was enacted in Sections 193 and 194 of the 1925 Act. A broader definition of common land would be allowed in respect of the limited number of urban commons to which a right of access would apply. However, the requirement for ministerial consent to any 'building or fence...or other work' in Section 194 was to be much more strictly, and narrowly, defined. Originally, then, a clear and logical relationship had been intended between the two Sections. Both would apply to the same (broadly defined) areas of land – the 'access' referred to in Section 194 being the general public right defined in Section 193. The latter would therefore guarantee the aim of preserving all common land. As finally enacted, however, with the restriction of the public right of access to urban commons, and with the opportunities for interpretation offered by both Section 193 and Section 194, the force of the 1925 Act has been much reduced in its practical application.

The initial proposals for reform, then, had defined a crucial role for the public. They had also stipulated a relationship between public concerns for access and for preservation and protection that was complementary in its nature. This, in itself, despite the failure of the 1925 Act to provide for the future management of the commons, would have represented a substantial achievement and a culmination of previous attempts to secure the legitimacy of the public interest claims in respect of common land. It was, therefore, to this point in time, and to the preceding campaigns for public rights in the nineteenth century, that the Royal Commission looked back when it considered its *Report*.

It will be worthwhile, at this point, to quote in full two of the relevant paragraphs of the *Report*.[26]

> 315. The recognition of a universal right of public access on common land is moreover a guarantee of the continued inviolability of the land. In some schemes of management (particularly for reclamation or improvement as woodland, as described in paragraphs 360 and 365) a common or a part of a common might have to be fenced for a few years. Despite the details and maps in the Commons Register, it is conceivable that where no holders of common rights survived any active memory of the land as common might in time be lost. So long, however, as the existence of a right of access was recognised and the intention to restore it was known and recorded, then whatever temporary restrictions might be necessary, there would be no danger of the common becoming for all practical purposes alienated permanently. *In a sense, the interest of the vanished commoners in keeping the land open would be bequeathed to the public by virtue of the latter's possession of a right of access.*
>
> 316. The extension generally of the public right of access is indeed a prerequisite to our other recommendations. *It is no innovation but rather the logical conclusion of the long process over the past century of widening and establishing more firmly the free access over common land which the public has enjoyed in fact, though not generally in law, for a much longer period.*

(Italics added)

The 'other recommendations' of the Commission, for which access was 'a prerequisite', included not only the preservation of the status of common land, but also a comprehensive provision for its future management. It was the 'statutory restrictions on...development' and its consequent 'immunity from man-made change' that had given common land 'its unique character'. Its 'recognised uses' had, however, not undermined but 'served to protect' this and should therefore be upheld.[27] This would be the aim of the proposed schemes of management. They would also 'encourage those uses' where they 'now appear to have declined'. The concern for common land had been incidental to the central aims of the 1925 Act. It should now be made the focus of reform.

The Commission's proposals for reform

The basic objective of the Royal Commission may be thought of as a recasting of Sections 193 and 194 of the 1925 Act in a way that would recognise the original intentions which lay behind them but would also comprehend the need for the positive management of common land to conserve its valued characteristics. The

Commission's first proposal, therefore, was that there should be a public right of access to all common land.[28] This should not, however, be an unqualified right, but would be subject to the regulations already applied in the case of Access Agreements under the 1949 National Parks and Access to the Countryside Act. To these, bye-laws might be added, as provided for in the 1899 Commons Act, where this was considered to be essential to any particular scheme of management.

The Commission's second proposal was to preserve all common land in existence at the date of the passing of the projected Commons Act.[29] The Inclosure Acts would be repealed, and any compulsory purchase by public authorities would be subject to parliamentary approval. Nor would any subsequent 'deregistration' of common land be permitted – on the grounds, for example, that land had ceased to be common because of the release or extinguishment of any rights that existed over it.[30] The preservation of the remaining commons would therefore be assured. It would also be necessary, however, in order to preserve their intrinsic value, to provide for appropriate regimes of management. Any measures with this aim must in turn depend for their effectiveness upon the possibility of establishing a definitive record of the rights attached to common land. As we have seen, the absence, in many cases, of formal management bodies would make such a task extremely difficult. For the same reasons, it would also be difficult, more often than not, to ascertain the actual extent of the areas of land involved.

The Commission further proposed, therefore, that a period should be determined for the registration of common land and of the rights attached to it, including rights of ownership. The registration process itself was conceived of both as a means and as an integral part of the proposed reforms. It would cover, in all, a period of twelve years. The first eight of these would allow for the provisional registration of common land, and of rights and ownership claims, in registers to be held by the commons registration authorities (local planning authorities). In addition to registrations made by owners and rights-holders, local authorities would themselves be able to register areas of land as common in the public interest, as would any interested member of the public. At the end of the registration period, a further four years would be allowed for objections to be recorded, though these might be made at any time subsequent to the provisional registration of a claim. Submissions concerning schemes of management and improvement would also be accepted by the registration authorities from the date of the opening of the registers. Any local authority, including the registration authority, might initially propose schemes related to public amenity. However, the registration authorities would also possess a reserve power, after two years, to put forward a scheme of management in any case where none had been proposed by owners or rights-holders, and where it considered this to be in the public interest.[31]

It was proposed, then, that the process of registration and that of establishing schemes of management would run in parallel – the areas of registered common involved would, for example, be officially mapped as part of the establishment of any management scheme. The registration authority would therefore exercise an overall control. It was anticipated, however, that it would also undertake a less formal facilitating role, arbitrating disagreements and disputes concerning registration.[32] In this capacity, the authorities could draw on their existing experience in relation to public footpaths and rights of way. The intention would be to keep to a minimum any formal procedures or resort to legal remedies. Indeed, it was hoped that, in many cases, commoners and owners would themselves be able to come to a mutual agreement of their rights on an informal basis. It should, however, be noted here that any informal negotiations of this kind would take place within the context of the wider aims proposed by the Commission. The intention of preserving existing areas of common land, that is, and of ensuring their future status, would be implicit, as it would in the case of any dispute requiring more formal procedures for its resolution. The importance of this point – that the registration process was merely a means to an end which must in turn be clearly defined, and that this end need not be the one proposed by the Royal Commission, but might indeed be its opposite – will become evident in Chapter 4, where the implementation of the 1965 Commons Registration Act is discussed.

Where the informal resolution of a dispute over the registration of land or rights proved impossible, it would be referred to the Commons Commissioners to be appointed by the Lord Chancellor.[33] A hearing would then be arranged, to be held locally, where a commissioner would adjudicate contested claims in public. This would be conducted 'with the minimum necessary formality', though the commissioner would have the power 'to summon witnesses, to call for papers and to take evidence on oath'. The commissioner would be required to state the reasons for any decision, and written copies of this would also be supplied to the parties involved. Once again, it should be noted that such hearings were intended to form part of a wider 'public interest' project, within the context of the objectives defined by the Royal Commission. They would need, as a consequence, to be similar in their conduct to a public inquiry, though the intention was that they should also be as informal as possible. Unlike a court of law, the aim in this case would be essentially one of clarification (rather than contestation).

Schemes for the management or the improvement of commons, which might be promoted by anyone with a legal interest in the land, would be subject to the approval and confirmation of the registration authority. There would be a right of appeal to the Minister, who would have the power to call a public inquiry. A local authority could also promote a scheme where the primary purpose was public amenity. As noted above, the registration authority could, after a two-year period, exercise a reserve power in all cases where private interests had failed to promote a scheme and where this was considered necessary in the public interest. This may be seen as part of a *public guardianship* role defined for the registration authorities who, in addition to their general responsibilities connected with registration and with the establishment of schemes of management, would be required to carry out ten-yearly reviews of the state of the commons in their area.[34] Local authorities would also be vested with the ownership, where this was unclaimed, of commons for which they had successfully promoted a scheme of management. More generally, unclaimed commons would be vested in the Public Trustee.

In essence, then, the core proposals of the Commission, from which the rest follow, are those related to access and preservation. Public access was conceived of as the basis for the preservation of certain valued areas of common. Preservation further implied a need to provide, through proper management, for the maintenance of their valued characteristics. This in turn would require a process of registration to ascertain the current facts about common land and rights; a process which would, itself, be well suited to the simultaneous institution of comprehensive schemes of management. The Commission, then, offered a coherent vision of the reforms necessary to the future preservation of the commons, drawing for its values upon a public-interest tradition whose legitimacy had received increasing recognition over the past century in a succession of acts of parliament. Its proposals would address the immediate problem of the widespread neglect and consequent deterioration of common land; and through the institution of a fundamental right of public access, together with the guardianship role defined for local authorities, would also assure its continued preservation and right management for the future.

The starting point or 'first stage' of the reforms was the process of registration. In the event, this was the one element of the Commission's proposals that actually became law in the form of the Commons Registration Act of 1965. There was, therefore, at the time of this Act, a widespread expectation of subsequent 'second stage' legislation that has been repeatedly resurrected in subsequent years. As will become apparent in Chapter 4, the Act itself offers few, if any, grounds for such an expectation. A more basic criticism, however, is that of the sense in which registration can be said to *be* a 'first stage' once detached from the process of reform proposed by the Commission. If it was presumed that the land was to be preserved, and that this in turn implied a need for schemes of management (which must themselves incorporate a fundamental right of access), then any negotiations with a view to registration (the first 'stage') would be determined by these presuppositions. Such negotiations would also naturally provide the basis for the local initiation of particular management schemes. Given the ends in mind, there would be no point (except in a purely *logical* sense) in separating out two 'stages', only to have to review or repeat the whole process at a later date. If, on the other hand, the objectives of registration were to be postponed into the indefinite future, there would exist no reason and no practical motivation – in short, neither a carrot nor a stick – for the process of registration to assume the desired character. Indeed, given that the Commission's proposals represented a considerable shift in favour of public concerns, there would be every reason to expect the very opposite. The public interest might well be perceived as a future threat to be anticipated rather than as a present necessity to be accepted. This in fact was what happened. As a piece of law, the 1965 Act had been stripped of the objectives, defined by the Royal Commission, that it was originally intended to serve. When the inevitable appeals reached the courts, therefore, the latter predictably took a view, natural to them, that was somewhat less progressive than that of the Royal Commission. What the Commission had conceived of as the public interest was seen by the courts as an 'encumbrance' upon private property rights – a view that, in turn, forced subsequent interpretations of the Act by the Commons Commissioners which deprived the registration process of an initially expansive notion of its objectives. The Act itself had failed to mention any second stage.

NOTES

1   *Royal Commission on Common Land 1955–1958: Report*, Cmnd 462, HMSO, 1958.
2   ibid, p 77, Para 225.
3   ibid, p 103, Para 314ff.
4   ibid, p 104, Para 316.
5   ibid, p iii, The Royal Warrant.
6   ibid, p 117, Para 365.
7   W G Hoskins and L Dudley-Stamp, *The Common Lands of England and Wales*, Collins, 1963, p 84.
8   Royal Commission, *Report*, Ch I.
9   ibid, p 14, Para 45.
10   For a full discussion of Sections 193 and 194 see pp 30ff below.
11   Howard Hill, *Freedom to Roam*, Moorland Publishing Company, 1980.
12   Marion Shoard, *This Land is Our Land*, 2nd ed, Gaia Books, 1998, pp 55ff.
13   Hoskins and Dudley-Stamp, op cit, Chs 5–6. *See also* E P Thompson, *Customs in Common*, Merlin Press, 1991, Ch III.
14   Hill, op cit, p 20.
15   Tim Bonyhady, *The Law of the Countryside*, Professional Books, 1987, p 139.
16   Hill, op cit, p 176.
17   Bonyhady, op cit, p 138.
18   G D Gadsden, *The Law of Commons*, Sweet and Maxwell, 1988, Chs 9 & 11.
19   ibid. The definition here is in signal contrast (as will become apparent in Chapter 4 below) to the close legal definition of 'waste land of the manor' adopted by the courts in respect of the 1965 Commons Registration Act.

20   Paul Clayden, *Our Common Land*, Open Spaces Society, 1992, p 53.
21   Kate Green, *Land Law*, 3rd ed, Macmillan, 1997, p 5.
22   Bonyhady, op cit, p 134.
23   The wider definition of common land that was finally applied, in Section 193, to 'urban' commons.
24   Bonyhady, op cit.
25   Shoard, op cit, p 342.
26   Royal Commission, *Report*, p 104, Paras 315–6.
27   ibid, p 74, Para 219.
28   ibid, pp 103–4.
29   ibid, p 78, Para 230.
30   ibid, p 92, Para 276.
31   ibid, p 136, Para 406.
32   ibid, Ch VII.
33   ibid, pp 96ff.
34   ibid, p 124, Para 393.

4

The Commons Registration Act

The failings of the Act

It has often been suggested that the purpose of the 1965 Commons Registration Act was the preservation of surviving areas of common, but that it failed in achieving this end. This is not so. Or, at least, the objective of preservation is not evident from a reading of the Act itself. Another frequent criticism, in this case justifiable, is that the time allowed for the registration process was too short. The Royal Commission had proposed a period of twelve years: eight for registration, and a further four to record objections. Registration under the 1965 Act ran for three years, divided into two periods of eighteen months. Another two years were allowed for objections. And a final period of just over a year was specified during which applications or objections could be withdrawn. Cases still in dispute would then be referred to the Commons Commissioners by the registration authorities.[1]

In effect, the Act more than halved the time allowed by the Royal Commission for the registration process. The work was therefore rushed. And the registers it created were far from perfect.[2] Extensive areas of common land were omitted from the record. They therefore ceased to be common under the provisions of the Act. At the same time, certain areas of land that were not common (as defined by the Act) were in fact recorded as such. In respect of common rights, the sub-division, in many instances, of larger areas of common land into smaller 'CL' units[3] encouraged multiple registrations by rights-holders (i.e. the registration of the original level of rights over *each* of the sub-divisions). At the other end of the scale, the amalgamation of smaller commons as larger units permitted applicants to claim rights which now extended over a much wider area. In either case, the results, combined as they often were with the over-quantification of rights claims by applicants, could be unrealistic or nonsensical. Both land and rights registrations, however, no matter how anomalous they might be, were subsequently allowed to stand where they were not the subject of a formal objection.

	Period I	Period II
Table 2.		
Registration periods under the 1965 Commons Registration Act		
	Period I	Period II
Provisional registration	2/1/67–30/6/68	1/7/68–2/1/70
Registration authority	land 'without application' up until 31/7/70	
Objections	1/10/68–30/9/70	1/5/70–31/7/72
Withdrawals	up until 17/12/71	up until 31/7/73

The period for the settlement of disputed cases by the Commons Commissioners, from 1972 onwards, was equally fraught with difficulties – though the problems encountered here were not only those presented by the imperfections in the registers. The Act contained a number of other anomalies. Legal loopholes had been identified, for example, whereby private agreements to prevent the registration of common land, now in disputed cases referred to a commissioner, might pre-empt an official hearing. These were widely exploited by the interests opposed to registration. It was also soon evident that the decisions of the Commons Commissioners might themselves be successfully contested by appeals to the courts. As a result, court rulings in 1976 and 1979 undermined principled intentions to preserve disputed areas of land by disallowing any consideration of their historical status. The question now was not to be whether land was common at the time of the passing of the Act (as proposed by the Royal Commission) or at the time of its initial registration (as assumed in certain decisions of the Commons Commissioners). The matter at issue must be whether or not land could be deemed to be common at the date of any hearing. The Commons Commissioners were subsequently obliged to follow these rulings – which, in effect, validated private actions and agreements intended to prevent registration. But the intervention of the courts had also established a precedent with much more far-reaching implications. The status of a registered common might now be subject to legal challenge, and the common to deregistration, if at *any* future date it ceased to satisfy the definition of common land specified in the Act.

Detailed criticisms such as these of the provisions of the Act – that it failed in its purpose because the registration process was rushed or because of anomalies and legal loopholes resulting from poor drafting in the original Bill – are valid in so far as they go. But they also miss the point. They imply that the faults of the Act were those of an instrument unsuited to its ends. But they assume, by this same token, ends that were never given legal force. The fundamental imperfections of the 1965 Act are not to be found in its detail, but are a result of the legal context in which it was implemented. The existing law of property afforded no recognition to unenforceable public aspirations. Which was, of course, the reason for the comprehensive legal reforms proposed by the Royal Commission. It was as a direct result of the failure to implement such wider reform of the law that the Act not only undermined the special status of common land, but also provided a legal precedent, and a much-simplified procedure, for its loss through deregistration. The Act, in short, achieved the opposite of the objectives proposed by the Royal Commission.

The Act as 'first stage' reform

In spite of this, the 1965 Act was widely seen at the time as the 'first stage' of further reform. The second stage would comprise legislation bringing into force the earlier proposals of the Royal Commission. Though it has proved remarkably robust, this expectation was totally misconceived. The registration process proposed by the Commission could not simply be lifted in the way that it was (as a kind of neutral instrument) from its intended context of legislative change. It could not, at any rate, then be expected to serve the purposes originally defined for it. The Royal Commission considered a universal right of public access to be a prerequisite of its proposals. This would provide the basis for the preservation of surviving areas of common. Preservation would further imply a need to provide for conservation management; which would in turn require a process of registration to be instituted. The 1965 Act made no mention of rights of access, of any intention to preserve or of a need for the positive management of common land. It therefore gave such aims no legal force at all. Had it done so, the loopholes in the Act could not have appeared, since they depended upon the *absence* of a legal recognition of these principles.

Similarly, the registration process could not have resulted in the kind of documentary shambles that required the passage of two further acts of parliament 'reconstituting' – or remaking from scratch – the registers of Dyfed and Glamorgan.[4] The Royal Commission's proposals implied, and defined, an active guardianship role for the registration authorities. They also described a close relationship between the process of registration and that of the institution of management schemes. The two processes were to run simultaneously under the supervision of the registration authorities in a way that would ensure the creation of 'living' registers as a practical means to securing the ends of access, of preservation and of conservation management. The 1965 Act failed even in this. It produced no such registers – though this is surely the one thing it should have done if it were to be conceived of, in any meaningful sense, as the first stage of further reform. In effect, the registers created by the Act were formed in a vacuum. They possessed no 'living' relationship, at the time or subsequently, to any practical schemes of management. The provisions made for their future amendment were, to say the least, inadequate. And in any case, such amendments were to be entirely voluntary. In this light, it is difficult to see in what sense the registers created by the 1965 Act could be of any practical use, let alone how they might provide the basis for second stage legislation.

Implementation

The Royal Commission produced its *Report* in 1958. The Conservative government of the time, however, was little disposed to contemplate the radical reform, even in such an obscure area, of property law. At the same time, it seems to have felt the need for a response to the Commission's work. As a result, it proposed the idea of registration as a first stage. This itself would involve no radical change, whilst the prospect of any wider-reaching reform could be postponed into the indefinite future. Unfortunately, in legislating for the Act of 1965, the new Labour government simply adopted the proposals of the previous administration.[5]

No second stage legislation has in fact been seriously considered at any time since – though it seems that the Labour administration of 1964–8 did at least intend that the 1965 Act, as far as it went, should serve some kind of positive end. Moreover, the Act itself retained certain residual features reflecting the original concerns of the Royal Commission. Thus, individual members of the public, or interested organisations, might register areas of land they believed to be common. There was no requirement that they possess any legal (property) interest in the land. Local authorities could therefore act in this way, including those appointed as registration authorities. The latter were in fact given specific powers under the Act to register land they thought to be common where no application had been received.

That the government encouraged the use of these rights is evident from an official Circular produced one year prior to the opening of the registers:

> The Minister asks all registration authorities and other local authorities (including parish councils) to use these powers to the full and to regard themselves as the "long-stop" against the possibility of land which is common or a green failing to be brought on to the registers. The Minister appreciates that with this object in view many local authorities have already

carried out preliminary surveys of commons and greens in their areas, or are in process of doing so. Where such a survey has not yet been embarked upon, the Minister would urge the registration authority to take such steps as it can, in collaboration with all other local authorities in its area, to ensure that no commons or greens are allowed to remain unregistered.[6]

Local authorities should set a lead by registering land owned or managed by them that they believed to be common. The early registration of such areas by the authorities, whilst it would 'help to reduce enquiries and applications from the public', would also give the whole exercise 'a flying start'.[7]

The motives of the Labour government of the time, then, cannot simply be seen as cynical – though it is difficult, with hindsight, to understand how the shortcomings of the Act could have been overlooked. There was clearly the intention that the Act should succeed in 'bringing land on to the registers'. How this could have been expected to serve anything other than private ends, however, in the absence of a comprehensive reform of the law, remains something of a mystery. It was not enough, for instance, simply to encourage the good intentions of the registration authorities. The Act itself afforded them no legal basis for a role of the kind that had been proposed for them by the Royal Commission. What they might attempt on an informal basis must, then, necessarily be constrained by the existing law – not to mention the attitudes of the registration authorities themselves, who in many cases would prove to be more sympathetic to private interests than to public aspirations.

The Commons Commissioners, once appointed, were placed in a similar position when they came to adjudicate decisions on disputed cases. It is clear that at least some of the commissioners had in mind the principles proposed by the Royal Commission when they were first required to exercise their powers. Their intention, simply put, was that areas of land that could be shown to be common ought to be preserved in the public interest. This end, however, was not necessarily shared by the owners of private interests in common land. Inevitably, the possibility of further second stage reform was widely seen by these interests not as an anticipated good but as a potential threat to private property rights. This was especially so in upland areas where rights of common were still an essential part of the farming economy and where, as in the case of Northern England, extensive areas of common land had been exploited for driven grouse shooting since the middle of the nineteenth century.

To prevent registration of the land was an obvious means of avoiding this perceived threat. However, the interests of rights holders and those of private landowners might often be found to be at odds in this respect. If land failed to be registered under the Act the rights over it would cease to exist and the land would lose its status as common. If, on the other hand, rights of common were registered, the registration of the land would follow automatically. Owners or others wishing to avoid registration must often be ready, then, to negotiate a conflict of interest with holders of common rights. At the outset, any such negotiations took place in a context where they might be considered to be contrary to the spirit of the Act – or rather, to the intention that it should in fact serve public ends. As we have seen, however, this intention failed to survive an early resort to the courts, whose determination of the substance of the Act altered the whole complexion of the registration process.

The court decisions

Commons continued to enjoy the protection afforded by Sections 193 and 194 of the 1925 Law of Property Act. Within this legal context, it is the persisting importance of common grazing rights that has probably been the most important factor in securing the preservation of the upland commons. This is so despite and not because of the 1965 Act. At the same time, it was the definitions laid down in the Act which now determined the status of the land.[8] Thus, common land included those areas of land subject to rights of common. Alternatively, land not subject to such rights, to qualify as common, must be 'waste land of the manor'. It must, that is, be part of a manor. It must belong to the lord of the manor. And it must be land that is open (unenclosed), uncultivated and unoccupied. To be registered under the 1965 Act, then, land had to satisfy one of these two definitions. The registration of rights would thus secure the land in question. As a corollary, however, the withdrawal, or the failure, of such rights claims would mean that the land could only be common if it were waste of the manor. In this case, it must not only possess the required physical characteristics (open, uncultivated, unoccupied), but must also be proven to be 'of a manor' in the required sense.

The issue raised by the court cases referred to above was, in effect, whether or not land must continue to satisfy these definitions in order to retain its status as common land.[9] Should areas that were known to have been common or waste land – for example, at the time of the passing of the Act, or at the time of its initial ('provisional') registration – continue to be recognised as such, simply by virtue of this fact? Or where rights had originally been registered but the registration was then withdrawn, should this be accepted as *prima facie* evidence of the actual status of the land? With reference to waste land of the manor, should the 'severance' of the title and the land at any point – by, for example, the sale of either – affect its status as common? Or if it ceased at some point in time to be 'open', or unimproved, or unoccupied – should this have a similar effect? In short, were the criteria for registration to be historical? Or was there to be a strict requirement that land which, for whatever reason, no longer satisfied the legal definition would lose its status as common?

It was these questions that had opened the loopholes in the Act. Thus, they had suggested the possibility of avoiding registration before the Act was passed. Or, after the registration process had begun, that of proving any provisional registration invalid. Alternatively, a proper registration might be invalidated by negotiating the release of rights that had already been registered – for example, by buying them out – and their subsequent cancellation in the register. Or land that was waste of the manor might cease to be such by deliberately bringing it outside the definitions laid down in the Act.

The judgement of the courts in the *Clwyd* case (1976), and in *re Box Hill* (1979),[10] settled these issues in favour of a strict legal requirement. The former related specifically to land defined as common by virtue of the rights that existed over it. The latter extended this judgement so that it also clearly applied to waste land of the manor. In simple terms, the courts decided that land, to be registered as common, must satisfy the definitions under the Act at the time of any hearing – with, in effect, the further implication that a registration might similarly be brought into question, and potentially subject to deregistration, at any time in the future. The judgements therefore validated previous negotiations intended to circumvent the Act. As will become evident from the cases to be examined below, they also set the tone of subsequent hearings. It was, however, not only the decisions of the Commons Commissioners that were affected.

The role of the registration authorities

Registrations of land and rights under the Act were initially defined as 'provisional'. Where not subject to an objection, they would become 'final' automatically. Where an objection was lodged, and where the application was not withdrawn, or a modification negotiated, the disputed case was to be referred to the Commons Commissioners on the closure of the registers. The registration authorities were closely involved in these matters – for example, in notifying applicants of objections, or in advising on and facilitating the modification or the withdrawal of disputed claims. The stated intention here was to avoid the delay, and the possible expense, of referral to a commissioner for a formal decision. An additional practice, that of 'Decisions by Consent', was developed out of this role in the period after the registers had been closed to further applications. In this case, disputes that had actually been referred to a commissioner and were awaiting a hearing might yet be resolved by bringing the opposed parties together. The registration authorities might encourage and facilitate such negotiations. Where agreement was reached, a formal request could then be submitted to the commissioner that he confirm this as a Decision by

Consent. No hearing would then be necessary and no public record of the negotiations would be involved.

Though it was certainly widely used, it is difficult to assess the significance of this practice or of its consequences. It was off the record, as were the many other private negotiations that surrounded the registration process. For the same reason, it is unclear to what extent the registration authorities were in fact actively involved, whether in negotiating Decisions by Consent or in their role, at an earlier stage, of facilitating the modification or withdrawal of disputed claims before referral. Since, however, they were (i) obliged under the Regulations to further attempts to resolve the earlier disputes; and since (ii) in all the relevant cases of Decisions by Consent they were 'entitled to be heard', it is clear either that they were involved, that they were complicit, or that they were negligent, in all such informal negotiations.

The significance of the role of the registration authorities will become clearer in the individual cases that are to be examined below. However, three related points should be kept in mind. The first is the basic question of the legitimacy of this role. The second is the matter of the blanket of secrecy, or confidentiality, with which these affairs were surrounded – as they continue to be to the present day. The third is that of the motives of those registration authorities who quite plainly favoured private agreements resulting in the loss of common land from the registers. In fact, the Royal Commission had itself stressed the importance of the informal negotiation of claims. It had also advocated an active role for the registration authorities in this area – though with rather different ends in view. The crucial point here is, once more, that of the context in which these activities actually took place – a context in which they were, in legal if not in moral terms, completely legitimate. More specifically, it is to do with that context as it was redefined by the court judgements in *Clwyd* and *re Box Hill*. By these decisions, the courts signed the death warrant of the Act as a public interest project, making a mockery of any informal intentions that might lie behind it. In doing so, however, they merely underlined the consequences of an original failure to afford any kind of legal status to the public interest.

Case studies[11]
(A) Muncaster Fell, Cumbria (Cumberland) (CL 330)[12]

Muncaster Fell is atypical of Cumbria, where most common land was registered with relatively little dispute – though certain parts of the south-west fells of
the Lake District, of Scafell and of the hills above Buttermere and Ennerdale seem
to have been lost to the registers, despite the fact that they were considered to be
common land in the early 1960s.[13] The overall success of the registration
process in Cumbria as a whole, however, can be attributed to a number of factors.
One of these was the involvement of organisations such as the Friends of the Lake
District. Another was the substantial public and National Trust ownership
interest in common land – though this need not necessarily imply a willing
compliance on the part of the bodies concerned. Perhaps the most significant
factor, though, was a typically high level of rights applications, most often
supported by commoners' associations. This was of particular importance in
those areas, such as East Cumbria, where there was a strong sporting interest.[14]
In contrast, a number of quite extensive areas claimed as common along the
Solway Coast of Cumbria failed to be registered in the face of opposition from
commercial peat and wild-fowling interests. The rights claims here were in nearly
all cases low.

Muncaster Fell is a small, detached area of upland on the western edge of
the Lake District fells, close to, and north of, the estuary of the River Esk. The
area provisionally registered included approx 3.6 sq kms of open hill, separated
by a fell wall from the surrounding lowland. The land was registered by the
Friends of the Lake District in December 1969. Four rights claims were subsequently made, for grazing. Ownership was claimed by the Muncaster Estate,
which also objected to the application. The land was sold in 1970, soon after
it was registered, to the Eskdale and Ravenglass Railway Company. The four
rights claims were withdrawn about ten weeks before the commissioner's
hearing, which was held in September 1981. The rights claimants did not
attend.

At the hearing, the original owner, Sir Pennington-Ramsden, claimed that the
land had never been common. Though it was open land, and was grazed *in*
common, the rights were leased (or 'tenant') rights. Since only freehold rights
could be registered under the Act, the land did not therefore qualify as land
'subject to rights of common'. As the land had also been sold away from the
manor, and thus 'severed' from the title, neither could it be considered to be
'waste land of the manor'. The commissioner, in his decision, declared the application void. Because the land now qualified as common under neither of the
definitions in the Act, he was obliged to do so. He strongly indicated his belief,
however, that the land was common land – noting specifically its sale subsequent

to registration. He also obviously had in mind the very recent withdrawal of the four rights claims, quoting not only *re Box Hill* but also the *Clwyd* case (with direct reference, that is, to the absence of rights) as the reason why he was obliged, against his better judgement, to dismiss the application.

No deliberate attempt to avoid registration could have been proved, of course, without wider powers of investigation. Why the sale of the land at that date, though? And why the original claim for rights if the land was 'never' common? And why was it that the rights claimants, with their continuing interest in the land, failed to appear at the hearing? The central point here is that the judgement of the courts had now made such questions irrelevant. What was to be decided was the state of affairs at the time of any hearing, regardless of how this had come about, or what historical truth it might conceal.

Four other commons owned by the Muncaster Estate in SW Cumbria – Birkby Fell (5.6 sq kms), Corney Fell (5.4 sq kms), Birker Fell (13.6 sq kms) and Waberthwaite Fell (2 sq kms) – were registered under the Act. In each of these cases a large body of rights holders was represented by the South Cumbria Commoners' Association.

(B) Boulsworth Hill, Lancashire (CL 134/183/258/261)[15]

Another instance illustrating the consequences of the court decisions of 1976 and 1979 is that of a group of four commons covering the Lancashire side of Boulsworth, above the town of Trawden. Three of these were owned by the Bannister Estate, which was also part-owner of the fourth and the lessee of sporting rights over much of the remainder (which belonged to the North West Water Authority). The attitude of the commissioner here contrasts strongly with that shown in the case of Muncaster Fell. In a series of hearings (1981–82), the Chief Commons Commissioner, Mr Squibb, confirmed an agreement to the exchange of rights of common for leased rights. Since the latter could not be registered under the Act, most of land involved, covering about 15 sq kms in all, was lost to the register.

The Executors of the Bannister Estate objected to all four applications. The latter were made in 1969, one of them (Combe Hill) as an application for the registration of the land by the Ramblers' Association. There were also five rights claimants, including the local Water Authority, the owner of one of the farms. Joseph Parker claimed rights over all of the areas, whilst the remaining claims were each restricted to a single CL unit. Three of the latter, including the lessee of the NW Water Authority, accepted the restriction of their rights to two small areas of land covering 68 hectares and 84 hectares. These small areas were consequently registered as common. Joseph Parker, however, together with the remaining single-area claimant, surrendered the common rights he had claimed. In return, the Deed of Surrender granted to them both leased rights for 999 years 'at a peppercorn rent'. Parker's rights would cover 'most of the area originally claimed' – i.e. three of the CL units, including that originally registered by the Ramblers' Association. Between them, then, the five rights claimants had signed away roughly 15 sq kms of land that would, had it been registered, have had the status of urban common.

The agreements – to the surrender of claims to all but small parts of the land, and to the release of rights – were negotiated prior to, or as a result of the adjournment of, the commissioner's hearings. These were held in 1981 and 1982, and were therefore subject to the *Clwyd* and *re Box Hill* judgements. In this case, however, as is clear from the register and the written decisions, the commissioner was obviously quite happy to acknowledge, and even to facilitate, private negotiations which directly resulted in the loss of large areas of common land. The four claimed commons each included summit areas covered by heather moorland that was also grouse moor.

As in the case of Muncaster Fell, then, a large landed estate experienced no difficulty in avoiding registration when faced with only a small number of rights claimants. There is little doubt that all four of these areas had always been urban commons (their registration would, in effect, have clearly confirmed this for the first time). The aim of the owners was to avoid this eventuality – an aim that was quite happily facilitated by the Chief Commons Commissioner, Mr Squibb. In strictly legal terms, perhaps, the subterfuge adopted was a failure. Since the rights over the land were not extinguished by statute, but were surrendered by private agreement, Section 193 might still be claimed to apply.[16] This would depend, of course, upon proof of the status of the land as 'waste, or a common' in the period prior to the commissioner's hearings – though this in turn is clearly implied by the need to negotiate deeds of surrender, no matter how these may have been worded to avoid the implication. The ineffectiveness of the 1925 Act, in this as in other cases, is only underlined by the fact that, though access had been vigorously sought over these urban commons for many years by local ramblers, it had been consistently denied in the interests of sporting. The area was, for example, the subject, in 1956, of the first-ever Access Order under the 1949 National Parks Act. The Minister refused to confirm the Order.[17]

(C) Hepton RD, Calderdale (Yorks W Riding) (CL 139/397/497)[18]

Hepton Rural District includes the Yorkshire side of the Boulsworth hills. It is unusual, in a sense exactly opposite to that of the Lakes Urban District, in that it forms an enclave in an area – i.e. the former West Yorkshire Metropolitan County – where all the other local authorities are urban in status. Virtually all of the district was, until relatively recent times, in the ownership of the Savile Estate.

Over about 70%, ownership is now shared with Yorkshire Water. The latter owns the greater part of the land,[19] though the Savile Estate has retained its sporting rights. All of the unenclosed upland area of Hepton (>50 sq kms.) was claimed as common. Most of the 70% referred to – including Widdop and Wadsworth Moors, Black Moor and Flask and the greater part of Stansfield Moor – failed to be registered as a result of owner opposition and low rights claims. The other 30% comprises the eastern part of the district. It is all registered common. Oxenhope and Midgely Moor, which covers most of this area, is an urban common by virtue of the fact that it straddles the boundary with Bradford Metropolitan District to the east. It was registered 'without application' by the registration authority.

One area that was the subject of dispute included three claimed commons in the extreme south-west of the district, lying to the west of Hebden Water – Black Moor and Flask (5.5 sq kms), Heptonstall Town Moor (6.7 sq kms) and Hoar Side Moor and Park (1.8 sq kms). All three were considered as a group at a single hearing in December 1981. The objectors were Baron Savile and the Yorkshire Water Authority. Black Moor and Flask they claimed not to be common. This was true also of all but small parts of the other two areas. However, they proposed to allow the registration of the latter two, excluding certain areas they had excepted, in return for the surrender of Black Moor and Flask. A tenant of the objectors claimed the exclusive use of leased rights over this last area – confirming the claim that no common rights existed.

The four original rights claimants for Black Moor and Flask unfortunately (?) failed to appear at the hearing. There were, however, sixteen rights claimants for Heptonstall Town Moor and seven for Hoar Side Moor and Park. The objectors, apparently, were therefore conceding little in their proposal to allow the greater part of these areas to be registered. Despite all of this, the commissioner accepted the proposal; which had, in effect, been presented to the hearing by the objectors as a *fait accompli*. Black Moor and Flask, the rights claimed over it, and the other areas specified, were declared void.

Again, then, a large estate with a sporting interest is the principal objector, this time in alliance with a public owner, the Water Authority. In some respects, however, the case is atypical. The parties involved, their motives and the nature of their 'informal' agreement prior to the hearing are all quite evident – though the commissioner himself seems to have been unclear, not to say confused, about who exactly owned what. The reason for the failure to appear of the four original rights claimants to Black Moor and Flask is not apparent. Nor is the role of the registration authority, which was 'entitled to be heard'. On the other hand, the sense of *fait accompli* encapsulates the consequences of the 1976 and 1979 court judgements. The matters to be considered now had little to do with the public interest, but were those that pertained at the time of the hearing.

(D) Nidderdale AONB, North Yorkshire
(CL 232–4(NR); CL452/476(WR))[20]

Nidderdale lies to the east and north of the River Wharfe, its western watershed forming the boundary of the Yorkshire Dales National Park. It was confirmed as an AONB in 1994, covering an area of 603 sq kms. The role proposed for this area, in the *Draft Management Plan* of Sept 1997, is remarkably similar to that of the other two large AONBs in the north of England, The Forest of Bowland (800 sq kms) and The North Pennines (2000 sq kms). The most obvious of these similarities is a recognition of 'the immense significance' of private landownership.[21] Of particular importance are those large estates which control a 'substantial proportion' of the land – including Yorkshire Water, which owns 15% of the AONB. (NW Water also owns 15% of Bowland.) Another similarity is the importance of the sporting, or grouse-shooting, interest. (The official emblem of both Nidderdale and the North Pennines AONBs is a red grouse. That of the Bowland area is, ironically, a hen harrier). Closely linked to these are attitudes concerning public access. The focus of policy is upon (lowland) rights of way, on the supervision of potential 'recreational damage', and on the 'selective' use of information to protect 'sensitive' sites (crucially, heather moorland).[22] Whilst access is thus defined in terms of its adverse 'environmental impact', farmers and landowners ('the local community') are, on the other hand, depicted as 'the fashioners of our beloved landscape'; or, less assertively, it is suggested that 'our natural landscape is anything but' (sic).[23] A further resemblance, then, lies in the assumption of a necessary conflict between public access and private landownership and in the conflation of ownership interests with both 'the local community' and 'conservation'. Thus, in respect of heather moorland, the 'central objective' of conservation policy is 'the maintenance of [its] sporting use'.[24]

The foregoing – the quotations are taken from the *Draft Management Plan* – gives a fair impression of the relative strength of public and private interests in the areas covered by the northern AONBs, and of the terms of the relationships that exist between local authorities and private owners. It also underlines the importance of the role of large estates *in all those instances where applications under the 1965 Act involving significant areas of land failed to be finally registered.* Another of the AONBs, the North Pennines, will be examined below. The immediate relevance of the foregoing discussion, however, is with reference to Decisions by Consent, and to the part played in these by the registration authorities and other concerned local authorities. As parties 'entitled to be heard' they were, or ought to have been, actively involved in all such decisions. As has already been suggested, Decisions by Consent extended an earlier mediating role played by the registration authorities. They were introduced in 1971 by the then Conservative government under regulations concerning the Commissioners' hearings.

Two of the significant private interests involved in the registration process in the Nidderdale AONB were the estate of Countess Swinton, which included extensive land-holdings, and that of G S Bostock of Tixall, Shropshire. The Swinton Estate lies in the extreme north of the AONB. Land owned by the estate that was claimed as common under the Act includes four areas at the head of the River Burn, looking down on Colsterdale and the town of Masham – Colsterdale Moor (13 sq kms), Pott Moor (14 sq kms), Ilton Moor (10.5 sq kms) and Grewelthorpe Moor (2.1 sq kms).

Grewelthorpe Moor was registered without dispute as the result of a rights application by the Parish Council. The three larger areas, all of them heather moorland noted for their sporting, were registered as commons by the Ramblers' Association. All three applications were declared void, in 1975–6, by the Chief Commons Commissioner, Mr Squibb. Since these were Decisions by Consent, no hearing was necessary. Having the support of all parties entitled to be heard, the decisions could simply be confirmed by the commissioner. As a consequence, no details are available as to why the registrations were declared void. The records of any negotiations that were involved, where they exist, continue to be considered as confidential by the registration authority, North Yorkshire County Council.

To the south of the Swinton Estate are several smaller areas owned by G S Bostock. These include Kirkby Malzeard Moor (3.8 sq kms) and Stock Beck Moor (3 sq kms), both of which were registered as common under the Act. Adjoining these, again to the south, are Dallowgill Moor (14.4 sq kms), provisionally registered as CL 476; and an area to its east of 10 sq kms, in the parishes of Laverton and Kirkby Malzeard, that was provisionally registered as CL 452. Dallowgill Moor belonged to G S Bostock. He also held the sporting rights over CL 452, whose owner was Leeds City Council. The registrations for both areas were considered at the same hearing in March 1981.

The two areas of land involved are contiguous, the moorland of Dallowgill falling away to the lower ground of CL 452. The latter included within its boundaries several farms to which all the rights claimed over both areas (excepting one additional claim over Dallowgill Moor) were attached. Again, excepting this one farmer, all were tenants of Leeds City Council. The council therefore claimed the rights over its own land to be leased, and not common, rights. Furthermore, a release of all of these tenants' claims, over both areas of land, had been negotiated between the claimants and the owners prior to the hearing. The decisions were therefore made on the basis of a withdrawal of rights claims that had already been agreed.

The application for the registration of CL 452 was declared void. There were now no rights claims, and there had been no suggestion that the land was 'waste of the manor'. The same conditions applied to Dallowgill Moor. All rights claims, including that of the single claimant who was not a tenant of Leeds City Council, had been withdrawn. In this case, however, no specific objection had originally been made to the land registration. It had therefore become final, in August 1972. There was no reason why it should not remain so.

As is clear from those cases involving the Swinton Estate, a Decision by Consent required no formal hearing. But given the recognition of the legitimacy of the kind of prior agreement arrived at over CL 452 and Dallowgill Moor, any hearing might itself be rendered a formality. In this particular instance, however, the proceedings were complicated by the confirmation of Dallowgill Moor as a 'zero-rights' common. In the case of CL 452, objections had been made to both the land and the rights registrations. There was therefore little difficulty in declaring the former to be void when all the rights claims were withdrawn – there had been no suggestion that the land was waste of the manor. In the case of Dallowgill Moor, however, the land registration stood. Because no specific objection had been made to it, the registration had become final in August 1972. It would remain so because no relevant legal 'event' had subsequently occurred which would effect a change in its status under the 1965 Act. The rights over it, for example, had not ceased to exist, despite the fact that the claims for them had been cancelled, because they had only ever been provisionally registered.

Here, then, an anomaly in the Act, confirmed by the courts in the *Corpus Christi* case,[25] had actually secured the registration of the land as a result of a simple procedural omission on the part of the objectors. It would also now be very difficult, despite its zero-rights status, to obtain the deregistration of Dallowgill Moor. In effect, it could not 'cease' to be common, since there existed no good reason in law, except Section 10 of the Act, for its continued registration. It could not, for example, cease to be waste of the manor, since it had never been claimed to be such – the land had been registered as the result of a rights application. But nor could the rights over it cease to exist, because none had been finally registered.

It is clear that G S Bostock's aim was to prevent the registration of Dallowgill Moor as a common – a result he had already obtained for a smaller part of the moor (CL 612) that had been registered as a separate CL unit. Here, there was only one rights applicant. The provisional registration of the land followed automatically from the single rights application. But since the land registration was, in this case, *also* the subject of an objection, it had remained provisional. When the rights applicant failed to appear at the hearing, then, both the rights and the land registrations were declared to be void.

Given the date of the hearings (1981–2), no importance was afforded, in respect of either CL452 or Dallowgill Moor, to the principled preservation of common land. If, however, it was an anomaly in the Act that secured the registration of the latter, the rights that were claimed over it were clearly rights of common. The land was therefore common land. But the negotiated release of rights covered both Dallowgill Moor and CL 452. If it were true that *none* of the original rights claims covering CL 452 had been valid common rights, there would have been no need, it would seem, to negotiate their release.

(E) North Pennines AONB
Durham (CL81); (Yorks N Riding) (CL 285/323–5/343–4)[26]

As was suggested above, the area covered by The North Pennines AONB includes a number of large landed estates. It also includes 770 sq kms of heather moorland, of which 90% (700 sq kms) is 'used for sporting purposes'.[27] The question of leased rights – usually where an estate owns all of the land, including the farms to which any grazing rights are attached – also proved to be of importance here. The actual use of unenclosed land for common grazing under leased rights is, in many respects, similar to that of common land. Since leased rights are not common rights, however, they may be varied by the owner, most often in the interests of sporting.

The parish of Lunesdale lies to the south of the River Tees, in what was formerly the North Riding of Yorkshire. All of the higher land of the parish, covering about 80 sq kms, was provisionally registered as a single area of common by the Ramblers' Association in 1969. The registration was objected to by the Strathmore Estate. It was withdrawn in June 1973, just before the date on which it would have been automatically referred to the Commons Commissioners. The Ramblers' Association lacked supporting evidence for the application and wished to avoid any risk of an award of costs.[28]

90% of the parish is owned by the Strathmore Estate.[29] The rights, then, may well have been leased, and not common, rights. The land, therefore, if not waste of the manor, would not have been common under the Act.[30] The records held by the registration authority, however, contain no evidence as to whether this was so or not. The objection lodged by the estate simply records that 'the land is not Common'. This was, in fact, the required form for such an objection. Neither was any more evidence required by the registration authority for it to cancel an application such as this when the applicant (here, the Ramblers' Association) would not (or, as in this case, could not) pursue it further.

The Ramblers' Association was the organisation most often involved in such cases. And the threat of an award of costs, where an application was persisted in but sufficient evidence could not be produced at any hearing, was very real. Of course, much of the evidence that would be helpful might itself be 'confidential'. A further consideration – which has already been mentioned above – was the shortness of the registration period. The Ramblers' Association had, it seems, one person covering the whole of Durham and the North and West Ridings of Yorkshire, carrying out the work in his spare time.[31] Given this fact, what was achieved seems remarkable. The same, however, cannot be said for the actions of the registration authorities who, it will be recalled, had been 'asked' by the Minister to act, along with other concerned local authorities, as 'the "long-stop" against the possibility of land which is common…failing to come on to the registers'.[32]

The simple 'required form' of the objection ('the land is not Common') was presumably to avoid any conflict of interest on the part of registration authorities also actively pursuing the registration of common land. In this respect, it seems to have been unnecessary. The registration authorities involved here obviously invested little time or energy in pursuing such claims. The Ramblers' Association – or, rather, its one representative – was therefore acting unassisted in the many other cases covering the north of England where it was finally obliged to withdraw applications for the same reasons as those given above. The Strathmore Estate itself, for example, made identical formal objections to four other large areas provisionally registered by the Ramblers' Association – Holwick Fell (9 sq kms), Hunderthwaite Moor (8 sq kms), Mickleton Moor (5 sq kms) and Crossthwaite Common (2.1 sq kms). Again, all of these applications had to be withdrawn because of a lack of supporting evidence. An objection by the adjacent Raby Estate to the registration of 18 sq kms of Upper Teesdale took an identical form, and followed an identical course. Another local case of exactly the same kind was that of Lartington High Moor (6 sq kms).

Now, all of these areas of land had been identified in the surveys carried out by the Royal Commission on Common Land prior to its *Report* in 1958.[33] And all of them except Lunesdale and Holwick Fell, which had been indicated as possible common (or leased) grazings, were understood by the Royal Commission to be 'true commons'. The surveys had involved, amongst other things, a close consultation with the local authorities; who, as a result, held (or should have held) relevant information concerning their own areas at the time of the registration process under the 1965 Act. The information seems, in these cases as in most others, not to have had much use.

The only officially recorded reason for the failure of these and many similar areas to be registered as common, then, is the bare statement that 'the land is not Common' made by ownership interests who were opposed to registration. The period involved is that stipulated for the initial registration and withdrawal of applications – i.e. 1967 to 1973. The period, that is, *prior to* the court judgements which disallowed the possibility that the registration process might be seriously considered as one that should serve public rather than private interests.

(F) North York Moors, North Yorkshire (NR)

If a map of the commons that were initially registered in the North York Moors is compared with that of the 'Moor and Heath' which the National Park considers it 'important to conserve',[34] there will be seen to be very little difference between them. Missing from the former are Kepwick, Hawnby, Wheeldale, Moorsholm and East Moors – no applications were made to register these areas as common. Otherwise, there is an almost exact correspondence. Virtually all of this land is also heather moorland. It comprises, in fact, the single most extensive area of such moorland in the country. The sporting interest is therefore strong; whilst the entries of objections in the register of commons read like a *Who's Who* of the minor nobility.

About half of the land entered as common failed to be finally registered. The objectors, however, were relatively few. And the few CL units involved were relatively large. The latter form more or less continuous blocks of land, where adjacent areas claimed as common often also shared a single ownership, or sporting, interest. The Forestry Commission, for example, successfully opposed registrations in the east over extensive areas lying to the north and south of the main moorland watershed. A single interest, the Feversham Estate, achieved a similar result in Bransdale, of which it owned the greater part,[35] and in Farndale. In the west, applications covering nearly the whole of the Cleveland Hills failed to be finally registered as a result of objections lodged by Viscount Ingleby and Viscountess Pollington.

Virtually all of these cases sprang from applications made by the Ramblers' Association – though one or two of those involving the Forestry Commission were also contested by local people. In effect, the Ramblers' Association was fulfilling the role of 'long-stop' that had originally been advocated by the Minister for the registration authorities. Few of the cases, however, were actually referred to a commissioner (they were withdrawn, as were those in (E) above, because of a lack of supporting evidence). A central aim of such applications was to encourage rights holders to come forward. In the event, very few did – though, as the previous case studies will have suggested, the reasons for this are far from clear. The rights sections of the registers are, in fact, almost invariably empty. So also are the ownership sections.

In a large number of cases, moreover, the ownership sections, and sometimes the rights sections, are simply missing from the registers. Any related background papers, meanwhile, are treated as strictly confidential by the registration authority (again, North Yorkshire County Council). Few of these cases actually reached the Commons Commissioners for a decision. For the most part, therefore, the objections entries in the registers must be relied upon to make any sense at all of what went on, and of why it was that these areas were not registered as common land.

The blocks of land described above were identified in this way. Meanwhile, the motives of the Forestry Commission are clear enough. It has since planted half of the areas it contested with over 20 sq kms of conifers.

The extent of the land involved in the North York Moors is quite evident. The areas originally claimed as common that were not finally registered cover roughly 250 sq kms. The nature of the interests at work is also plain. Given the outcome elsewhere of the registration process and the reasons for its failure, it is hardly likely that the motives in this case of shooting owners were any different in kind. Perhaps this is the proper place to ask if motives such as these are quite enough. It may well be that 'the land is not Common'. Or is, at least, not common now. But perhaps now is also the time to acknowledge that land of this kind is so uncommon that it belongs to us all.[36]

NOTES

1   For a detailed examination of the legal provisions of the 1965 Act see Paul Clayden, *Our Common Land*, Open Spaces Society, 1992.

2   J W Aichison, E J Hughes, & S Masters, *The Common Lands of England and Wales: Report to the Common Land Forum*, Countryside Commission, 1984.

3   CL units: areas of common land as recorded in the registers.

4   Aichison et al, op cit, pp 10ff.

5   The Conservative government's proposals were first announced in Nov 1961. See W G Hoskins and L Dudley-Stamp, *The Common Lands of England and Wales*, Collins, 1963, p 86.

6   Ministry of Land and Natural Resources, *Circular No 2/65*, Nov 1965, p 2, Para 6.

7   ibid, p 2, Para 7.

8   Some areas, for example the New Forest and the Forest of Dean, were exempted from the Act. The immediate area under discussion – i.e. the northern uplands – was not affected by this provision.

9   Clayden, op cit, pp 24–6 and 44–5: *CEGB v Clwyd CC (1976)* & *re Box Hill Common (1979)*.

10   ibid.

11   The case studies that follow cover all of those instances in which larger areas of land claimed to be common in Northern England failed to be finally registered under the 1965 Act. The standard Decision Numbers are noted for each case. They are taken from *The Commons Registration Act 1965: Decisions of the Commons Commissioners*. A copy is held in the Countryside Agency's library at Cheltenham. Volumes by present counties.

12   Muncaster Fell, Cumbria (CL 330) 262/D/500–4.

13   D R Denman, R A Roberts and H J F Smith, *Commons and Village Greens*, Leonard Hill, 1967, Map No 7.

14   A point also of relevance in the case of the various stinted or regulated pastures to be found throughout the North Pennines area.

15   Boulsworth Hill, Lancashire (CL 134) 220/D/217–20. (CL 183) 220/D/206–7. (CL 258) 220/D/222–3. (CL 261) 220/D/212–6.

16   Law of Property Act 1925. Section 193(1)(d). On the wider question of the effect

of the 1965 Act on Section 193 see G D Gadsden, *The Law of Commons*, Sweet & Maxwell, 1988.

17   Howard Hill, *Freedom to Roam*, Moorland Publishing, 1980, Ch 10.

18   Hepton RD, Calderdale, W Yorks (CL 139/397/ 497) 220/D/122–33.

19   Michael Allaby, *The Changing Uplands*, Countryside Commission, CCP 153, 1983, pp 12ff.

20   Nidderdale AONB, North Yorkshire (CL 232)(NR) 268/D/148–9. (CL 233–4)(NR) 268/D/268–9. (CL452/476)(WR) 268/D/341–4.

21   North Yorks CC, *Draft Management Plan: Nidderdale AONB*, Sept 1997, Part A, Ch 2, p 19.

22   ibid, Part C, Access Policy.

23   ibid, Part A, Ch 3, p 31.

24   ibid, Part C, p 98.

25   See Clayden, op cit, p 30.

26   No decision numbers. These cases were not referred to the Commons Commissioners.

27   North Pennines AONB Steering Group, *The North Pennines AONB*, 1995.

28   Richard Harland, personal communication, Sept 1998.

29   Allaby, op cit, pp 7ff.

30   The leasing of rights over any such area of land would usually mean that it would be considered to be 'occupied', and therefore not 'waste'.

31   Richard Harland, loc cit, (note 28).

32   Ministry of Land and Natural Resources. See note 6 above.

33   *Royal Commission on Common Land 1955–1958: Report*, Cmnd 462, HMSO, 1958. For details see Hoskins & Dudley-Stamp, op cit, Appendix.

34   North York Moors National Park Committee, *Areas of Moor and Heath*, 1984.

35   Allaby, op cit, p 11.

36   Details of all of the areas covered in the preceding case studies are to be found in the Appendix below, where they are listed together with the (larger) commons that were finally registered under the 1965 Act.

5

A Changing Context: The Common Land Forum

As we have seen, the 1965 Act was not a 'first stage'. It provided no platform for further reform. On the contrary, it undermined the privileged status of the commons by establishing a simple procedure through which that status might be lost. This was a direct result of the failure to legislate for the principles defined by the Royal Commission on Common Land. But the failure to act had further important implications. The aim of the Commission had been to protect the 'unique character' of a 'national reserve' of land against the forces of change which now threatened. In the longer term, the legal status of the commons must be assured. But a more urgent necessity was to provide for their protection and management in the many cases where management bodies had ceased to exist. In the event, no such provision was made. As a result, the forces perceived as a threat by the Commission – including, most importantly, structural changes in agriculture – were allowed free rein. They adversely affected not only unmanaged commons but also those where management structures had survived.

The threat of deregistration

The court judgements of 1976 and 1979 led to the loss of common land during the course of the registration process, but they also made clear the circumstances in which the status of the land that had been registered might be brought into question at any time. This would no longer require a resort to the courts. The Act itself had provided for the amendment of the registers if land should 'cease' to be common.[1] Thus, if an owner bought out the registered rights, for example, or the properties to which they were attached, he might then apply to the registration authority for deregistration of the land on the grounds that it was no longer common. The application must be advertised and might then be subject to objection and to further appeal procedures. But there were few, or no, grounds on which an objection might be based. If the land, for whatever reason, ceased to

Table 3. Common land in 'highest risk' deregistration category

Region	ALL COMMONS		COMMONS WITH UP TO ONE RIGHT			
	Number	Acres	Number	% of no	Acres	% of area
South-east	2,238	75,275	1,960	88%	36,973	49%
South-west	1,172	158,422	771	66%	40,437	26%
East	844	19,041	721	85%	7,138	37%
Midlands	813	29,500	609	75%	6,453	22%
North	851	375,612	605	71%	15,775	4%
North-west	275	25,593	187	68%	3,540	14%
Yorks & Humbs	859	227,824	625	73%	41,536	18%
Total England	7,052	911,267	5,478	78%	151,852	17%
Wales	1,623	457,767	933	57%	38,016	8%

[Source: Countryside Commission/RSRU (1989)]

satisfy the definitions under the Act, it was simply liable on application to be removed from the registers.

The reality of the continuing threat of deregistration – particularly to low-rights commons – was underlined by the Countryside Commission in 1989, when it published information from a national database on common land compiled by the Rural Surveys Research Unit (RSRU) at Aberystwyth University. It was evident that the threat to the commons from development pressures (agriculture, housing, industry, roads) had increased. Land was, as a consequence, being lost from the registers. Moreover, 'the 1965 Act, designed to ensure that commons remained commons for good, has in fact become a means of doing away with them'.[2] The strongest threat was to low-rights commons. Thus, 78% of the English commons had no more than one right registered over them. Some of these areas might be protected by owners such as local authorities, trusts, or the Crown Estate, or by well-intentioned private owners. But it was clear that, if the continuing loss of common land was to be prevented, there was an urgent need for reform.

It is evident from Table 3[3] that the greater threat was to smaller commons and to those in the south and east of the country. In the event, very few of the commons of the uplands have been deregistered. An obvious explanation for this is the continued importance of rights of common over these areas. But it is also clear that the registration process, together with the decisions of the Commons Commissioners, had already acted as a filter in taking out areas claimed as common in cases where registration might be deliberately avoided by negotiation or by legal challenge. That low-rights commons were still under threat, however, is demonstrated by the case of the Gunnerside Estate in upper Swaledale.[4]

The estate lies at the northern end of a zone of heather moorland on the north and east margins of the Yorkshire Dales National Park. This includes all of Swaledale and the northern side of Wensleydale, together with the eastern marches of the Park round to lower Wharfedale and the adjoining Nidderdale AONB.[5] An area important for its sporting, it is also difficult of access, though the parts of its southern reaches covered by the Bolton Abbey Estate were finally opened up as Access Areas in the 1960s and 70s as a result of prolonged political pressure from the nearby cities of West Yorkshire. Upper Swaledale, however, is more removed from urban influence. Apart from the through route of the Pennine Way, its open uplands are more or less devoid of public rights of way.

A dozen commons were finally registered as belonging to the Gunnerside Estate, covering a total area of just under 100 sq kms and including the whole of the open land of the upper dale above the village of Gunnerside. All of the commons had been registered without dispute, and most of them had a substantial number of rights holders. This was not the case, however, with the areas deregistered in 1981–4 on the application of the 3rd Earl Peel, who had succeeded to the title in 1969.[6] Keld Side (CL 265), a small area of 60 hectares, was removed from the register in early 1981. Later in the same year, the Earl made a further application for the deregistration of the larger Ravenseat Common (CL 150). Though Ravenseat covers an area of about 6 sq kms, there was only one registered rights holder. The right was surrendered in July 1981. The Earl produced the relevant documents. The application then received 'the publicity required'. No objections were made. And the common was therefore removed from the register.

Three years later, a similar application was made to deregister East Stonedale Moor (CL 153), which covers 7.34 sq kms of upper Swaledale. Again the Deeds of Release were produced for the three rights that had been registered under the Act. In this case, however, further evidence was required by the registration authority that the land could not still be considered to be 'waste land of the manor'. The Earl held the Lordship. He was therefore obliged to prove that the land was not waste (i.e. that it was not unenclosed, unimproved, and unoccupied). The evidence produced was that (i) the land was enclosed on two sides; (ii) 60% of it was actively managed as grouse moor – it had been drained, the heather was regularly burned, and the moor was keepered; and (iii) though the land itself was not let, grazing rights were leased to two individuals, one of them a tenant of the estate. Though Richmondshire District Council made 'representations', there were no objections to the removal of the land from the register. Once more, the land was deregistered.

It seems from the authority's records, then, that the last application was examined more thoroughly – perhaps because the Common Land Forum (1984–6) was now in session discussing these very matters. The evidence is hardly impressive, however. The leased rights no doubt involved an exchange of some kind for the surrender of common rights. They were, nevertheless, enough to establish that the land was occupied[7] and that it was therefore not waste.

It was not, in the end, the Common Land Forum that put a brake on attempts to deregister common land. It was, perhaps surprisingly, a new judgement of the courts which now overturned the earlier rulings in *Clwyd* and *re Box Hill*. The *Hazeley Heath* case was brought by Hampshire County Council. An attempt had been made (the latest of a series of such attempts)[8] to deregister the common, which was waste land of the manor. The owner, Sir Anthony Milburn, had sold the manorial title, which was therefore 'severed' from the land. He then applied for deregistration in 1981. But the registration authority, Hampshire County Council, was determined to oppose the application. It therefore took the matter through the High Court to the Court of Appeal in the hope of having the judgement in *re Box Hill* overturned. The decision was given in 1990. The appeal was granted, on the grounds that the owner's attempt to deregister the land, if allowed to succeed, 'would defeat the reasoning of the recommendations of the report of the Royal Commission'. The word 'of' in the phrase 'waste land of the manor' should be taken to refer, not to present possession by the lord of the manor, but to the historical status of the land 'in the days when copyhold tenure still existed'. To allow deregistration 'as a result of a simple change of ownership' would 'make a nonsense of the Act of 1965'.[9]

Since the judgement goes behind the 1965 Act to its intended purpose, it is considered also to imply a similar interpretation in the case of commons registered by virtue of the rights that exist over them – in other words, the loss of such rights, since they could be shown to have once existed, would no longer put the status of the land under threat. If this interpretation holds good, the *Hazeley Heath* decision completely reverses the earlier interpretations in *Clwyd* and *re Box Hill*. It guarantees the status of commons on the register – albeit belatedly – against any future attempts at deregistration.[10] In strictly legal terms, however, the judgement is far from safe. Indeed it is a clear example of the courts creating what is in effect new law through judicial interpretation. The judgement not only goes 'behind' the Act; it also goes behind and beyond the wording of the Act, and in so doing it goes beyond the law. As has already been argued at length above, the 1965 Act gave no legal status to the intentions of the Royal Commission. The judgement, therefore, praiseworthy though it may be, is founded on a moral and not a legal interpretation. As such, it is all the more liable to be overturned by future judgements. The status of common land cannot, and should not, be left to the eccentricities of individual members of the judiciary.

The 'privatisation' of the commons

The legal threat of deregistration is not the only way in which the status of common land has been undermined by the failure to provide for its protection. If the upland commons have retained their status because of their continued agricultural importance, this very fact has also laid them open to a different kind of threat. The Royal Commission had proposed not only that the remaining commons should be preserved but that their valued characteristics should be guaranteed by the introduction and the support of formal management bodies. The 1965 Act contained no provisions related to the management of the commons. As a result, they have been profoundly affected by changes in the wider rural economy.

Since 1965 all marginal upland areas have undergone radical structural change. This has involved, on the one hand, a steep decline in the rural population and a consequent loss of rural services and facilities. On the other hand, a continuing influx of ex-urban migrants has itself exacerbated the problems experienced by declining local communities. Much of this change has resulted from massive job reductions in agriculture with the shedding of labour-intensive farm practices. The same period has seen a widespread amalgamation of farm holdings and an intensification of land use. These processes have in turn directly affected the management and use of common land.

The Upland Landscapes Study (1983) identified two specific developments of this kind, applying both to common land and to common grazing under leased rights.[11] The first involved an intensification of use, including enclosure and improvement, on areas close to the farm, with a consequent neglect of the wider moorland. The second was an opposite trend towards a greater use of the whole of the open moor – through, for example, increased stocking levels, and over-wintering of stock on the hill, often involving the use of supplementary feeds ('fothering' or 'proving'). It is the latter which has most affected common land.

Such changes are apparent in a study by Olivia Wilson of the commons of the Durham Dales.[12] Bowes Moor, for example, lies on the Durham side of the Stainmore Gap, covering 46.4 sq kms of land above the valley of the River Greta, a tributary of the Tees. It has 107 registered rights of common which, at the time of registration, were administered by the Lords in Trust of the Manor of Bowes. All of the rights, however, were found in the early 1990s to be in the hands of six farmers, who now determined the (intensified) use of the common for grazing. This example is all the more interesting because it is of a common (typical in the Pennine areas of Durham, North Yorkshire and East Cumbria) which is under the formal control of an organised body of rights holders. It would seem, then, that the changes in agriculture since the time of the Royal Commission have undermined the management of common land even in those areas where such bodies continued to exist.

Table 4. Registered common land 'not recognised' by farmers in the Cambrian Mountains ESA (1a) (N Section)

[based on figures taken from Olivia J Wilson & Geoff A Wilson, 'Common Cause or Common Concern? The role of common land in the post-productivist countryside', Area (1997), 29.1, 45–48]

Total commons finally registered	43.35 sk
Total recognised commons	7.05 sk (16.3%)
Total access commons	30.91 sk
Total access commons recognised	2.41 sk (7.8%)

Montgomery

CL 104	Cae-yr-Allt	0.05 sk	unclaimed	
CL 14	Commins	0.15 sk	unclaimed	
CL 117	Copa Shon	0.19 sk	unclaimed	not recognised
CL 45	Wylfa	0.22 sk	estate (urban common)	
CL 30	Tycerrig	0.33 sk	estate	not recognised
CL 119	Commins Pant Glas	0.35 sk	3 x farmers (no RoWs)	not recognised
CL 10	Bryn Wg	0.46 sk	estate	
CL 9	Cefn Modfedd	0.48 sk	estate	not recognised
CL 12	Fron Goch	0.54 sk	estate & farmer	
CL 37	Melinbyrhedyn	0.59 sk	estate	
CL 32	Parc	0.79 sk	urban common	GOLF COURSE
CL 76	Cwm Ednant	4.05 sk	4 x farmers	not recognised

Total finally registered commons	8.20 sk
Not recognised/status disputed.	5.40 sk
Recognised	2.80 sk
Access (urban) commons	1.01 sk
Access recognised (urban)	1.01 sk

Cardiganshire

CL 116	Pont yr Oerfa	0.06 sk	estate, farmer	
CL 75	Bank Bwa Drain	0.07 sk	CEGB	
CL 109	Pt Plynlimon	0.12 sk	Crown Estate	not recognised
CL 115	Disgwylfa Fawr	0.13 sk	unclaimed	not recognised
CL 110	Pt Plynlimon	0.19 sk	Crown Estate	not recognised
CL 83	Bryn Bras	0.42 sk	estate	
CL 62	Bryn Bras	0.44 sk	estate, NT	
CL 76	Mynydd Ffynnon Wen	0.53 sk	estate	
CL 42	Henriw	1.33 sk	estate, farmer, NT	
CL 25	Land nr Cwmsymlog	1.40 sk	Crown Estate	
CL 151	Nant y Moch	2.27 sk	farmer/pt unclaimed	not recognised
CL 27	Drosgol	2.46 sk	Crown Estate	not recognised
CL 26	Land SW Plynlimon	4.71 sk	Crown Estate	not recognised
CL 28	Plynlimon	21.02 sk	Crown Estate	not recognised

Total finally registered commons	35.15 sk
Not recognised/status disputed.	30.90 sk
Recognised	4.25 sk
Crown Estate	29.90 sk
Crown Estate recognised	1.40 sk
Access recognised	1.40 sk

The amalgamation of farm units has thus concentrated rights previously attached to smaller holdings in the hands of a few 'improving' farmers. The result has been an intensified sole use of the land. This process of 'privatisation' is even more evident in a study by the same author of the Cambrian Mountains of mid-Wales.[13] The areas of land involved here were often much smaller, low-rights commons. In practice, half of the commons (about 85% by area), though registered, were not recognised as such; whilst in many cases the land was actually claimed by individual farmers as a part of their holdings. Where there was more than one rights-holder, commons were typically sub-divided and assigned between individuals (see Table 4).

The general effects of overgrazing due to subsidies, together with the abject failure of Environmentally Sensitive Area (ESA) and other conservation schemes in halting or reversing this process, are explored by Graham Harvey in his book *The Killing of the Countryside*.[14] One of the specific examples he offers is that of the Cambrian Mountains ESA – including the area covered by the second Wilson study (above). But he also describes the same processes at work in the Lake District and in the Shropshire Hills ESA. According to Harvey, 'some of the worst environmental damage is done to common land'.[15] Most of the Long Mynd (22.5 sq kms) in Shropshire, for example, is heather common. In the past 'the rules governing such things as stocking levels and the removal of animals in winter were strictly enforced. But the management system that had sustained the heather moorland over generations failed to survive the coming of subsidies'.[16] Similarly, in the Lake District, much common land has been 'overgrazed for years' as a direct result of the agricultural subsidy regime.

Reforms in the Common Agricultural Policy (CAP) since 1992 – with the extension of various 'agri-environment' schemes, and the (supposed) enforcement of cross-compliance by the Ministry of Agriculture, Fisheries and Food (MAFF) and by DEFRA – have done little or nothing to reverse this.[17] From 1993, for example, MAFF had powers to withhold livestock subsidies in cases of overgrazing. And after 1996, it supposedly took a tougher stance in enforcing such cross-compliance. However, there are very few cases indeed in which farmers have actually been penalised by a loss of subsidy. Moreover, MAFF

> ...would only reduce or withhold livestock subsidies if the land affected by overgrazing or unsuitable supplementary feeding is of environmental importance. This is land which supports natural or semi-natural vegetation, for example moorland, unimproved grassland and some woodland. Grazing of animals on improved agricultural land will not be affected.[18]

As Harvey observes:

At the end of World War Two 40 per cent of farmland in Wales was classified as rough grazing. A little more than 40 per cent was listed as improved grass...By 1992, two-thirds of all Welsh farmland was classified as improved grass, while less than one-third remained as rough grazing...Since most upland grazing has already been 'improved' and is presumably no longer considered important, those farmers who have now destroyed their heather moorland will clearly receive favoured treatment under the subsidy system.[19]

ESA schemes have had as little effect. A five-year review of schemes for Wales in 1996, for example, showed

> ...that they [ESA schemes] had succeeded in reducing the entire Welsh flock of over 11 million animals by just 1,500 sheep. The cost to the taxpayer was £3 million, or £2000 per sheep removed. Other evidence suggests that the designation of ESAs in Wales merely intensifies grazing pressure on the surrounding land. The wild Welsh hills continue to resemble billiard tables.[20]

In the Lake District ESA, meanwhile, 'the uptake of many moorland protection schemes has been dismal...[and]...farmers entering agreements to restrict grazing in both summer and winter account for less than 2 per cent of the land area'.[21]

The case of the Long Mynd is more closely examined by the National Trust in its response to the government's (2000) consultation on commons reform.[22] Despite the actions of MAFF in the five years after 1995, 'annual monitoring which is carried out by FRCA (the Farming and Rural Conservation Agency) demonstrates a continuing decline in the condition of the vegetation'.[23] The causes of this were clear:

> The massive increase in sheep numbers and the damaging practice of overwintering stock, with supplementary feeding, was induced by the headage-based subsidies for sheep farming introduced in the 1970s. This has provided a financial incentive for the commoners to increase their stock numbers way beyond what the land can sustain...In the view of the National Trust which is supported by English Nature, the only way to halt the decline will require stocking levels to be reduced to 1.5 sheep per hectare in the summer and none in the winter.[24]

The rate of stocking in 1995 was 4.9 per hectare – with sheep being kept on the hill all the year round. But the major problem in implementing reform was the lack of any 'legally constituted framework for managing commoners' rights'. In fact, the situation was virtually identical to that described by Wilson in the case of Bowes Moor. Under the 1965 Commons Registration Act, rights were registered over the Long Mynd by 92 separate commoners. In 1995, however, there were only 17 active commoners, who 'between them were grazing up to 11,000 sheep on the hill'.

The Trust had encountered similar management difficulties in the Lake District. In the case of the Buttermere Commons (55 sq kms) the problems were related especially to the sale of rights quantified under the 1965 Act as rights 'in gross':[25]

> All of the rights originally registered on the Buttermere Commons under the 1965 Commons Registration Act were rights appurtenant [attached] to land. Since the mid 1980s there have been a number of successful applications to amend the register to allow the rights to be held in gross. Upon re-registration a significant proportion of these rights in gross have been leased or permanently transferred away from the original holding to which they were attached.
>
> Some of the rights in gross have been purchased by farmers with existing rights on the Buttermere Commons, thus giving them the capacity to increase their stock on the common should they so wish. Others have been transferred to landowners and farms not having traditionally had any connection with the Buttermere Commons. This increases the potential for difficulties in the future management of the commons and for increased grazing levels. The exercise of rights appurtenant is naturally restricted by land occupation whereas there is virtually no limitation on the exercise of rights in gross.[26]

The same effects were evident as in the case of the Long Mynd:

> The sustaining principles of levancy and couchancy[27] have been lost and need reinstating. If common rights existed under these principles, the numbers of animals which were grazed on the commons could not exceed the number of animals which could be overwintered – together with any stock which had not been commoned – on the commoner's own land-holding.[28]

It is not surprising, then, that the Trust was

> ...very disappointed that there are no proposals [in the Government's consultation document] for the day to day management arrangements for

commons…(including)…legally constituted commoners' associations and the operation of default associations where voluntary arrangements are not forthcoming… This is unfinished and unresolved business that needs tackling urgently…[29]

In short, the basic problem is to do with the breakdown or the complete absence of effective management structures. In the face of this, attempts to deal with the failings of the 1965 Act, or to reverse the effects of the subsidy regime, have proved fruitless. The government's consultation exercise (February–April 2000) ignored these facts, not least because it was based on a view of the present state of common land and commons management that was already thirty years out of date when the Royal Commission submitted its *Report* in 1958.[30]

Structural changes in agriculture, then, have resulted in the *de facto* privatisation of common land, affecting even those areas where use was previously regulated by formal management bodies. The failure to protect such commons has therefore seen them bereft of the institutions and the practices which guaranteed their unique status. This, however, is not the only change on the ground which has undermined the shared use of the commons for extensive grazing. Over the same period, owners of land or sporting rights have also sought to gain a closer control of common land, often in conflict with 'improving' farmers. This, again, is evident in the Durham Dales where, more recently, 'especially in the last twenty years, the reputation of West Durham and the other North Pennine grouse moors has grown, and demand is international'.[31] As has already been suggested, the 'balance' claimed to exist between sporting use and the extensive grazing of common land is a myth – it reflects rather the case of leased common grazing, where the owner may regulate any use directly. In the case of common land, the buying up of rights represents an alternative means of exerting control, even where the purchase of all rights (and the possibility, therefore of deregistration) is not an option. The improving farmer, however, may be unwilling to sell out where increased numbers of heavily subsidised sheep may be run on a common which is no longer regulated by an effective management body. More recently, then, the conflict between farming and sporting interests has intensified – a point of significance in considering the claims of those opposed to commons reform to represent both of these interests.[32]

The Common Land Forum

As was suggested in Chapter 4, the registration process under the 1965 Act was itself fundamentally flawed. In hindsight, it gave no grounds for any realistic hope of further reform. In spite of this, the Act was widely regarded as 'first stage' legislation. And the expectation of further reform proved remarkably strong. The reason for this, perhaps, lies less in the 1965 Act than in the force and coherence of the Royal Commission's original proposals. It was these which gave substance and meaning to any continuing commitment to positive change.

The Commission itself undertook comprehensive survey work. It also generated subsequent publications and preparatory research activity, including that by former members. W G Hoskins and L Dudley-Stamp, both members of the Commission, produced, in 1963, a definitive work on the history and geography of the commons which drew together and supplemented the original survey work.[33] D R Denman, in this case assisted by two former commissioners, undertook a detailed study based on new research of the 'use, management and conservation of commons', the purpose of which was to make recommendations on future management schemes.[34] A new text was also published in 1966 on the law of the commons.[35]

In 1978, the need for further reform was again considered, this time by an interdepartmental working party which 'broadly endorsed' the Royal Commission's proposals. Its recommendations 'formed the basis of the work of the Common Land Forum',[36] which was established by the Countryside Commission in 1984. Once more, much original work was carried out on behalf of the Forum. Independent reports were commissioned on the state of the registers[37] and on the form that future management schemes might take.[38] The Forum also consulted widely, receiving detailed responses from, for example, conservation groups. Subsequently, comprehensive surveys were to be conducted by the Rural Surveys Research Unit at Aberystwyth University. The RSRU's initial work brought together information held by the individual registers in a national database.[39] This, in turn, provided the basis for further studies. The most important of these was probably the *Biological Survey of Common Land*, which would finally be extended to cover all of the counties of England and Wales.[40] Meanwhile, the proposals of the Forum on management bodies for common land were put to the test in a project sponsored by the Lake District National Park in 1988–90.[41]

The Forum, then, revived the original enthusiasm surrounding the Royal Commission's proposals. It also generated renewed hope of second stage legislation by drawing together all of the interests concerned with its work and, seemingly, securing their agreement. It failed, however, for the same reasons that the Royal Commission had failed. And once more, proposals for reform were shelved. The reasons for their failure, however, were in this case to be made quite clear by a body which was established with the specific purpose of opposing them.

The Moorland Association, set up in 1986, represented the owners of grouse moors (the 'heather commons') and shooting interests in the north of England. Its *Comments on the Government's Consultative Proposals*[42] was produced in response to a government Green Paper based on the Forum's *Report*. At first glance, the Association's principal objection was to the proposal for a general right of access. But it went far deeper than this. As will become clearer below from a closer examination of the *Comments*, the objection was in fact to any reform that might incorporate a legal recognition of public rights. It was here, then, that the radical implications of the Royal Commission's proposals, now restated by the Common Land Forum, were for the first time openly considered and rejected. Previously, they had simply been allowed to gather dust. In this instance, however, a consensus did seem to have been achieved – for a short time, at least – that had the support of the national organisations representing farmers and landowners (the National Farmers' Union and the Country Landowners Association). Both the NFU and the CLA had been represented on the Forum.

This acquiescence was perceived by the grouse-shooting interest as a betrayal. It was, in fact, more apparent than real. For neither the NFU nor the CLA has ever behaved as though it were an active party to any such consensus. Nevertheless, it was to be the opposition of the Moorland Association alone which ensured that the proposals of the Forum, like those of its predecessors, would be laid to rest.[43] There can be little doubt that the Moorland Association and the interests it represents must depend, in the longer term, on the wider support which seemed in this case to have been lost. Their apparent betrayal, however, momentarily offered a glimpse of a mental set normally screened from view by the public discourse, to which conceptions of the public interest were, if not a nonsense, merely the sum-total of the private interests of a privileged few. Assumptions such as these do not normally need to be stated. They are common currency.

The Forum met from 1984–86 under the aegis of the Countryside Commission. As has already been mentioned, it carried out original work on the present state of the registers of common land and on the requirements for future management schemes. It also consulted widely. Moreover, its membership included the whole range of interests in common land – government agencies, local authorities, voluntary access, amenity, and conservation bodies, farmers and landowners. The proposals it produced were, in broad terms, a recapitulation of those of the Royal Commission. But they were subject to one fundamental constraint – that of the intervening period during which the 1965 Commons Registration Act had taken effect.

It was agreed, first of all, that the registers created by the 1965 Act should not be 're-opened', but that the threat of deregistration should now be removed by the granting of 'statutory' status. This would apply to any registered common which came outside the definitions of common land laid down in the Act. Certain small areas that were quite obviously mis-registered (including, for example, dwelling-places and their attached land) should, however, be removed from the registers.[44] There would also, necessarily, be a need for negotiation in many cases – on, for example, more realistic levels of rights. But with these provisos, the existing registers could serve as a starting-point for the creation of 'living' records.

For each common, an association would be established. This would draw up a management scheme based upon one of two models, for 'amenity' or for 'grazing' commons. All schemes must incorporate a public right of access. Whilst any significant variation of a scheme from that of the appropriate model (e.g. for farming or game management) must be subject to public scrutiny. The associations would include representatives both of the private interests concerned and of the local authorities. The proposed changes would also restore to local authorities something of the role originally proposed for them by the Royal Commission. They would, for example, have a supervisory function in the establishment and approval of management schemes. There would also now be a duty, on the part of the registration authorities, to protect commons under threat from inclosure. Unclaimed areas of common, meanwhile, would be properly vested in local or district councils.

In summary, then, it was accepted that the consequences of the registration process could not now be reversed. Within this constraint, the Forum agreed changes which at least included all of the *elements* of the reforms proposed by the Royal Commission – i.e. statutory status; a public right of access; management bodies with public participation; a 'living' register. It also defined a basic guardianship role for the local authorities and for members of the public. There were, however, two essential differences from the reforms advocated by the Royal Commission. The first was to do with the nature of the proposed right of access. Although approved management schemes were to incorporate a public right of access, it would constitute almost an add-on feature. In contrast, the Royal Commission had taken the principle of public access as its starting-point – as the 'prerequisite' of its other proposals.[45] Secondly, and perhaps even more significant, was the failure of the Forum to re-affirm the Commission's conception of the complementarity of access and conservation. It had, instead, fallen foul of the paradigm of a 'necessary conflict' between these interests, first popularised in the 1960s by Michael Dower's *Fourth Wave*[46]– although, as a defining idea, this was already implicit in the 1949 National Parks and Access to the Countryside Act.

In contrast, the views of the Royal Commission represented a distinctive and radical strand of the tradition, the origins of which were examined above in Chapter 3. It is all the more bizarre, then, that the strongest criticism of the Forum, on the part of the Moorland Association, should be not only that of its 'bias' towards access interests, but of its 'misrepresentation' of the Commission's intentions in this respect.[47] It will be necessary to examine the whole of this critique more closely in Chapter 6 below. For if the Common Land Forum went a long way towards restating the original proposals of the Royal Commission, the Moorland Association went even further in the opposite direction. It offered, indeed, a manifesto of private rights of almost equal force to that produced by the Royal Commission on behalf of the public interest. The latter conceived of access as the fundamental principle in the case for public rights. The Moorland Association saw it as an illegitimate desire that was intrinsically destructive of its object. But then the Association's *Comments* also denied the existence of any public interest that transcended private ends, or of any rights that were not private property rights. The suggestion may seem paradoxical that it is, in fact, this latter view that has determined the development of countryside law and policy. It is none the less true. The Moorland Association's case, therefore, has a much wider reference. And it demands, for this reason alone, a much closer examination.

NOTES

1   Commons Registration Act (1965), Section 13 (1966 Regulations).
2   Countryside Commission, *Common Knowledge...?*, CCP 281, 1989.
3   Table 3 incorporates revised figures supplied in June 2001 by Paul Johnson of the Countryside Agency.
4   Details of the deregistration of the Gunnerside commons are taken from extracts of committee papers made available by the registration authority, North Yorkshire County Council.
5   On the Nidderdale area, see Chapter 4 above.
6   After, that is, the commons of the estate had been registered. The 3rd Earl Peel was Chairman of the North of England Grouse Research Project, which reported in 1986. He was also a prominent member of the Moorland Association, established in the same year in response to the findings of the Common Land Forum.
7   On leased rights see Chapter 2 above.
8   Marion Shoard, *This Land is Our Land*, 2nd ed, Gaia Books, 1997, Ch 9, pp 346–8.
9   The account of, and quotations in, the *Hazeley Heath* case are taken from Paul Clayden, *Our Common Land*, Open Spaces Society, 1992, Pt VIII, pp 116–7.
10   The proposal that the major criterion for registration should be historical status also brings into question the disqualification of many areas of 'waste land' on the grounds that they were subject to leased rights.
11   Geoffrey Sinclair, (ed), *The Upland Landscapes Study,* Environment Information Services, 1983. The *Study* found that such 'common grazings' in the uplands covered an area almost equal in extent to that of true commons.
12   Olivia J Wilson, 'Common lands in the Durham Dales', Area, 1993, 25.3, pp 237–45.
13   Olivia J Wilson & Geoff A Wilson, 'Common Cause or Common Concern?', Area, 1997, 29.1, pp 45–58.
14   Graham Harvey, *The Killing of the Countryside*, Jonathan Cape, 1997, Ch 6, 'The View from the Hills'.
15   ibid, p 85.

16   ibid, p 87.

17   A contention that is supported by the Countryside Commission's *CAP Reform and the Countryside,* Research Notes, CCRN7, 1997.

18   MAFF, *Your Livestock and Your Landscape. A guide to environmental conditions attached to livestock subsidy schemes,* 1996.

19   Harvey, op cit, pp 80ff.

20   ibid, p 84.

21   ibid, p 89. That little has changed in the five years since Harvey's book was published is evident from the Papers presented in December 2002 to the Stakeholder Working Group established by DEFRA following the publication of its *Common Land Policy Statement 2002.* The subject of cross-compliance, for example, is covered in Paper 8. More than half of the cases actually brought against farmers under the cross-compliance rules have simply been dropped. Whilst, 'up to the present [i.e. since 1993]...' only 92 cases '...are either under prescription or awaiting field investigation' (see Paper 8.28ff). The Stakeholder Working Group was set up to consider issues related to the 'agricultural use and management' of common land. Details of the Group (including an Internet source for the Papers) are given in Chapter 8 (note 34) below.

22   DETR, *Greater Protection and Better Management of Common Land in England and Wales,* Feb 2000. The response of the National Trust is important, not only because of the organisation's aims, but because it manages 12.5% (660 sq kms) of the total area of registered common land in England and Wales.

23   'Greater Protection and Better Management of Common Land in England and Wales', *Response by the National Trust,* April 2000, Pt I, Sect 1.

24   ibid.

25   Rights 'in gross' are rights that are not attached to a property holding. Excepting the case of 'sole' rights, the existence of rights in gross will almost invariably be the result of a sale of common rights away from the holding to which they were originally attached. On this, and on the effects of the quantification of grazing rights under the 1965 Act, see Chapter 2 above.

26   National Trust, *Response,* Pt II, 4.2.

27   The quantification of rights with reference to the number of stock maintainable (*levant and couchant*) on the commoner's holding.

28   National Trust, *Response.*

29   ibid, introductory Summary and Conclusion.

30   See Ch 8, pp 103ff below.

31   Olivia Wilson, 'Common Lands in the Durham Dales', p 238.

32   See Chapter 6 below, where the suggestion that game management has conserved the land in the face of subsidised agriculture is also discussed.

33   W G Hoskins and L Dudley-Stamp, *The Common Lands of England and Wales,* Collins, 1963.

34   D R Denman, R A Roberts and H J F Smith, *Commons and Village Greens,* Leonard Hill, 1967.

35   Brian Harris and Gerard Ryan, *The Law Relating to Common Land,* Sweet & Maxwell, 1966.

36   Paul Clayden, op cit, Ch VII, p 75.

37   J W Aitchison, E J Hughes and S Masters, *The Common Lands of England and Wales,* Countryside Commission, 1984.

38   Land Use Consultants, *Management Schemes for Commons,* Countryside Commission, 1985.

39   See Countryside Commission, *Common Knowledge...?*
40   RSRU, *Biological Survey of Common Land.* Commenced 1989 as part-survey. The DETR funded its extension to all counties. Work was completed in 2001.
41   LDSPB, *Lake District National Park Commons Project*, 1990.
42   Moorland Association, *Comments on the Government's Consultative Proposals for further Legislation on Common Land*, 1987.
43   Nigel Curry, *Countryside Recreation, Access and Land-Use Planning*, E & FN Spon, 1994, pp 71–3.
44   Rectification of Registers Act (1989).
45   *Royal Commission on Common Land 1955–1958: Report*, Cmnd 462, HMSO, 1958, p 104, Para 316.
46   Michael Dower, *Fourth Wave*, London: Civic Trust, 1966.
47   Moorland Association, op cit, Section B.

6

The Moorland Association

On the face of it, the objections of the Moorland Association to the proposals of the Common Land Forum were centred on the issue of public access. The attempts of the Countryside Commission to resolve this dispute proved unsuccessful. Thus, a series of discussions was held in 1988 with the Commission as mediator between, on the one hand, the Moorland Association and the Moorland Gamekeepers' Association, and on the other, the Ramblers' Association and the Open Spaces Society. According to Curry, it was 'because of the intractable positions of the two groups in the fight for access, this time conducted around the committee table rather than on open moorland as it was in the 1930s, [that] the issue of common land remains unresolved'.[1] This is not so – though it expresses a misrepresentation that lies at the heart of the discourse. It is quite clear, from the Moorland Association's earlier response (1987) to the government consultation based on the Forum's *Report*, that the 'intractability' of the issues needs to be seen in much broader terms. The Association's *Comments*[2] offers a detailed criticism of the proposed right of access in so far as it applied to the 'heather commons' of the uplands.[3] However, it also includes a statement of principles that is elaborated – as the title suggests – in a number of comments and observations. These define the context for the more detailed critique of access. But they also carry with them much wider implications. The dispute over access was not (as has so consistently been asserted) the only point at issue. It was merely the most salient feature of a more fundamental disagreement.

The Association, the Forum and the Commission

The Forum's intention that 'living' registers should be created as the basis for the future management of common land was broadly welcomed by the Association.[4] Management concerns were also acknowledged, at least to some extent, as a legitimate public interest – as was 'the public concern…to ensure that the upland open spaces are kept as open spaces'.[5] No principle of preservation is implied here, however. Nor is there the implication of any right of access. The suggestion is, on the contrary, that the representation of local authorities on management bodies would in itself be sufficient to secure the objective of 'proper' management.[6] In short – and this is represented as the Royal Commission's view – it is accepted 'that proper management of [a] common is a pre-requisite of public access. It does not follow however that public access is a pre-requisite of proper management'.[7] Access, of course, is not a prerequisite of game management. Though no-one has ever suggested that it was. But then, nor is conservation management (the implied meaning of 'proper' management) in itself a prerequisite of access. The relevant term here is not conservation but preservation. The use of this term, however, is carefully avoided by the author of the Comments.[8]

The misquotation of the word 'prerequisite' in this context is both deliberate and characteristic. The *Comments*, in what is a blatant subterfuge to anyone familiar with the Royal Commission's *Report*, inverts the Commission's priorities whilst claiming to offer their 'true' meaning. The latter is taken to be what the Commission would have intended had it referred directly to the case of the heather commons.[9] The Forum, meanwhile, is castigated for its 'bias' and its 'ignorance'. It had, in fact, merely attempted to restate the Commission's case, omitting its more controversial aspects, in circumstances that had been created by the 1965 Act. The overall strategy of the *Comments*, then, is to undermine the authority of the Forum whilst claiming that of the Royal Commission for its own. The *ad hominem* argument of bias and ignorance is one that is invariably brought to bear whenever countryside 'traditions' such as hunting and shooting are brought into question. The corresponding claim of a privileged insight into matters concerning the public good (represented here by the 'true' intentions of the Royal Commission) is perhaps even more characteristic. The Comments is not an exceptional text, nor does it present, in the end, an extreme position. It represents a point of view which is, for example, happily shared by many conservation bodies and which enjoys the acquiescence of most local authorities. It is unusual only in the fact that it states openly what are otherwise unquestioned assumptions. To quote Marion Shoard:

> The countryside of Britain is controlled by a small, tightly-knit group of individuals dedicated to retaining their power over what they believe that they own absolutely and ought to continue to own absolutely, *not only for their own good but for ours as well*.[10]   (Italics added)

As we have seen, what the Royal Commission in fact considered to be the 'prerequisite' of all its other recommendations was *a public right of access*.[11] This was, specifically, a necessary condition of the principle of preservation. The latter in turn implied a need for 'proper' (i.e. conservation) management in order to preserve the valued characteristics of the land. The *Comments*, however, rejects any idea of a public right of access. It also dismisses the idea that common land possesses any kind of special status, in recognition of which it ought to be preserved. What exactly is intended by the term 'proper' management will become apparent from a closer examination of the arguments below.

Public 'asset', private property

The *Comments* is divided into two parts. Part I consists of an introduction, a detailed criticism of the proposed right of access and a summary of the Association's counter-proposals for access and management. Part II covers matters to do with the registers and the status of common land. The aspect of the argument most clearly stated is that to do with access in so far as it affects the heather commons. In one sense, this implies a compromise of principle, in so far as it engages with the proposals on their own terms. If, however, the possibility of a public right is entertained, the conclusion arrived at is that it would undermine existing public goods in the form of conservation interests and the welfare of the rural community. Though this is often considered to be the core argument of the *Comments*, and though it is widely accepted as a powerful case, it is in fact spurious. As will be demonstrated below, it reduces to an argument from self-interest. It therefore fails to establish the conclusion that is intended.

The other major strand of the argument develops a principled position clearly opposed to that of the Royal Commission. It frames the more detailed critique of access, defining its context in Part I ('Access and Management'). It then reappears in Part II ('Registration and other matters') as a coda dismissing the idea of preservation without ever quite mentioning it. Essentially, the argument is an attempt to draw out the implications of the private ownership of common land, which is considered to be the same as 'any other sort of private land, or indeed any other sort of private property'.[12] Private ownership implies an exclusive control of the land and of the benefits that flow from it. The centrality of this notion of strictly private entitlement is quite evident from the Association's stated objective 'of the conservation of heather moorland in England and Wales for the lasting benefit *of all persons entitled to enjoy it*'.[13] The owner, then, is entitled to use as he will his own private property. Or it might be disposed of by sale, for example, or by lease, gift or bequest. He 'has no obligation to take the needs of the local community into account when making management decisions'[14] – or, indeed, in making any other kind of decision. Ownership rights are 'exclusive'.

Two points are of immediate relevance here. First, these exclusive powers of control, benefit and disposal are particularly relevant in the case of rural land, because planning regulations have never imposed significant control on development or change of use to do with farming or forestry. Second is the question of lesser legal interests in land. Ownership (including long leasehold) is considered to be an 'estate' in land. There may also exist certain lesser rights or interests – for example rights to do certain things (e.g. rights of way) or to take certain things (e.g. rights of common). In theory, they are derivative of ownership. But since they are 'attached' to the land they limit the owner's freedom of action. Because the exclusivity of ownership rights is itself an asset, they also reduce the market value of the land. They are consequently referred to as a 'burden' or an 'encumbrance' on the title. In this sense, common land is a very special case. This is largely to do with the nature of the rights involved – most importantly, rights of grazing. But it is also because such rights are to some extent underpinned by statutory provisions (e.g. Section 194 of the Law of Property Act). Because of these two factors, the limitation on the owner's freedoms in this case amounts to a *separation* of ownership and control.

The existence of common rights therefore involves a *shared* use and management of the land. Though the interests directly concerned may nowadays be purely 'private' interests (owners, individual rights holders), this was not so in the past when the well-being of whole communities might be affected. It is this communal aspect of the institution of common land that lies at the root of the tradition drawn upon by the Royal Commission. It had originally suggested the thought, in the mid-nineteenth century, that common rights might provide a model for public rights in a rapidly-changing society that was trying to redefine its relationship with the countryside. This strand of the tradition, and the values it supports, are of equal relevance today in the context of the changes at present affecting rural policy. The institution of common land in this sense offers a model for the future, as a means of redefining the nature of public concerns related to access and conservation. Nor is this need for structured reform merely a national concern, given the widespread acknowledgement (at least in formal terms) of the global issues surrounding the 'Earth Summits'.

The assertion of private rights, then, with the implication that common land is 'like any other sort of private land', is a falsehood in both a practical and a legal sense. The uniqueness of the institution itself cannot be so easily dismissed, nor can the Commons Acts and the relevant Sections of the 1925 Act be dismissed as mere exceptions,[15] applying only through specific provisions or to specific areas of land. But the same assertion of private rights is also, and perhaps more significantly, intended as a denial of the legitimacy of the tradition from which the Royal Commission drew inspiration. What is being argued here is that, given the exclusivity of private property rights, public rights of the kind proposed by the Commission and the Forum do not and cannot exist. Though the 'theory' may be weak at this point (rights of this kind might well be legislated for) the 'facts' support the case overwhelmingly. Thus, the state, or public bodies, may purchase private rights for public ends. Or private rights may be appropriated for the same purpose by bodies such as the National Trust. Alternatively, agreements of various kinds may be negotiated in return for compensation – if the owner so wishes. But the appropriation of private rights to public ends in this way does not imply a different *kind* of right in the sense proposed by the Royal Commission and the Forum. The outright purchase of land, together with its further, and explicit, dedication to stated ends – as in the case of the National Trust – is the closest approximation to this within the constraints of the existing law. But even this does not encompass the matter of public interests in private land. In effect, it fences off areas seen to be of exceptional value to the public with boundaries drawn from a body of law that is hostile to the end desired – though the extent to which Trust ownership achieves this end should not be overestimated. To quote David Riddle, the National Trust's Head of Land Agency:

> Most of the Trust's farming tenancies are subject to post-war agricultural law which gives tenants a high degree of freedom to farm as they wish in order to maximise food production. This same law gives tenants great security of tenure, allowing them to occupy their farms for life and usually to pass their holdings on to a second or a third generation if certain conditions are met. In these circumstances the Trust cannot influence farming practices as of right but depends upon discussion and negotiation with tenants.[16]

Over 80% of the National Trust's holdings are farmland or land that 'depends upon farming'.[17] In this case, land and conservation management policies may well also depend on the 'voluntary' agreement of tenants.

One way of looking at this fundamental divergence of values is to compare the actual meaning of the words employed, on the one hand by the Royal Commission and on the other by the Moorland Association. Thus the former refers to the commons as a 'national reserve' of land which *ought* in some sense to *belong* to the public because of what it is and what it represents – though this by no means excludes the possibility of co-existing private rights. The Commission also employs, in relevant contexts, the phrase preferred by the Moorland Association, describing common land (or in the latter case the heather commons) as a 'national asset'.[18] However, the Association's use of the phrase, and its intentions, could not be more different. In this case such a 'national' asset does not (though this is what is implied) 'belong' to the nation, except in the sense that it lies within the national boundary and that it is therefore one of the (private) assets which (when added together) comprise the nation's total 'wealth'.

Now it might well be that the worth of a particular asset of this kind could be enhanced – in the case of land, perhaps, by a change of use; or in the case of common land by its 'improvement' for forestry or farming. As a consequence, both the value of the asset and that of the *national* wealth (as the sum total of private assets) would be increased. The 'good' involved here is convertible. Indeed it takes its value solely from its convertibility – in the case of land, from the 'exclusive' right of sale. The value is the price it can command in the market-place. This is the exact case of common land in so far as it is considered to be private property in the sense intended by the *Comments*. Indeed, the surer the status of the land as common, the less would be its (market) value and its value as a national asset – the more, so to speak, it would be a 'frozen' asset. The conservation of the heather commons for game, whatever it implies, is no cold commitment of this kind. But, then, nor can the intention of preservation in the public interest be adequately described as the freezing or fixing of an asset whose value is intrinsically related to its marketability.[19]

The case for public rights rejected

This economic view of common land as private land and of the property rights attached to it as exclusive rights determined the Association's response to the Forum's proposals for reform. As is evident from Chapter 4 (above), this was also the view confirmed by the Courts in the *Clwyd* case and in *re Box Hill*. These judgements had in turn redefined the nature of the registration process under the 1965 Act. Deliberate attempts to prevent the registration of land were recognised as legitimate (since registration would be a 'burden' on the asset which would reduce its market value). As a consequence, much land that was common failed to be finally registered. It therefore ceased to be common under the provisions of the Act and was lost from the registers. Furthermore, the judgements implied that registered commons which, in the future, ceased to satisfy the definition of common land under the Act would also be liable to be deregistered. In effect, the Forum negotiated a bargain in this matter. The registers would not be re-opened. That is, the results of the registration process would be allowed to stand. But in return, land which might now be threatened with deregistration should be protected by being granted 'statutory' status.

The Moorland Association rejected this compromise – there was nothing amiss with the court judgements, or with the way they had affected the subsequent course of the registration process. There were, however, some cases where land had been finally registered that did not in fact satisfy the definition of common land under the Act. Such land should be removed from the registers.[20] By the same reasoning, land that ceased to be common should continue to be liable for deregistration.[21] Again, the interests concerned here were purely private interests. There was therefore no justification whatsoever for the proposal that common land should be protected by any kind of special status.[22] The proposal for the creation of statutory commons was, in fact, merely 'an attempt by the Forum to obtain as much common land as is possible for the purpose of obtaining public control and public access to it'.[23]

The proper management of common land was, similarly, to be a strictly private affair. Thus, there was no reason why 'if the object of the Forum's proposals is to ensure that commons are managed and maintained as open land for the benefit of the public at large, the public interest cannot simply be protected through representation on management committees, without any need for public access over the common'.[24] The local authority representative would act, in effect, as an observer. However, there was 'a distinct risk of antagonism to sporting interests on the part of politically orientated Local Councils'. Any provision for the vesting of land where ownership was unclaimed should therefore not involve local authorities.[25] In short, neither the public authorities nor the public itself had any legitimate 'guardianship' role of the kind originally proposed by the Royal Commission. But nor was there any admission that the management of common land should have preservation as its determined end.

This *might* be the case. That is, private and public ends might (happily) coincide. And indeed this *was* the case. The heather commons were, it was suggested, a 'semi-natural habitat formed by careful management over at least a century by the owners and occupiers of the land'.[26] The continuation of this 'balanced' regime of sporting and farming use was therefore the best way to assure their conservation. As has already been suggested (and as is apparent from pp 64-9 above) this picture of natural harmony is a myth. It seems odd, to say the least, given the supposed balance of sporting and farming use, that 'members of the Association [had] been working for some time....to improve co-operation between...owner[s]... and the various types of person exercising rights of common'.[27] It was this very matter upon which the Forum had been most blamed for its 'ignorance'. But if the supposed balance was a fiction, it was clearly the imposition from outside of *any* management requirements that was at issue. The control of the land, its management and its use were matters solely for the private interests involved. If 'the public concern is to ensure that the upland open spaces are kept as open spaces this is a consideration that applies to all such open spaces and not only to common land and should not be dealt with by legislation on common land'.[28]

Similarly, it was the prerogative of the owner to grant or to withhold access. The proposed right of access would therefore be a 'compulsory derogation from the rights of the owner'.[29] In the form proposed, it would also be incompatible with the management of the land. Any provision for improved access should take the form of clearly defined linear routes. Furthermore, 'the owner and the commoners affected should not be deprived of the right to decide in what circumstances the public at large should be allowed access on to their common'.[30] Once more, however, there was no good reason why a public *right* of access 'should extend to [common] land rather than any other sort of private land'.[31] If, however, any improvements to access were to be contemplated, these must be regulated by the private interests involved.[32] In this case, access might be quite adequately provided for by 'an extension and rationalisation of the network of public footpaths and by the creation where appropriate of access areas under Access Agreements'.[33]

Access and the right to roam

Common land, then, could be said to have no special status. Proposals for preservation were therefore without justification. Its management was a matter for the determination of private interests, as was any access that might be granted. The principle that the commons were no different from 'any other private land' was therefore fundamental. There were no grounds for legislation. If, however, there were to be reform, the heather commons must be treated as a special case. In particular, the proposal for a general right of access was unacceptable. Where 'a common in practice amounts to "a reserve of uncommitted land"…uncontrolled access…may be of little significance'.[34] In the case of most heather commons, however, 'the land is very heavily committed to shooting and to agriculture'.[35] The proposal for a right of access which was (supposedly) 'without significant restriction'[36] would therefore 'ultimately destroy the asset which it is sought to preserve and to enjoy'.[37] For this reason, the *Comments* offers a detailed criticism of the proposed right.

The basic argument is quite clearly stated.[38] First, there was no need for a general right of access to common land. There already existed adequate means for the improvement of access which had never been properly tried. Such a general right, moreover, would be impracticable in the case of the heather commons. Attempts to enforce it would either be so restrictive as to render the right meaningless or they would be destructive of the 'balanced' management of the land for farming and for sporting. The latter outcome would have further unacceptable costs. The present management of the land already provided for its conservation, creating a valued habitat which supported, for example, many threatened species of bird. It also made a vital contribution to the rural economy in marginal upland areas, not only in purely financial terms but also in terms of the employment opportunities it created, which would otherwise not exist. Aspirations to a general right of access of the kind proposed, then, were not only illegitimate; they were unnecessary, unworkable, and would be destructive of the existing public goods which were supported by the present management of the land for farming and for sporting. Clearly, if all of this were true, for the Forum to continue to press for a general right of the kind proposed would be proof enough of its 'bias' and 'ignorance'. The fact is that very little of it is true.

First, then, it is suggested that there already exist adequate mechanisms for the improvement of access in the form of access agreements of various kinds and in the possibility of negotiating concessionary footpaths. The obvious question here is why these have never been used to any significant extent. A prior consideration, however, is why they should be needed. It is hardly an accident that the uplands are for the most part devoid of public rights of access, given the role of landowners in determining the implementation of post-war rights of way legislation. But this itself is merely one instance of a wider case, which has both local and national dimensions. In implementing countryside policies, including more recent countryside management initiatives, local authorities have been almost entirely dependent on the 'good will' and the co-operation of landowners. It is therefore disingenuous to suggest, as the *Comments* does, that the reason for the failure to employ existing access mechanisms is a matter of 'unwillingness' on the part of local authorities. In the negotiation of Access Agreements, for example, Lancashire County Council reports, in respect of the Forest of Bowland AONB,[39] 'an uneven balance in the negotiating position of the parties, with landowners and particularly shooting tenants having an absolute veto'.[40] It is only in the Peak District National Park, where the will of owners has been opposed by an equal and opposite force ready to commit resources unavailable elsewhere, that significant agreements of this kind have been negotiated. But even here, 'a study by Gibbs and Whitby (1975) showed that fewer than half of them [i.e. the Peak's Access Agreements] were used primarily to obtain or safeguard access, the remainder being used to obtain greater control over visitors, or for amenity purposes'.[41] Here as elsewhere, that is, access concessions and particularly Access Agreements have been used not as a means of extending but of controlling or denying access. If, as is also suggested,[42] local authorities have balked at such agreements because of their cost, this is not a matter that is determined at a local level. The under-funding of access policies is merely one aspect of the marginalisation of access concerns in the national political process. Thus, it was the concerted opposition of landowning interests which determined the exclusion of the original proposal for a right to roam in the 1949 National Parks and Access to the Countryside Act. In the same way, landowners had ensured that the right of access would be confined to 'urban' commons in 1925.

If the voluntary approach to access has produced no significant improvements, this is not because of the unwillingness of local authorities to act, or because of any absence of demand. It is because the piecemeal approach defined by the 1949 Act embodies the interests of private landowners and their fundamental opposition to public access rights. In this, it simply reflects the present laws and

institutions of private property. The latter are in turn the source of the characterisation of a general right of access as 'without limit', and therefore as necessarily
destructive. Almost without exception, the courts have denied the very possibility
of such a general right (a *jus spatiandi*) in English law. It would *necessarily* be
'destructive' of the exclusive rights of property if people had a right to 'wander'
(or 'roam', or 'ramble') wherever they pleased. Imagine, say, a large number of
rights-holders entering the land each day and trampling all over its surface, or
simply having the right to do this whenever they pleased. A freedom of this kind
would effectively 'sterilise' the land. What value or productive use could it then
possibly have to the owner?[43]

The picture is, in effect, a legal figure. It does not imply – even though the
judges concerned with these rulings may well have privately entertained the idea
– that, in fact, people would necessarily *behave* in this way. This, however, is
exactly what it has been taken to mean. This is, in other words, the picture's *ideological* force. But it possesses this force only as the obverse of exclusive private
property rights which conceive of a mountain or an unenclosed moor as 'like any
other sort of private land, or indeed any other sort of private property'.[44] In short,
the picture of lordly solitude and solitary dominion implies the picture of the
unruly mob. If the owner can (irrespective of its nature) 'do as he will' with his
own private property then, in legal terms, any general right of access *is* an anarchic 'right to trample'.

But a mountain is not like 'any other kind of private property'. It is not like a
factory, say; or a farm; or a private garden; or a handkerchief. When stated in this
way, the obvious questions that are raised – of kind, proportion and scale – reveal
how ridiculous, or rather how *archaic*, are claims to such exclusive rights in this
case, both in their substance and in their intent. Yet it is only within the framework of rights such as these that a right to roam can be considered to be both
illegitimate and inherently destructive. In reality, no general right of access has
ever been conceived of or attempted that was not defined by corresponding
responsibilities. A right to roam would therefore carry with it no physical threat
to the land or land management. There may be a threat – albeit a threat that is not
physical in the sense that is implied. But then, nor are the interests opposed to it.
The matters in question here are legal, ideological and above all political. And it
is in these matters that are to be found the reasons why existing access mechanisms have not worked. They were never intended to work. Or not, at least, in
such a way as to extend public access. They were in fact intended to achieve the
opposite. They cannot, therefore, be expected to 'work' now.

What then of the contention that, in so far as it was applied to the heather
commons, a general right of access would be 'impracticable' and ultimately
destructive? It will come as no surprise that public access is presented in the

Comments as inherently damaging in just the way suggested above. Any access, it is contended, is necessarily destructive;[45] though what is described in substantiation of this is not the inherent difficulties of managing public access, but a catalogue of criminal or criminally negligent acts – fire, litter, egg-stealing, vandalism, disruptive political protest, poaching, sheep-rustling. Such acts are in turn insinuated as being characteristic of public behaviour. Though, in this latter case, the acts themselves may more usually be unwitting, ignorant or careless – in a way that is, again, implied rather than described. This, then, in support of the supposed 'inherent' conflict. But these are only the existing problems. In the form proposed, of a general right, the threat of access to proper management would be increased immeasurably, in a way that would be 'impracticable' and ultimately destructive.

It is not only the threat of access that is misrepresented in this way. The existing use of the land is presented as a 'natural' balance of farming and sporting use, which is vital to and closely integrated with the local economy and which offers conservation benefits that are obvious. The 'traditional' use of a 'semi-natural habitat formed by careful management over at least a century'[46] supports, then, not only private but public benefits. The destructive results of open access are, by way of contrast, equally evident in the case of the Peak District National Park where, as a result of such access policies, there had been 'a break down of proper moorland management'. The 'discipline of privately owned upland moor management disintegrated. Grouse interest declined. Sheep were uncontrolled. Moors were over grazed. Fires started accidentally'.[47] It is interesting that the effective agents of destruction described here do not include public access – though this is presumed to have set the whole train of events in motion. The chief agent of anarchy would seem to be (subsidised) farming. Indeed, the process could simply be seen as a reversal of that which took place in the nineteenth century, when farmers were shifted from the hills of the Peak for those 'who could afford much more to shoot grouse than farmers could pay to graze sheep…The old native will point to 50,000 sheep on the moorlands between Longdendale and Baslow sixty years ago, but who could find 5,000 there today?'[48] Thus Royce, writing is 1935, with reference to the establishment of grouse moors in the mid- to late nineteenth century, when 'the first to suffer were the farmers, already feeling the pinch from the agricultural depression'.[49] As has already been suggested, the picture of an harmonious balance of farming and sporting has never been anything but a myth. The more recent intensification of farming in the uplands, and the *de facto* privatisation of common land,[50] have served only to exacerbate pre-existing conflicts between farming and sporting interests.

In this context, an alternative picture is often presented – that of sporting as a bulwark against the threat of subsidised agriculture. Thus, heather moorland

managed for sporting provides a refuge for wildlife, and in particular for threatened species of bird. There is of course some truth in this, though it is hardly the
truth that the purpose of sporting management is the conservation of natural habi-
tats. Heather managed for game is in fact a degraded habitat, where 'regular
burning leads to a dominance of heather at the expense of various lichens and
mosses, as well as a loss of the intimate mixture of dwarf shrubs'.[51] In most cases
it is a virtual heather monoculture – though it is the grouse which are more often
referred to as the 'crop'. But even if there are conservation benefits of a kind, these
are purely contingent effects. There exists no *commitment* to such benefits. They
are incidental to the private benefits of sporting use. But then the same consideration applies to any benefits that sporting may provide to the local economy.
Once the (timeless) picture of a balanced, traditional use closely integrated with
the local rural 'community' is removed, the nature of these benefits suddenly
seems less certain, and it becomes clearer that, in actual fact, any benefits are very
limited indeed.

Access, sporting and land conservation

Both the threat, then, and what is actually threatened, are shown for what they
are once the veil of ideological misrepresentation is lifted. Public behaviour is not
typified by criminal acts. Nor can a general right of access be characterised as just
such behaviour as this raised to a level of anarchy by a licence to go anywhere at
will. But neither can game management be seen as essential to the conservation
of the uplands or to the prosperity of marginal rural areas. Nor can any threat to
such management be counted as a threat to conservation or the rural economy.
The only real threat here, in fact, is that of an intrusion upon a privileged leisure
activity which has no vital connection with either the environment or the local
community. It is physical, not in any terms relevant to the management of the
land, but only in the sense that it is *spatial*. And only in so far as that space is
defined as an exclusive *social* space, *belonging* to a particular group – as for
example a private room or, perhaps more relevantly, a country mansion or a
stately home. The value of sporting is that of a positional good. It is not the
activity itself but the exclusive nature of the activity that is brought into question
by the proposed right.

In its present form, the sport of grouse shooting originated in the mid-nineteenth century. It relied on the existence of a modern transport system (the
railways) to get from the south of the country to the northern moors. It relied also
on modern gun technology, employing new (breach-loading) guns that could be
rapidly reloaded. Its development was typically financed by profits from urban
rents and mineral rights. It was, in other words, a product of the Industrial
Revolution.[52] Indeed, its origins are reflected in the nature of the sport itself. The

'guns' are static in a line of butts. The birds are rounded up by groups of beaters and driven *en masse* over the butts to be shot. The sportsmen are kept in continuous action by loaders who service a 'pair' of guns. (A concession to tradition here. It would be 'unsporting' to use an automatic gun that provided for more that two shots. But then this would also obviate the use of a servant to reload). The aim is to slaughter and 'bag' as many birds as possible.

As a countryside tradition, then, the sport in its present form has remarkably urban-industrial characteristics. By way of contrast, 'rough' shooting, the form from which the present sport was derived, involves the guns ranging the moor with dogs to walk up the prey. It is 'rough' in the sense that it involves some physical exertion and some contact with and knowledge of the surrounding environment – even though the 'guns' are as likely nowadays to have been brought to the moor in four-wheel-drive vehicles over tracks constructed at public expense. If the end were in fact *sporting*, then, this would be the preferred activity. And any actual physical problems concerning the management of public access, including those to do with closure periods, would be rendered insignificant. Most often, the position of those supporting public rights would be that of Howard Hill, 'that the needs of the few will have to take second place to those of the majority'.[53] But there is clearly a simple alternative to the complete extirpation of grouse shooting. Rough shooting has, at least, intrinsic value as a sport. It also has a closer affinity with the natural environment. That affinity would extend to the management of heather moorland for conservation ends, since the 'rough' sport does not require a heather monoculture of the kind necessary to the production of an overplus of grouse. This alternative, however, could not offer the luxury product in exclusive surroundings that is presently maintained at the cost of common values and of the public purse.

NOTES

1   Nigel Curry, *Countryside Recreation, Access and Land-use Planning*, E & FN Spon, 1994, Sect 3.6, p 73.
2   Moorland Association, *Comments on the Government's Consultative Proposals for further Legislation on Common Land*, 1987.
3   According to the Open Spaces Society, the heather commons (i.e. those commons actively managed for grouse shooting) include about 1500 sq kms, or more than a third, of all English commons. They cover approximately 60% (by area) of the commons of Northern England. The Moorland Association, meanwhile, claims a membership managing 2400 sq kms of heather moorland, out of an estimated 2800 remaining in England and Wales.
4   Moorland Association, op cit, Sect J.1.
5   ibid, Sect I.4.
6   ibid, Sect D.1.
7   ibid, Sect C.6.

8   ibid, Sect B.6.

9   This is in fact the case, critical of the Royal Commission, that was argued twenty years earlier by D R Denman, in his *Commons and Village Greens*. An extract from this book is included as an appendix to the *Comments*. It is characteristic, in its attitude to access, of a period which also saw the publication of Michael Dower's *Fourth Wave*. On the latter see Ch 5, pp 72-3 above.

10   Marion Shoard, *This Land is Our Land*, 2nd ed, Gaia Books Ltd, 1997, p xviii.

11   *Royal Commission on Common Land 1955–1958: Report*, Cmnd 462, HMSO, 1958, p 104, Para 316.

12   Moorland Association, op cit, Sect C.5.

13   ibid, Sect A.1 (italics added).

14   Olivia J Wilson, 'Landownership and Rural Development in the North Pennines: a Case Study', Journal of Rural Studies, Vol 8, No 2, pp 145–58, 1992.

15   Moorland Association, op cit, Sect C.4.

16   David Riddle, 'The National Trust and Agriculture - An Overview' at NT website: www.nationaltrust.org.uk (as at Jan 2003).

17   ibid.

18   Moorland Association, op cit, Sect A.1.

19   A seemingly more cultivated version of this piece of sophistry is offered by Roger Scruton in a book recently produced by the Countryside Group, an offshoot of the Countryside Movement (the book is ironically titled *A Countryside for All*). The landscape, apparently, 'owes its beauty and its fertility to the fact that it is privately owned'. It is a national asset 'only in the sense that Shakespeare is a national asset'. If Shakespeare 'belongs' to anyone, he belongs to the public. His work belongs to individuals in so far as it has shaped their lives, in providing a discourse whose meaning lies in the fact that it is shared by others. If ever there was a literary landscape in which a right to roam may be said to exist by virtue of the values it represents, it is that of Shakespeare. This is not what Mr Scruton intends, but it is the only way his words can be taken to *mean* anything. Just the same is true of the phrase 'a national asset', not excepting the linguistic mystifications of private landowners and their apologists.

20   Moorland Association, op cit, Sect K.1.

21   ibid, Sects K.4–K.7.

22   ibid, Sect C.5.

23   ibid, Sect K.4.

24   ibid, Sect D.1.

25   ibid, Sect L.2.

26   ibid, Sect B.6.

27   ibid, Sect I.5.

28   ibid, Sect I.4.

29   ibid, Sect C.9.

30   ibid, Sect C.7.

31   ibid, Sect C.5.

32   ibid, Sect I.10.

33   ibid, Sect I.2.

34   ibid, Sect C.8.

35   ibid.

36   ibid, Sect A.1.

37   ibid, Sect B.9.

38   ibid, Sections D–H.

39   On the other northern AONBs, see Chapter 4 above.

40   Lancashire County Council, Response (June 1998) to the DETR *Consultation Paper* on access.

41   Curry, op cit, 3.64, p 65.

42   Moorland Association, op cit, Sect D.3.

43   The attitude of the courts to the possibility of a right to roam *(jus spatiandi)* is discussed in Tim Bonyhady, *The Law of the Countryside*, Professional Books, 1987, Part II, Chap 2.

44   Moorland Association, op cit, Sect C.5.

45   ibid, Sect I.1.

46   ibid, Sect B.6.

47   ibid, Sect G.8.

48   Howard Hill, *Freedom to Roam*, Moorland Publishing, 1980, Ch 3, p 46. Quoting Royce, *Clarion Handbook, 1936–7.*

49   ibid.

50   See Ch 5 above, pp 64 ff.

51   ITE/NERC, *Heather in England and Wales*, HMSO, 1989. Quoting Pearsall, 1968.

52   On the nineteenth century origins of the present sport of 'driven' grouse shooting, see Ch 2, pp 21ff above.

53   Hill, op cit, p 115.

7

Public Rights and Private Interests

In its response to the Common Land Forum, the Moorland Association offered a detailed critique of the Forum's proposals for access in so far as they applied to the heather commons of the north. It was this which came to be seen as the crux of the disagreement over commons reform. If, however, the analysis in Chapter 6 is accepted, what was at issue here had little to do with the physical problems of access or of access management. The Association's opposition to a public right of access was merely one aspect of a much broader case which opposed private to public interest claims. Its perceived importance as the major obstacle to reform was in fact a reflection of the view that was now a commonplace of the discourse of access as a threat to the countryside and of its incompatibility with conservation ends. The access 'problem' was therefore doubly misrepresented.

If the *Comments* is seen for what it is – as a statement of the case for private property rights – it defines a position that is more clearly opposed to the original proposals of the Royal Commission. The Commission had offered a coherent and wide-ranging definition of public rights that had far more radical implications. It had not only conceived of access as a fundamental principle, a 'prerequisite' of both the preservation and the conservation management of the commons; it had also proposed a strong 'guardianship' role for the public authorities, a role that was itself seen to be derived from basic rights belonging to the public. In a very real sense, these radical proposals implied much more than a simple legislative reform. They defined what was, in effect, an alternative discourse – a different way of conceiving of the public interest in respect of the countryside. The prioritisation of access and the recognition of its complementary relationship with public concerns for preservation, protection and conservation, represented a fundamental shift of emphasis, away from a paradigm of private stewardship and towards one of public guardianship. It therefore implied a redefinition not only of the elements of public policy but of the way these elements related to each other. If access was not in conflict with land or conservation management then the 'stewards' of the countryside could no longer be conceived of as protecting the public against itself.

Property rights and public policy

This assertion of public rights constituted a direct challenge to exclusive ownership claims. But it also served to undermine accepted notions which attributed a privileged insight to private interests even in matters concerning the public good. In some part, this alternative view reflected the 'special' status of common land. Thus, the Commission had drawn upon, and proposed extensions to, existing legal provisions related to the commons. It had done so, however, in a way that consciously incorporated a more radical strand of the tradition lying behind the earlier acts of parliament. This alternative view has already been referred to.[1] It reflected, for example, the more progressive aspirations of the organised working class, with its alternative political vision of the countryside. The proposals of the Royal Commission, then, might well be understood in this much broader sense. If, as the Moorland Association claimed, common land was like any other private land, this would itself imply a much wider applicability of the principles defined by the Commission.

This alternative view, however, should by no means be taken to be incompatible with the rights of private property. It should be seen, rather, as inimical to a particular *conception* of these rights. The institution of common land is itself often seen as archaic – as an anachronism from 'the time when much of our land was wild [and] ownerless' involving quaint 'odd-sounding rights like herbage and pannage, turbary and piscary, estovers and brakes'.[2] Clearly, this is untrue of the shared grazing of the uplands where, in so far as neither has been affected by the more recent process of privatisation, both common land and a comparable area that is not common continue to be managed under a regime of shared use that is as relevant today as it was in the past. But what is *remarkable* about this view of common land as an 'archaism' is that it is considered to be *exceptional* in this sense. The Royal Commission had drawn inspiration from a tradition which, in its origins, constituted an attempt to redefine the institution of common land in terms that would express the modern conception of a *public* good. No such process of redefinition can be said to have been applied to the archaism of the 'exclusive' rights attached to private land. The proposal that common land, for example, or 'open country', is 'like any other sort of private property' ignores obvious differences of kind, proportion and scale that make a literal nonsense of the statement. As an expression of power and privilege, on the other hand, private rights of this kind are not only inadmissible in a democratic society; they are also incompatible with any idea of a common good transcending that of private interests. Yet it is this conception of private rights that currently prevails in property law and that has determined the development of countryside law and policy.

The most obvious, and perhaps the most important, example of this is the National Parks and Access to the Countryside Act of 1949, which incorporated a resolution of public and private interests that has been definitive in the post-war period. As in the case, already examined, of the 1965 Commons Registration Act, the legislation of 1949 remodelled original proposals for change that had been far more radical in their implications. Two major aspects of the resulting 'post-war settlement' are of immediate relevance here. First, the 1949 Act institutionalised a division between public concerns for access and for conservation that was grounded in a perception of conflict between the two. The more obviously *political* conflict here was that between access interests and the interests of farmers and landowners. The latter, however, had already been proposed as the future guardians of the landscape and of the traditional countryside by the Scott Report on rural land use (1942). Farming and forestry had, on this basis, been largely exempted from development control under the provisions of the Town and Country Planning Act of 1947.[3] Specific concerns for nature conservation, meanwhile, would also be 'removed from the realms of land-use planning'.[4] They were to be defined in strictly scientific terms, in a way that offered little threat to ownership interests. On the contrary, the exclusivity of private property rights was to provide a legal basis for exclusionary policies on the part of nature conservationists, who in many cases held to a view of 'natural' ecosystems which also saw access, and indeed any human presence, as intrinsically damaging.

A second major aspect of the 1949 reforms was that public concerns for both access and conservation were to be defined in terms of existing private property rights. Any extension of public rights, that is, must be achieved through agreements arrived at voluntarily with individual owners. This might involve the purchase or lease of property rights; or the negotiation of some kind of contractual agreement incorporating financial compensation. The proposals of the Royal Commission, limited though they were to a particular category of land, were clearly opposed to both of these aspects of (what was now) mainstream countryside policy. They implied the possibility of new legal forms which would need to incorporate a radical redefinition of the balance of public and private interests. In contrast, the approved forms and values faithfully reflected the existing laws and institutions of private property. They therefore placed the development and the implementation of public policy firmly under the control of private interests. It is hardly surprising, then, that the 'stewardship' of public concerns by these interests should have had the extremely limited results that it has.

De facto rights and the law of trespass

The limited extent of public rights of access is evident from the work of Tim Bonyhady.[5] Thus, the primary means of access to the countryside is the network of public rights of way (RoWs) – though this is less evident as a 'network' in upland areas. There also exist limited statutory rights of access attached to specific areas of land. These include urban, and certain other, commons; land owned by the National Trust that is covered by statutory provisions for public access; and those areas now owned by the water companies in the Lake District and mid-Wales over which public access was secured by nineteenth century legislation. For the rest, public rights of access depend upon various kinds of market mechanism. This may involve, more certainly, ownership or long leasehold on the part of public bodies, or it may consist of more limited rights secured under short-term contractual agreements.

For much the greater area of open country, however, the public must rely on *de facto* rights of access. The fact that such rights exist is, according to Bonyhady, a result of a refusal on the part of the courts strictly to enforce the exclusive rights of owners in instances considered to be trivial or 'vexatious'. The interpretation of private rights by the courts, then, has acted as a balance to their otherwise exclusive nature. As is evident in the case of Scotland, however, the extent of the land involved may be of equal importance, given the practical difficulties this presents of enforcing any legal claims.[6] Over more manageable areas, however, there also exists the more effective right '...of English landowners...to use self-help measures to exclude the public'. In contrast, for example, to Norway, '...there are [no] restrictions on the circumstances in which landowners may fence [around] uncultivated land'. But '...apart from erecting fences, English landowners and their employees – notably gamekeepers – may warn off and then use reasonable force to expel intransigent trespassers. Through these means, members of the public, especially over the last hundred years, have been and continue to be excluded from large parts of rural England'.[7]

De facto rights are not only uncertain. They are also problematic in the sense that they tend to benefit only those few with the knowledge and the confidence to exercise them; who may, to a greater or lesser extent, imply or express a complicity with the exclusionary policies of landowners. Meanwhile, the contingent nature of such rights has more recently been underlined by the enactment in 1994 of the Criminal Justice and Public Order Act. In effect, the Act criminalises *de facto* rights of access by defining the new offences of 'aggravated trespass' and 'trespassory assembly'. The former might apply to any knowing or 'deliberate' interference with the lawful aims or activities of an owner or occupier. It therefore means that *de facto* access (i.e. trespass) may now be treated as a criminal rather than a civil offence. The offence of 'trespassory assembly', meanwhile,

'extends protection of private property rights against those expressing commu-
nity-regarding values'[8] – including groups protesting against the exercise of
'exclusive' private property rights.

The market as value: 'commodification'

As with the existing civil law, the way this legislation will be applied is a matter
for the courts. However, the re-definition of trespass as a criminal offence must
be seen in the context of current economic trends involving the 'commodification'
of the countryside. Thus, the development of payment schemes for public
'goods' such as access and conservation has itself further entrenched the notion
of exclusive private ownership, whilst simultaneously undermining the legitimacy
of public interest claims. The more recent extension of these schemes, under the
agri-environment measures introduced in 1992, was proclaimed as, amongst
other things, a 'new access initiative'. Such schemes have also been widely seen
(currently as part of the Rural Development Regulation) as a model for the
projected major reform of the European Union's Common Agricultural Policy
(CAP). Yet:

> these new proposals really do little more than confirm the continuation
> of traditional values and the asymmetric [nature] of public subsidies for the
> maintenance of the libertarian freedom of farmers and landowners...
> Having supported, certainly in financial terms, the destruction of the coun-
> tryside and its subsequent reinstatement, the public is now being
> committed to pay yet again for the privilege of viewing what all its subsi-
> dies have achieved: a legal means of diverting public funds into the income
> and capital worth of landowners and some farmers... Rather than signi-
> fying the acceptance of public rights in the countryside as a legitimate aim
> of public policy...the dualism of purchased access 'rights' to pre-deter-
> mined areas combined with punitive consequences [i.e. under the 1994
> Criminal Justice Act] for those who fail to adhere to the new market imper-
> ative, is more redolent of a return to the class schisms of the past... Public
> access to the countryside has [once more] been appropriated by public
> policy and packaged as an enhanced citizen 'right', while actually reaf-
> firming the hegemonic power of property and its owners at the expense of
> the wider citizenry.[9]

In short, the continuing trend of a shift towards market mechanisms in the
securing of public goods, and the potential for the further development of these
mechanisms as a major element of future CAP reform, has redefined the context
in which the provisions of the Criminal Justice Act will be interpreted by the

courts. The power to exclude informal *de facto* access, for example, is essential to the sale of access as a commodity. Such developments suggest that the courts may well in the future take a much stricter line in applying the new laws of trespass. This shift towards market values is, meanwhile, equally evident in the case of conservation policy. In this case, regulated access may form a part of the commodity, or *de facto* access may be excluded by virtue of a presumed conflict. More generally, the employment of market mechanisms in all of these cases reflects wider changes affecting countryside policy as a whole, which are the consequence of existing and projected structural reforms in the agricultural industry.

Property rights and common interests

The nature of existing rights in relation to the countryside, and the more recent shift towards the commodification of public goods, may be more clearly understood with reference to Table 5. The table is adapted from a study carried out by the Centre for Leisure Research (CLR) for the Countryside Commission in the mid-80s.[10] The study was concerned with the nature of access, and with how it might be seen in terms of the relative accessibility of the countryside to a range of social and interest groups. The latter included recreationists, conservationists, local authorities, countryside managers and ownership interests, each of whom was seen to express differing, though related, 'ideologies' of the countryside. Each of the groups, that is, started from a different set of assumptions, attitudes and values which involved a characteristic way of 'seeing' the countryside. This in turn defined what were and what were not accepted to be legitimate uses of countryside 'resources'. The different ideologies could be related to each other along a scale of values ranging from the public to the private. These in turn were closely correlated with 'preferred' mechanisms through which provision for access might be made.

The scale of values is shown in Table 5, together with the corresponding mechanisms. In its original form the table included only policy mechanisms related to access.[11] Quite clearly, though, the correspondence also extends to conservation provision. In the context of the present discussion, then, Table 5 indicates the range of existing types of provision. It also shows how the shift towards market provision may be seen both in terms of the mechanisms employed and of the ideological values they imply.

In relation to access, the weighting of provision towards market mechanisms is clear, with recent policy developments overwhelmingly at this end of the scale. Proposed changes in the CAP would push the imbalance even further in this direction. *De facto* rights are placed at the opposite extreme, reflecting the ideology of a freedom, or right, to roam. A general 'right to roam' might alter-

Table 5. The countryside: policy mechanisms, rights and ideology

Access mechanisms	Ideology	Corresponding conservation mechanisms
	Non-market	
de facto access right to roam	common interests expressed as land rights	public guardianship of a common possession
rights of way rights of open access	public rights over private land	protected species and immediate living-space (Wildlife and Countryside Act 1981) C&RoW Act provisions for SSSIs
	Market	
access agreements management agreements with access element 'agri-environment' schemes public/quasi-public ownership	public intervention in the market	management agreements (local authority) 'negotiable' agreements (eg English Nature) 'agri-environment' schemes National Nature Reserves/trust ownership
ownership rights sporting rights permissive access (e.g. clubs/groups under lease, licence, day-ticket)	private property rights	private conservation bodies game/estate amenity conservation voluntary initiatives on private land

[Adapted, with the permission of the Countryside Agency, from: Centre for Leisure Research, 1986, *Access to the Countryside for Recreation and Sport*, Countryside Commission].

natively be placed under the next category of 'public rights over private land'. However, in so far as it implied that the land in question had some kind of special status, it should be placed in the same category as that afforded to *de facto* rights. The suggestion might be, for example, that the land belonged to the public in some sense, or that there ought to be some kind of public/private co-ownership defined in terms of the rights attached to it. Or that, in effect, the land 'belongs' to no-one. The proposals of the Royal Commission are of relevance here, in that they bring together concerns for access and for conservation management in a relationship to land that is seen to warrant preservation because of its special characteristics. Such land might still be 'private' land. But there would also be a real sense in which it belonged to the public. In contrast, the so-called right of access legislated for in the Countryside and Rights of Way Act 2000 (C&RoW Act) carries with it no such implications.

In the case of conservation provision, contractual and other market mechanisms have enjoyed a virtual monopoly. In this area, then, proposed CAP changes would be largely a matter of an increased coverage. Existing provision which falls into the 'public rights' category is limited to that covering protected species and their 'home' sites – though similar protection has recently been extended by the new provisions for Sites of Special Scientific Interest (SSSIs) in the C&RoW Act. Planning law is not included here because of its very limited applicability to rural land. Existing categories of designated land (other than SSSIs) are also omitted because, in so far as they are effective, they rely not on 'public rights over private land' but on market mechanisms. Again, proposals such as those of the Royal Commission would be placed at the extreme (rights) end of the scale. In contrast to planning law, for example, they imply not only the negative powers of development control, but also the positive management of the land for determined ends.[12]

The concept of ideology is very loosely applied in the CLR study. It is clear, however, from Table 5 that it might be usefully employed in a wider sense to describe a *dominant* ideology of private property rights, expressed largely in terms of a market philosophy; and a corresponding, though distinctly marginalised, ideology of public rights. The general shift of values noted above can be seen in these terms, as can the overriding importance of private property rights in determining the nature of public policy as a whole. In this latter case, the idea of 'dominance' carries with it a number of implications. The ideology of private property rights should be seen not only as having determined the form and much of the content of public policy. It has also determined the discourse of the countryside – in a way that defines how policies are conceived of and discussed, or problems debated and resolved.

This is evident, for example, in the relative weight of the opposed ideas, discussed above, of private 'stewardship' (Moorland Association) and public 'guardianship' (Royal Commission). It is not simply that the suggestion of a public role in this context would be considered to be marginal, or 'radical', or merely eccentric. It is that the discourse of stewardship *incorporates* the public values expressed in the distinction made here, projecting them as a mask of intentions or activities which most often serve only private interests. The same kind of analysis may be applied to other key words, such as 'nature', 'natural', 'traditional', or 'local community'; or, for example, to the doctrine of 'voluntarism' ('the voluntary principle') as defining the application of public policies to private land (where apparent claims to a democratic right of voluntary agreement imply exclusive private property rights of a kind that are anti-democratic). Though the employment of such terms carries with it the force of a legitimate public concern, they almost invariably obscure what are purely private ends. Yet they define the way people think about, discuss and debate the countryside and rural policy.

The prospect for reform

Both the paucity of public rights and the importance of policy mechanisms embodying a market philosophy are a reflection of the way private property rights have determined the development of countryside policy. The very limited extent of provision for access and conservation, however, is more obviously a consequence of their relative unimportance in an area of policy that has been largely defined by the interests of the agricultural industry. Thus, it is the existing and projected structural changes in agriculture that have provided the dynamic for the more recent elaboration of market mechanisms listed in Table 5. All of the market mechanisms of this kind may in fact be thought of as derivative of agricultural policy – though in a rather odd sense. They are, in effect, a buying back of agricultural subsidies which, because of the nature of the subsidy regime, may be seen as rights attached to the ownership or occupation of the land. The form of this regime is itself a reflection of the dominance of private property interests. In turn, it is subsidies such as these that, in the post-war period, have determined the value of land, both as a capital asset and as a source of income. In the same way, the 'market price' of access and conservation policies is completely artificial. 'Since most farm income comes by one route or another from support, compensation for profit foregone is, in effect, compensation for that loss of support'.[13] But the nature of the 'product' is equally artificial. What is 'for sale' is little more than a short-term contractual agreement to refrain from, or to set a limit to, environmentally destructive activities that are also subsidised by the state.

If market mechanisms are derivative in this way, the sense in which the agricultural industry may itself be said to be governed by a market philosophy is similarly misleading. Under the CAP regime farmers have enjoyed a guaranteed market for whatever they could produce. No other industry has ever been subsidised in this way or to this extent. And though the level of support for production has been reduced by the imposition of various types of quota since the mid-1980s, such policies have themselves only been imposed at the cost of further 'compensation'. In the UK, 'governments have chosen to direct European [production] subsidies to the largest farmers. This is why the policy has been uniquely damaging to the British countryside'.[14] The profits, then, even of these larger-scale and supposedly highly efficient agri-businesses, have been totally dependent on state subsidy. As in the case of access and conservation 'products', the 'market' is a creature of the state (or of the EU).

It is a measure, then, of the strength of their ideological *representation* that farmers and landowners are still confidently (and successfully) asserted to be, on the one hand, highly efficient entrepreneurs, and on the other, the natural stewards – or even the 'creators' – of the countryside. Each of these representations, despite their mutual incompatibility, carries with it the force of legitimacy in its relevant context of use. Yet their power, as facets of a dominant ideology, depends in turn upon two basic facts. First, that the values and assumptions they assert reflect, or are embodied in, existing laws and institutions. And second, that any changes in the latter will continue to carry these same values and assumptions. For such an ideology to enjoy a continued dominance, in other words, depends on political power of a kind sufficient to determine the nature of the law.

That the landed interest does continue to exercise power of this kind in the area of countryside law and policy will already be apparent from the preceding chapters. The question of immediate importance here, however, is whether or not this interest group will be allowed to dictate the form of the large-scale changes in countryside policy which now seem inevitable. And, if not, what should be the form of any alternative? The present study has sought, as a central concern, to clarify the kinds of issue that are at stake in this case, and to establish the nature and the terms of any wider debate. It has also suggested that there does exist an alternative model defining the relationship of public and private rights – though its adoption would involve changes that went beyond a simple legislative reform. It would require, most importantly, a shift of political power towards the representation of public interests of a kind that would clear the way for legal and institutional change. But the significance of such changes would in turn depend on the extent to which they could provide a framework for a new discourse of the countryside, embodying public ends in a way that was not simply a veiled representation of private interests.

If such a prospect seems unlikely, it is changes of just this scale that are projected in the proposed reform of the CAP. The kinds of reform that have been most widely discussed, in the case of the UK, involve an end to the present regime of agricultural production subsidies and a more or less comprehensive shift of resources into environmental and social support policies. That something of this kind must now happen is considered to be inevitable for two reasons. Firstly, the proposed enlargement of the EU to include a number of East European countries would mean that the existing regime of production subsidies could not be sustained in the longer term at present levels. Secondly, the CAP regime has come under increasing attack for its effects on world trade, first through the General Agreement on Tariffs and Trade (GATT) and more recently from the World Trade Organisation.

The scale of the changes that will be required implies a corresponding need for a comprehensive reassessment of the aims of public policy. This should also be seen as an opportunity for the first time to define a coherent vision of the future of rural areas in terms of clearly stated public objectives that are not open to manipulation by private interests. In the past, the support of agricultural development has dominated rural affairs. But if the present system of agricultural subsidies is to come to an end, there exists no reason, other than a failure of political will, for the continuation of policies that are mere derivatives of a discredited regime. As we have seen, however, the forces of inertia are deeply rooted – in the existing structures of political power, in the laws and institutions of private property, and in the countryside discourse itself. A piecemeal approach to reform is therefore not enough, nor is the kind of negotiated change that has in the past invariably been turned to the service of private ends. What is needed is a wholesale revision of law and policy of a kind sufficient to engage with the private interests opposed to change.

What has happened is the opposite of this. Thus, the DETR *Consultation Paper* on commons reform, and the subsequent *Common Land Policy Statement* produced by DEFRA,[15] follow, in their crucial aspects, a model based on 'the voluntary principle' that was adopted by the preceding Conservative government. The reforms they propose are remarkable only for the lack of insight they display into the issues surrounding the future of the commons. An identical failure of vision is apparent in the provisions for access to open country and registered common land in the C&RoW Act. The notion of access as a fundamental expression of public concerns lies at the heart of the debate over commons reform, but it is an idea that is present in neither the *Common Land Policy Statement* nor the C&RoW Act. On the contrary, the right proposed by the C&RoW Act incorporates a conception of access as inherently disruptive and destructive that is the very opposite of this. Whilst – but for a brief reference in an introductory paragraph of the consultation paper to 'complementary' provisions in the C&RoW Act – the question of access has barely been mentioned in the course of the commons consultation.

There is little evidence here of the much-vaunted 'joined-up' thinking, let alone of any comprehensive reassessment of public policy. On the contrary, the government's proposals exhibit a striking lack of internal coherence – almost as if a menu of options had been consulted, with the aim of concocting a legislative melange whose separate ingredients were individually selected for their 'customer appeal'. The so-called right to roam, in particular, may be seen as a half-formed gesture in the direction of a John Smith Memorial Bill that was proposed before the making of 'New' Labour. The resulting provisions for access in the C&RoW Act are not the citizenship right they are claimed to be, but a token exemption conceived of as a consumption good. In short, there is little or nothing in what the government has done, or proposes to do, that demonstrates any commitment to principled reform. Individual measures – for example, those related to SSSIs in Pt III of the C&RoW Act – may imply (or seem to imply) a radical shift, but the idioms, the ideology and the frame of reference have changed by not one whit. The kinds of outcome that may be expected are therefore predictable. For if there is little evidence in the government's thinking of any principled commitment to reform, or indeed of any principles at all, the opponents it will face suffer from no such moral or political blindness.

NOTES

1   See Chapter 3 above.
2   Countryside Commission, *Common Knowledge…?*, CCP 281, 1989.
3   Ann and Malcolm MacEwen, *National Parks: conservation or cosmetics?*, George Allen & Unwin, 1982, p 11.
4   ibid, p 8.
5   Tim Bonyhady, *The Law of the Countryside*, Professional Books, 1987.
6   The position on trespass in Scotland is somewhat complex. It is considered in Chapter 9 below.
7   Bonyhady, op cit, Part I, p 16.
8   Gavin Parker in Charles Watkins (ed), *Rights of Way: Policy, Culture and Management*, Pinter, 1996, Ch 5, p 85.
9   Neil Ravenscroft, 'New Access Initiatives', in Watkins (ed), op cit, Ch 3, pp 44–5.
10   Centre for Leisure Research, *Access to the Countryside for Recreation and Sport*, Countryside Commission, CCP 217, 1986.
11   ibid, Fig 17, p 139.
12   Again, as a result of the C&RoW Act, the same may now be said of SSSIs (which include most or all SPAs and SACs). The effectiveness of the new provisions, in a policy context defined by payment schemes for environmental 'goods', is yet to be proved.
13   Graham Harvey, *The Killing of the Countryside*, Jonathan Cape, 1997, Ch 4, p 53.
14   ibid, Ch 1, p 15.
15   DEFRA, *Common Land Policy Statement 2002*, July 2002.

8

Common Land and Open Country

Common land is special because it is largely untouched. It provides a vital resource in maintaining the viability of upland farms. Much of its open character and special biodiversity survives because it has been used in a traditional way.

Michael Meacher, Ministerial Statement, February 2001.[1]

The recent DETR consultation on commons reform (Feb–Apr 2000)[2] was undertaken independently of that for related proposals in the Countryside and Rights of Way Act. In so far as this was justified, it was because of the 'special' nature and status of the commons. If common land is not special in some sense, there would seem to be little reason for its preservation and protection, let alone for the kind of repeat registration process ('re-registration') that is suggested as a possibility in the consultation paper.[3] But if it is a special case, and if, as it seems, this is accepted by the government, the consultation paper itself offers little reassurance on this score. It contains a number of important proposals previously made in the context of commons reform, but a core element – that of public involvement in the management of common land – is missing. Without this key provision, any reform would lose much, if not all, of its substance and meaning.

Commons reform

Common land is indeed essential to the viability of upland farms. But it is for this very reason that it has not survived untouched and that its traditional use has all but disappeared. Had the proposals of the Royal Commission on Common Land been adopted forty years ago, then the Minister's statement (above) might well have been true. But the Royal Commission's proposals were not adopted; and the uplands – as the Commission itself had anticipated – have changed substantially since that time under the impact of agricultural subsidies, the intensification of farming practices and the extensive amalgamation of farm holdings. As a result of changes such as these, the upland commons (comprising, by area, much the greater part of the commons of England and Wales) have undergone a progressive *de facto* privatisation. Even in those areas where collective management bodies have survived the longest, the amalgamation of holdings has concentrated common rights in the hands of 'improving' farmers, who have shown little interest in the management of the land beyond the running of large numbers of subsidised sheep upon it. At the same time, private sporting interests, in competition with amalgamating farmers, have attempted to secure control of common rights for their own purposes. Nor should sporting use be thought of as a conservation boon. The management of heather moorland for grouse shooting produces, more often than not, a degraded habitat.[4]

Despite the implications of this progressive privatisation,[5] the picture of the collective 'traditional use' of the commons has retained its force. On the one hand, it may represent the unfulfilled aspirations of past and present reformers – perhaps most often now associated with the aim that such use might be restored through a radical reform of the CAP. It is an image, however, that has been far more powerfully deployed by the interests opposed to any changes incorporating public rather than private ends. Hence the strength of the mythic picture proposed by the Moorland Association of a 'balance' of 'sporting' and 'traditional' farming use as an 'integral part' of the society and economy of marginal rural areas - masking what is, in fact, a privileged and exclusive leisure activity which bears no intrinsic relationship whatsoever to the environment or the local community.

This fiction has been allowed – as so often in the past – to determine the 'hands-off' approach that is evident in the government's consultation paper. This may or may not be the result of a pragmatic decision to let well alone. But if it is, the decision was totally misguided. The present government has all too clearly succumbed to the same influences as the Wilson administration of 1964–68, which adopted the Bill that became the 1965 Commons Registration Act from its Tory predecessors with the disastrous consequences that are detailed above in Chapter 4. A similar origin for the DETR consultation paper is described in the introduction to the text:

> The 1995 White Paper "Rural England" ruled out comprehensive legislation. It announced that the [Conservative] Government would instead commission a management guide to identify and publicise best practice in managing common land.[6]

The *Good Practice Guide*,[7] produced by the Countryside and Community Research Unit at Cheltenham and Gloucester College, was published in June

1998. The approach it defines has determined the present government's proposals for commons management. The Guide takes as its starting point the mythic picture described above:

> The essential character of many commons has remained unchanged through many centuries and common land is widely recognised as a vital national asset because of the limited extent to which man has exploited it.[8]

The implication is that all is well with the commons, and with commons management, for those 'many commons' that have 'remained unchanged' under practices that are claimed to have been 'handed down through nine or more centuries'.[9] If there is any truth in this picture at all, of course, it begs the question of why there is a need for a Good Practice Guide. Not to mention the additional problem, repeatedly stressed by the Guide as of paramount importance, of the 'highly localised patterns of common land [management] over most of England and Wales' that have their origin 'in local custom'. (It is difficult indeed to see what 'good practice' could have to offer in the face of centuries of such locally-rooted experience). In fact, the Guide is based, and based deliberately, on a picture of the commons that was made redundant over 75 years ago, with the abolition of the manorial courts by the 1925 Law of Property Act. How could it be, then, that a fiction such as this was adopted as the foundation of the government's consultation proposals?

The straight answer is given in the consultation paper itself, though it involves yet another mythical entity. Agricultural use and management are issues 'which are important not only to the DETR and the National Assembly for Wales, but also involve the Ministry of Agriculture, Fisheries and Food'.[10] In other words, the question of commons management impinges directly upon the private property rights of farmers and landowners. It therefore involves issues that have been 'traditionally' dealt with by MAFF in terms of 'countryside stewardship' – a myth of equal proportions, and with a very close family resemblance, to that of the 'unchanging' commons.

If common land has retained its special characteristics to any extent, it is as a result, not of any (fictional) private stewardship, but of the public concerns that have been progressively secured by protective legislation from the middle of the nineteenth century. In 1958 the Royal Commission clearly stated the need for the reform of this legislation with the aim of assuring the public interest in the future of common land. The re-establishment of 'traditional' management was to be an integral part of this reform. But the Royal Commission was ignored. And it was because it was ignored that the 1965 Commons Registration Act had the effects that it did in furthering not public but private ends.

'Traditional' management and use is the very substance of any public interest claims in respect of the commons. It is what ought to be, or ought to have been, preserved and protected. The guarantee of this, however, as was perceived by the Royal Commission over forty years ago, is the concept not of private stewardship but of *public guardianship*. This, the Commission proposed, should be secured, in part, by the role it had defined for the local authorities. But any such role must in turn be seen to derive from the public itself. The public right of access was fundamental ('a prerequisite') in this respect, as a tangible expression of 'the public interest'; but, more importantly, as an embodiment of the special sense in which these areas *belong* to the public. Common land is 'special' not only in a purely practical sense, but as an historic focus of public aspirations in respect of the countryside; and, today, as a potential model, or paradigm, for the future expression of those aspirations. Most importantly, it embodies a perception of the *complementarity* of public concerns for access and for conservation, and of the fact that public access is essential to the preservation of those characteristics of the countryside that are valued in and for themselves. In the case of the commons, both public aspirations and the valued characteristics in terms of which they are defined attach to certain historic areas of land. It is this, above all, that is unique, and that makes the commons so important.

If public access is essential to the protection and right management of the commons, however, this is afforded little recognition in the consultation paper. Common land (or, more exactly, registered common land, excepting those areas defined in Section 15(1)) will be subject to the new right of access defined in the C&RoW Act. There is no recognition in the consultation paper that this has any management implications for the commons. Yet, in relation to both land and conservation management, the general right of access in the C&RoW Act is itself conceived of (in so far as the relationship is conceptualised) as a threat. If this is truly the case, it is hard to understand how such a general right can be justified or why it is to be legislated for, or in what sense it may be seen as 'complementary to'[11] the proposals for commons reform contained in the consultation paper.

If, on the other hand, the proposed right of access is to be seen in a positive light, as an integral part of 'the public interest' – as, in its *special* relationship to common land, it has since the middle of the nineteenth century – it is equally difficult to understand why the principles articulated by the Royal Commission, and reaffirmed in some part by the Common Land Forum, are so conspicuously ignored in the consultation paper. The reforms that are projected by the present government include, or derive from, the specific proposals of these bodies in respect of access, of preservation and protection, and of the vesting of unowned commons. These proposals, however, were originally related to each other in a way that was intended to determine the context in which the traditional management of common land would be secured. In contrast, the consultation paper suggests that there should be no provision, in the absence of public ownership, for any public involvement in the management process. In short, the *proposals* in the consultation paper bear no relationship whatsoever to the *principles* which originally determined their purpose. It is because of this that they lack any coherent intention.

Thus, in place of the kind of management schemes defined by the Royal Commission and the Common Land Forum – established under public supervision and incorporating public representation – the formation of private associations is to be 'encouraged', with the specific aim of facilitating entry into agri-environment schemes (an approach that has already been attempted, and proved to be inadequate). The extent to which this 'voluntary' solution will succeed is to depend, in turn, upon the general changes that (it is hoped) will flow from the reform of the Common Agricultural Policy. As in the case of the right of access, this is a general, non-specific proposal. In other words, it ignores the *special* nature of common land. Most importantly, it ignores the extent to which the valued characteristics of the commons have been undermined by their *de facto* privatisation, with the actual disappearance of the institutions and the practices that have supported shared management in the past. In effect, there no longer exists a viable 'private' base upon which to build a 'voluntary' reform.

But if public involvement in the management of the commons was a necessity in 1958 – after what was perceived, even then, as over thirty years of neglect – it is all the more so now. Indeed, the public interest in the future of common land *consists in* the on-going management of the land. The figures produced by the Countryside Commission in 1990[12] – though they relate less to the upland commons than to smaller (lowland) areas of common land, and to commons in the south and east of England – are of obvious relevance here. 70% of the commons in England and Wales (and 78% of the English commons) are subject to no more than one right of common. Many of these are amenity commons which may already be subject to some kind of regulation, but many are not. They may therefore require something more than the kind of solution projected in the consultation paper. But this is also true, to an infinitely greater extent, of the kinds of upland common described by the National Trust in its response to the consultation paper[13] – where, in the absence of effective management structures, a significant number of rights holders (together with any number of other interests that may be involved) possess no means of co-operative action or of dispute-resolution. As the government concluded in the case of access to registered common land and open country, the voluntary option is insufficient to the end that is desired (i.e. 'traditional' management).

The Common Land Policy Statement

This misrepresentation of the history of the commons, and of their present state, is sustained in the *Common Land Policy Statement* issued by DEFRA in July 2002 in response to the consultation:

> Over the past 40 years, various initiatives have been taken to protect common land, to ensure it is effectively managed and to increase the ability of the public to enjoy it. The Commons Registration Act of 1965 established registers of land and the rights held over it. In June 1998 the "Good Practice Guide on Managing the Use of Common Land" was published. More recently, this Government introduced landmark legislation – the Countryside and Rights of Way Act 2000 – to give the public a right of access on foot to all registered common land where such a right does not already exist...So, a great deal has been done, but more action is needed...[to build] a sound foundation on which to base the future protection of what the 1958 Royal Commission described as the "last reserve of uncommitted land in England and Wales".[14]

As a summary of 'the past 40 years', nothing could be further from the truth. The Commons Registration Act of 1965 gave no 'protection' to common land. Its effect was exactly the opposite. Neither did the *Good Practice Guide* do anything to 'ensure effective management'. It was, at best, a piece of fiction. Whilst the projected right of access, if it can be said to be a 'landmark' in any sense, is anything but the sound foundation proposed by the Royal Commission as the prerequisite of its proposals for reform. On the contrary, the so-called right of access conferred by the C&RoW Act is conceived of as a threat to the protection and right management of the land.

Clearly, there is no intention on the part of the government that public access should play the kind of foundational role proposed for it by the Royal Commission on Common Land. But the policy statement also lacks a coherent framework for reform of the kind articulated by the Commission. The Commission had conceived of access as the fundamental element of a group of interrelated principles and values which defined the *meaning* of the commons as an object of public concern. In the policy statement, questions of meaning and intention are (once more) displaced by a fiction, in which 'a great deal has been done' over 'the past 40 years' to assure the continuation of a state of affairs in which 'common land is special because it is largely untouched'.[15] In this light, of course, there already exists a 'sound foundation' on which to build, and the obvious need is to strengthen existing provisions – there is simply no case for radical reform. Accordingly, the policy statement adopts a piecemeal approach to the issues that is not only inadequate in itself, but has produced a rag-bag of proposals that are barely compatible. The stated aims are clear enough. Common land 'should in the present day and age be regarded principally as a public resource'.[16] It must therefore be protected from 'any uses that would reduce its value to the community as a whole'.[17] But there is little evidence of any commitment to these ends in the policy statement.

The crucial proposals for the voluntary reform of 'agricultural use and management' are considered below. But the speciousness of the government's position, and the emptiness of its commitment to public ends, is more immediately obvious in the measures that will supposedly ensure the 'special' status of the commons. On the one hand, it is suggested that ('generally') common land should not in future be subject to deregistration – its status should be assured (excepting only the case of compulsory purchase, where 'exchange land' would be given to replace any common that was lost). But it is difficult to reconcile this commitment with the proposal to allow, without any limit of time, the removal from the registers of land that was 'wrongly' registered 'according to the definition of common land under the Commons Registration Act 1965':

> The scope of this provision will cover not only dwellings and gardens that have been wrongly included, but any land that should not have been registered, including agricultural land and public highways. There will be no time limit on applications for deregistration and eligibility to apply will not be confined to landowners only but is likely to be restricted.[18]

What this means – and the implication is clearly emphasised – is that areas of land that fall into the categories described above in Chapter 2 as 'the common lands' (excepting those subject to rights of common, or sole rights) may now be removed from the registers, on the grounds that they do not satisfy the definition of common land under the 1965 Act. This includes regulated pastures; but it also covers the many other instances where land subject to rights of taking is held under a trust – for example by a town, or parish, body.[19] These are not, however, the only areas that will be affected. The provision applies equally to land that was registered where the rights over it were leased, and not common, rights. There are a significant number of cases of this kind – though registration, most often, was a voluntary act on the part of the interests involved at the time. But since land subject only to leased rights does not satisfy the 1965 definition, it may now be 'removed from the registers'.[20]

The provision is curious, given the government's commitment to the preservation and protection of the commons, and given the extensive areas of land that are involved. (The policy statement even offers an inducement under this measure; whereby land that is deregistered, in so far as it is not 'open country', will cease to be subject to the access provisions of the C&RoW Act). But stranger still is the apparently even-handed proposal to allow a parallel 're-registration' process for certain provisional registrations which failed under the 1965 Act.

The justification given in the policy statement for this proposal concerns the waste land that failed to be registered as a result of the court decision in re Box Hill (1979) because it was not 'of a manor' in the required legal sense.[21] The judgement in re Box Hill was overturned by the courts in 1990, through the Hazeley Heath decision – which, though it is not mentioned in the policy statement, is the implied source of the present proposal. The ruling in Hazeley Heath was made on the grounds that the interpretation in re Box Hill 'would defeat the reasoning of the recommendations of the report of the Royal Commission'. The word 'of' in the phrase 'waste land of the manor', it was decided, should be taken to refer, not to present possession by the lord of the manor, but to the historical status of the land 'in the days when copyhold tenure still existed'.[22]

If, however, the question is one of the historical status of the land, then the definition of 'common land' under the 1965 Act is completely overturned. And, if this is the case, it is impossible to understand how the government can simultaneously propose that areas subject to leased rights (all of which are historically common land)[23] may be removed from the registers on the grounds that they do not 'satisfy' the 1965 definition. Indeed, the question of historical status opens a whole can of worms related to the common lands (why, on these grounds, should a regulated pasture, or land subject to rights held under a trust, be liable to be removed from the register?). And this is not even to mention the wider implications of the fact that the Hazeley Heath decision is based on 'the reasoning of the recommendations of the report of the Royal Commission'. Because if the policy statement as a whole is subjected to reasoning of this kind, it becomes impossible to justify.

The position on the protection of the commons that remain on the register is somewhat clearer. Section 194 will be extended to cover all registered common land (at present, it applies only to land that was subject to rights of common in 1926). But it is also to be made more 'flexible' – so that the fencing of commons may be allowed, in strictly defined circumstances, in the interests of animal welfare or conservation management. (The possibility of imposing a speed limit on unfenced roads over common land is not even considered, despite the fact that it would, in many cases, make the fencing of the land unnecessary). Meanwhile, local authorities will be encouraged to use their enforcement powers under Section 194 by the provision of a simpler means of putting them into effect. As now, however, the authorities will have no *duty* to act, in circumstances where they have often failed in the past to take the initiative.[24] In a signal omission, a related 'guardianship' role for members of the public is dismissed, on the grounds that action should be left to 'the discretion of the democratically elected councils' – a justification singularly at odds with a provision of just this kind for rights of way in the C&RoW Act.[25]

There is little evidence in any of these proposals of a commitment to 'the future protection of what the 1958 Royal Commission described as the "last reserve of uncommitted land in England and Wales"'.[26] The 'reasoning' of the Commission was grounded in a notion of the intrinsic value of the commons that transcended the rights of private property owners and was expressed in a principled definition of the rights of the public. In contrast, the policy statement has a surface agenda that is defined in these terms – an impression that is mirrored in the superficial 'reasonableness' of the government's 'focus-group' approach to consultation. But if there is one thread that runs through the text of the policy statement it is that of the primacy of private property rights.

Thus, the areas of land that may be considered for re-registration are to be limited on the grounds that landowners are 'entitled to assume that the outcome of the original registration procedure...constituted a final decision...[especially] where the land [is] now used for arable or other purposes not consistent with the character of a common'. They should not now, therefore, be subject to 'the burden [sic] of common land status'.[27] But the Commons Registration Act of 1965 produced no certainty and no 'final decisions' for the land that *was* registered. On the contrary, it opened up the new possibility of deregistration – thus ensuring the very opposite of finality. But if private owners are entitled to certainty and finality 'now', the same is surely true for members of the public? The answer to this question in the policy statement is quite clear. They were not then. And they are not now. For if re-registration is to be a strictly limited exercise, deregistration is to be open-ended; it will be subject to no time-limit; and it will apply to *any* land that does not satisfy the definition of common land under the 1965 Act.

The priority afforded to private property rights is nowhere clearer than in the retention of the voluntary principle in relation to commons management. The policy statement is presented as a tentative document that will be subject to 'further consultation and consideration'.[28] But this was especially true of the issues surrounding agricultural use and management, which would be put to a 'Stakeholder Working Group' made up of 'the interested parties'. The question of commons management, then, was seen to be particularly intractable, not least because it is here that the government's belief in the sanctity of private ownership runs up against practical issues to do with a shared control of the land. The matter, however, is further complicated by the need to make principled provision for the wider public good (a kind of double whammy, then, for an administration with a distinct preference for the 'hidden fist' of market economics). The solutions proposed in the past to these problems have assumed that there should be public

representation on statutory management bodies. The proposal in the policy statement is that there should be statutory provision for two distinct kinds of body; the
one to represent the wider public interest, the other 'agricultural use and management' – though the latter may involve two, or even three, separate tiers of
organisation. The establishment of neither group of structures, however, will be
required. Each must be created 'voluntarily'.

Briefly, the proposal is that there should be a framework of law through which
statutory management bodies ('associations') might be established for each
common (or each local group of commons) by 'those involved – i.e. those with
rights to graze animals on the common'.[29] In addition, a further tier of regional
bodies, elected by members of the local associations, would have powers
(perhaps with administrative support from local authorities) to compile graziers'
registers, to make regulations related to management, to resolve any disputes and
to review rights registrations for possible referral to the Commons
Commissioners. This two- or three-tiered model 'could be instituted in a region
by the existing associations', though it must be done in such a way that 'the role
of [the existing] associations…should not be prejudiced'. The 'involvement' of the
public, meanwhile, would be in the form of representation by the County
Councils and National Parks; who would (if they chose to do so, and if they could
find the necessary resources) be 'empowered to convene broad-based management advisory bodies'.[30] Any statutory management body would be obliged to
'have regard to' the advice of the relevant advisory body – though the latter might
be given stronger powers in the case of a 'protected site' (SSSI, SPA, SAC).[31]

In short, the statutory management bodies – where such bodies existed –
would, between them, be directly responsible for *all* of the key issues that will
determine the future management of the commons. They would control the regulation of use, the maintenance of a 'living' register and the prevention of
overgrazing and supplementary feeding. They would take the initiative if any revision of rights in the commons registers were to be attempted; and might also be
considered the 'suitable body' for the vesting of commons where the ownership
of the land was unclaimed. The government, meanwhile, would exercise 'reserve
powers' where these were necessary, which might also be applied where a statutory management body did not exist (if, that is, a point of application could be
found). So that the government might, in either case, and 'if necessary' 'regulate
the activities of the commoners, and…hold them jointly responsible for any
conditions and penalties that might apply'.[32]

Interestingly, it is the Commoners' Council established under the Dartmoor
Commons Act of 1985 that is taken as the model for the proposed management
structures. But Dartmoor is not an exemplar. It is an exception. Not only are the
commons of the area unique. They exhibit just the kind of historical continuity

that is falsely assumed in the government's proposals to be the general case. The Forest of Dartmoor is registered under the 1965 Act as a single common of over 110 square kilometres. Surrounding it are the 'Commons of Devon'. The latter cover an area of approximately 250 square kilometres. Up until the 1950s, both of these areas of land were considered to form one vast common taking in more than thirty of the surrounding parishes. The Forest itself, moreover, has been in the ownership of the Duchy of Cornwall since the early fourteenth century. And the Duchy also laid claim, until comparatively recent times, to the ownership of the Commons of Devon. All of this great area was included in the National Park that was designated in 1951 – it comprises, in what is more or less a single block of land, nearly 40% of the Park. And though the Commons of Devon were subsequently divided up along the lines of parish and manorial boundaries under the Commons Registration Act of 1965, the Dartmoor Commons Act drew on this longer history of shared identity, ownership and rights.[33] It is this history that is the basis of the Commoners' Council and its constituent associations, whose relationship with the relevant public body – the National Park – is grounded in pre-existing relationships that were also built into the 1985 Act. These determining factors could hardly have been wished into existence. But if the Dartmoor Commons Act, or something like it, is to be a model for the government's proposals, this is exactly what would have to happen. Because the government is not proposing to legislate for them. They must come to pass 'voluntarily'.[34]

The reader is invited, at this point, to refer back to the evidence presented in Chapter 5 of the 'privatisation' of the commons, and to consider, in the light of this evidence, whether proposals of this kind for voluntary change are anything but a fantasy. As is clear from Section 5 of the policy statement, what is intended to drive these changes is reform of the Common Agricultural Policy through the progressive withdrawal of production subsidies, a shift of resources into agri-environment payments and the enforcement of cross-compliance on those in receipt of support. But if CAP reform is to be the driver of change, it simply will not work if an engine of change does not exist. In actuality, the present state of affairs is a 'tragedy of the commons' of the kind described by Garret Hardin.[35] In the absence of effective management institutions, a common resource is there for the taking. In the absence of a price mechanism, the 'hidden hand' can give no guidance. The resulting subsidy-driven free-for-all necessarily has a perverse and destructive effect. In a very real sense, the government's proposal to buy a voluntary solution through the further commodification of public goods is equally perverse.

There are matters of detail to do with the nature of any kind of management body (membership, structure, functions, powers) that are of importance in themselves. They are given a good deal of space in the policy statement, and are also to be a subject of discussion for the Stakeholder Working Group – though perhaps the more important concern should be that the bodies proposed in the policy statement will inevitably be seen by private interests as a means of securing (voluntary) compliance. To focus upon these matters of detail, however, is to be blind to the prior considerations that will determine their meaning and effect. What is so obviously lacking in the government's proposals is a coherent framework of law and policy of a kind that would give legal recognition to the intrinsic value of the commons and would therefore encompass, and give *legitimacy* to, the public interest claims in respect of commons management. It is only within a framework such as this that a shared discourse of common aims and values could exist.

The Countryside and Rights of Way Act 2000

The policy statement discards the values that have attached historically to common land in favour of voluntary market solutions. On the face of it, this kind of approach was rejected for the access to open country and registered common land that was legislated for in the Countryside and Rights of Way Act. On closer examination, however, what is represented as a right is once more seen to be defined as a commodity. The more radical conception of access developed in the context of the commons debate has, even in this case, found no place on the government's agenda. In the C&RoW Act, the projected right of access is conceived of not as a foundational principle but as a (land) use that is in conflict with both land and conservation management. The conflict, in the case of common land and open country, is assumed to be less severe or, at least, capable itself of being 'managed'. Indeed, it is presumably for this reason that a partial (as opposed to a universal) right of access was considered appropriate. But, to this partial allowance has been added a catalogue of exceptions, exclusions and restrictions, to the extent that it is glaringly obvious that what is involved is not a right at all, but the permitted use of a private resource – a commodity which is to be supplied, in this instance, free of charge to the consumer, though under strictly defined conditions. The *right* continues to lie with the owner, of whom the Act requires, in effect, a toleration of limited public 'use'.

If a 'partial' right such as this is not a right at all, this is nevertheless exactly what it has been represented to be, both by the government and by those opposed to public interest claims of this kind. But if this is the case it must also be seen as an exceptional provision, in an area of public policy that was well along the road to agri-environmental commodification. The perception, then, has been of a single, isolated measure, seemingly unrelated to the wider context of law and policy. The kinds of factor potentially at work in such a case, of legislative change placed in an environment completely hostile to its ends, have already been identified in the preceding chapters of this book – in the examination, for example, of the registration process under the 1965 Commons Registration Act. This should be borne in mind in the discussion that follows.

The DETR, in its consultation paper *Access to the Open Countryside in England and Wales*,[36] specified two options for reform. The first involved an extension of existing access provision on a voluntary basis. It was the second option, however, of 'compulsory' legislation for a public right of access, that was finally confirmed in March 1999 in a Commons statement by the Minister of State for the Environment, Michael Meacher. The new right, it seemed, was to form part of a comprehensive 'package' of access proposals which would also include reform of current rights of way provision. The intentions here, at least in respect of the right of access, seemed clear enough. It should be seen as an 'entitlement' belonging to 'all of us'.[37] Legislation for a right was also 'the only way to make sure that people will be free in perpetuity to explore open countryside'.[38]

The proposals for rights of way (RoW) reform would follow lines that had already been laid down by the Countryside Commission.[39] A new, more flexible approach to RoW policy was to be adopted, involving a rationalisation of current provision in the interests of identifiable recreational demand and of the changing needs of private landowners. This new perspective would also see a shift of policy from the securing of historic rights to a more active focus on the utility of the network through rights of way improvement plans. The problem here is that, though the production of the improvement plans is to be funded, there will be no new funding for their implementation. The reasoning behind this omission is to be found in a paper presented by the Countryside Agency to the National Countryside Access Forum in September 2000:

> The Government have consciously decided that there will be no duty on highways authorities to implement their improvement plans because this will:
>   a Encourage more imaginative and forward looking plans;
>   b Allow authorities to bid for funds from other sources to fund the improvements.[40]

The reasoning is certainly eccentric. Local authorities will have a duty to draw up rights of way improvement plans and to report on their implementation. They will not have a duty to put them into effect and will receive no new funding to do so. But this will encourage them to be more 'imaginative and forward-looking'. It is surely more likely that all of the imaginative effort will be invested in the paperwork?[41]

It is clear that the improvement plans are intended to be *in addition to* existing duties. But the latter have been consistently under-resourced; and despite the extra funding provided in recent years by the Countryside Agency (which is now to be withdrawn), most authorities are a very long way behind in their work on both the Definitive Map and the paths network itself. It is also clear, from the government's statutory guidance,[42] that rights of way improvement plans are to be very wide-ranging – and would, perhaps, be better referred to as 'access improvement plans'. They are intended to be integrated not only with the new provisions for open country access (by securing 'linking paths' over enclosed farmland), but also with improvements projected in a range of other plans related to rural development, transport, leisure, tourism, health and disability. It might well be that one or two of the more competitive local authorities will take up this new 'challenge' – at the expense of the less 'imaginative' majority. But the question of funding – or rather the lack of it – is crucial in every one of these policy areas.

Given the lack of committed resources, it is difficult to see how proposals of this kind for the reform of RoW and access provision could, as a general case, have any significant outcome in securing public rights other than through an extension, by *central* government, of an associated market provision (through existing agri-environment schemes, for example, or through some kind of new 'access incentive scheme'). The suggestion that this might be the case, however, should be understood in the broader historical context described above.[43] An increasing reliance on market mechanisms, reinforced by the more recent redefinition of trespass as a criminal offence in the 1994 Criminal Justice Act, has served only to undermine the concept of public rights. But this once more raises the point that, as part of a 'package' of reforms that will otherwise be defined in these terms, the proposal for a public right of access to 'open country' stands out as an obvious anomaly. It goes against the grain of existing policies and more recent trends towards market provision. But exactly the same is true if it is compared with the other (RoW) elements of the reform package. The so-called flexible approach to RoW provision, for example, is totally inconsistent with the criteria of acceptability (e.g. clarity, certainty, permanence) that are suggested as definitive of the value of access in the case of common land and open country.[44]

A month before the Minister's statement on access reform, in February 1999, the government had also released a discussion document[45] on the proposed *Rural White Paper*. The White Paper would involve a comprehensive review of the whole of rural policy, to be carried out jointly by the DETR and MAFF. The package of proposals for the reform of access provision, it seemed, though part of a separate process of consultation, would take its place in this wider-ranging programme. Given, however, that neither the discussion document nor the subsequent *Rural White Paper* suggest any radical changes of law or policy, but rather a shift of resources within the present system, involving relative adjustments in the scale rather than in the kind of provision, the so-called right of access stands out as an anomaly in much the same way as in the previous case. Thus, although 'the reform of both the Common Agricultural Policy and the Structural Funds Regulations...are likely to have important consequences for rural England', in which both the new Regional Development Agencies and Countryside Agency would play an important part,[46] there is no suggestion that this would involve any kind of radical change. The only really new departure of any kind was the suggestion in the discussion document that the DETR and MAFF would 'develop a more cohesive approach to policy development [sic]...taking forward joint planning of countryside programmes'.[47] Given the reported turf wars between MAFF and the DETR, however, and the actual scale of the changes in the whole range of rural policies implied by CAP reform, the suggestion of 'joint working' between the two Departments raised more questions than it answered. Nor, it would seem, has the situation improved much since June 2001, under the stewardship of DEFRA. The latter has more recently (2003) been the subject of an inquiry into its internal workings.[48]

If the right of access is to be introduced as an isolated measure – in a way that might well be seen as a token gesture – it is clear that it will face all the obstacles of political, legal and ideological inertia that have already been examined in detail above. It is obviously in anticipation of this that the proposed right has been considerably watered down, and that the tone of statements concerning access reform has been extremely conciliatory, underlining the extent of the qualifications to which any access over common land and open country will be subjected. Hence the Minister, in confirming the government's choice of the legislative option (rather than that of a 'voluntary' approach) was careful to stress that the 'policy is not of compulsion but of maximising consensus'.[49] The proposed local access forums, which will meet to discuss and advise upon the implementation of the right, would 'be able flexibly to take account of local circumstances, which vary dramatically'.[50] Owners and occupiers would, moreover, 'in general, still be free to use their land [including, for example, common land], subject to the same constraints as at present'.[51] It was, indeed, 'the limited nature of the new right of access' (and not, for example, a matter of principle) that was the basis for the government's refusal to consider any kind of general compensation payment.[52] Not only would the right be closely defined and regulated. The 'right of access will cease for anyone who breaches any of the range of restrictions under the National Parks and Access to the Countryside Act 1949 or who commits a criminal offence. Such a person will automatically lose any statutory right of access and *ipso facto* be subject to the civil law of trespass'.[53]

The proposed right, then, is seen by the government itself as so limited, and so hedged round with qualifications, that the opposition to it will be small in scale.[54] There seem, however, to be two possible outcomes to this approach, neither of which would achieve its stated end. On the one hand the qualifications of the new right – including, amongst other things, a close regulatory regime, a catalogue of permanently exempted areas, and provisions for permanent, long-term, recurring or temporary closures of various kinds – may be so 'successful' that they will simply reproduce the present restricted access regime under a different name. Alternatively, and perhaps this is the more likely outcome, there may be a concerted campaign by owners and occupiers, at both a national and a local level, against the enforcement of a gratuitous derogation of private property rights. In neither of these cases, that is, will the limited nature of the proposed right disarm the opposition in the way that is intended. It will not avoid but will *invite* such opposition. This might take the form of a quiet manipulation of the procedures for the regulation and control of the right or, if this were to prove unsuccessful, it might be expressed in a more overtly political refusal of compromise.

There is, in short, an obvious fallacy in the expectation that a consensus might be achieved in the legislative imposition of a right that is clearly perceived as an anomaly in terms of both present and proposed law and policy. Once more, however, the reasons for expecting an adverse outcome go much deeper that this. It is not only that every opportunity afforded by the qualified nature of the right – over the period of four years or more that implementation is expected to take – will be exploited in the defence of existing rights of property. It is that any such opposition, in the absence of wider reform, will be perceived to be *legitimate*. This is, in essence, the case – derived from existing laws and institutions – that was stated by the Moorland Association. But it is not simply a matter of the attitudes and assumptions of landowners. The proposed reform will leave existing laws and institutions untouched. Not the least of these is the notion of access, that is of *any* access, as inherently disruptive and destructive. As has already been argued at length, this is a keystone of the mainstream discourse of the countryside, which has determined not only basic policy development, but also the institutional forms of provision for both access and conservation. It therefore carries with it the force of 'common sense', or of an inherent necessity. To require, or to impose, an opposite understanding is not quite the case of Alice who, when she protested that she could not believe *impossible* things, was advised half an hour's practice each day. ('Why, sometimes I've believed as many as six impossible things before breakfast'.) It is, though, a close enough approximation. For a positive conception of access to be considered *admissible* would require changes of a completely different kind and scope to those that are at present in train.

Public access as a pivotal issue

It may be helpful here to return for a moment to the idea of access as a focus of the countryside debate, and to examine a little more closely how it has been defined and the implications that such definitions might have. Thus, the Royal Commission conceived of access as the vehicle of a fundamental right of public guardianship. On the other hand, the definition of public access as essentially destructive has provided the basis for a range of alliances of convenience between groups whose interests might otherwise be quite divergent. This has been true, for example, of the relationship between conservationists and landowners, though the former might express their (elitist) views more often in cultural or (supposedly) scientific terms, rather than in the idioms of private property rights. An adverse view of access has also provided the rationale for restrictive policies on the part of local authorities and countryside managers – who might well find common cause with landowners in supporting the legalistic characterisation of any right to roam as necessarily involving the 'sterilisation' of the land.[55]

The simple contrast here is between a negative and a positive conception of access. On the one hand, it is regarded as illegitimate and destructive; on the other, it is seen as the foundation of legitimate public concerns. The reforms and reform proposals of the present government include contradictory elements derived from each of these conceptions. On the one hand, the positive benefits of the right of access to common land and open country are described in terms of physical and spiritual 'enjoyment' or 'refreshment'. On the other, the legislative option is acknowledged to be an imposition, interfering with the 'enjoyment' in a strictly legal sense of the rights of private property. Whilst it is described as a new 'entitlement', however, what is actually proposed is a closely regulated and extremely conditional exemption, which leaves untouched the notion of private property rights as 'exclusive'. Furthermore, it is openly acknowledged that 'the protection of wildlife and environmental crops [sic] is our priority; and…will not be overridden by public rights of access'.[56] There is a recognition, that is, of the essentially destructive nature of the right, which perhaps also has its origin in the legalistic figure of 'sterilisation' – though it more obviously reflects the 'common sense' notions of the mainstream countryside discourse.

The weakness of the proposed right, however, and the way it is hedged round with negative qualifications, are equally an effect of the definition of its 'benefits' as essentially to do with 'enjoyment'. Whether such enjoyment is considered to be physical or 'spiritual', what is implied here is a *consumer* good rather than a right of citizenship. But it is by virtue of such a definition that the right may also be (mis)represented as a species of envy, or destructive *desire*, by the interests opposed to it. A right, however, is not, or does not involve merely, a desire. It is the opposed discourse, that of market economics – including under this heading the definition of citizenship in terms of consumption, and of citizenship rights as, in effect, goods and services purchased with 'the taxpayers' money' – which describes human individuals, not as rights-bearers, but as a bundle of appetites. Though they may be relevant in the context of the 'right' legislated for in the C&RoW Act, notions such as these fail to express the kind of legitimacy, embodying a full sense of the rights of the public, that was intended by the Royal Commission. The values implied, on the contrary, are those of an arbitrary, consumable (and disposable) use. They represent, that is, yet another image of destructive effect. What is clearly at work here is a reduction of the concept of 'rights', and its re-expression in terms appropriate to a market philosophy. But it is philosophies of this school which *define* the individual in terms of greedy appetite; and it is from this definition that the destructive consequences of the (parodied) right of access are deduced. The legal figure of the necessary 'sterilisation' of land by any right to roam has a similar (economic) origin in eighteenth-century theories of political economy, which in turn have their roots in earlier empiricist theories of the rights of private property.

In summary, then, two points should be noted. First, that both the negative and the positive conceptions of access are ideological in their nature. They represent, that is, completely different *systems* of value; the one based on rights of citizenship, the other on market values and private property rights. Secondly, criticisms of any right to roam as inherently destructive are a misrepresentation of the nature of the right that is claimed. It is market theory which conceives of the individual as a bundle of appetites. And it is this conception of the individual, not that of rights theory, which carries with it the implication of 'destructiveness'. The criticism therefore assumes what it pretends to prove. It carries with it the force that it does, however, because it is rooted in the mainstream discourse; and because this in turn reflects the rejection of a *jus spatiandi* by the courts (albeit by a further misrepresentation of the actual judicial interpretation).

What then of the *positive* aspects of a right to roam? First of all, it must imply something more than a right of way. More, that is, than the simple right to pass over the ground with the intention of going somewhere else. It is, therefore, necessarily an assertion of something about the land itself. What it is *not*, though this is what it is invariably implied to be, is the assertion of a right to wander up and down all over the surface of the land (driven, presumably, by unsatisfied 'desire') careless of the consequences. As has already been suggested above (pp 84-5), such a conception of the right to roam (or ramble, or wander) as a 'right to trample' is a figment of the legal imagination: a kind of shadow cast by the legal definition of 'exclusive' private property rights – which indeed do include the right to do just this (i.e. to dispose of the 'exclusive' possession by destruction) on the part of the 'owner'. What is asserted, however, in claims for a right to roam, is not a licence to wander at will, up and down, back and forth, here and there, but the right to *be* in a place by virtue of the characteristics it possesses – as a member of a society which affords recognition to the value of those characteristics, both as a shared possession and a shared experience. 'The land',[57] then, must in some sense, necessarily be recognised to be 'special'; but in a way that implies not only rights attached to the land itself, but also to any member of 'the public'. The latter is seen as a 'rights-bearer', not as a destructive 'consumer', or a thief, or as a trespasser whose presence is 'destructive', in a purely legal sense, of 'exclusive' private property rights.

Given closer analysis, then, the right to roam, taking the concept of 'rights' in the sense in which it is intended and not in the degraded form that is suggested by market theories, is seen to carry with it the kinds of implication that were stated explicitly by the Royal Commission on Common Land. If the land in question possesses 'special' characteristics in the way that is implied, then these ought to be preserved. But if this is the case, the way the land is to be managed is equally delimited. Any right to roam must therefore necessarily be defined in terms of the valued features of the land to which it is to apply. But the definition of such features also entails a reciprocal relationship with the community of rights-bearers, since it is they who endow the land with this value. If this suggests the kind of principles expressed by the Royal Commission, the same considerations ought now to be applied equally both to common land and open country. But they also have a much wider applicability. The assertion of a right to roam is not a threat, driven by destructive desire. It is a statement of common ownership.

NOTES

1   DETR, Press Notice 0091, 10th February, 2000.
2   DETR consultation paper, *Greater Protection and Better Management of Common Land in England and Wales*, Feb 2000.
3   ibid, 1.12.
4   ITE/NERC, *Heather in England and Wales*, HMSO, 1989.
5   See Chapter 5 above.
6   DETR, *Greater Protection and Better Management of Common Land*, Introduction, p vi.
7   Countryside and Community Research Unit, *Good Practice Guide on Managing the Use of Common Land*, DETR, 1998.
8   ibid, Ch 1, p 3.
9   ibid, p 4.
10   DETR, *Greater Protection and Better Management of Common Land*, 4.1.
11   ibid, Introduction, p i.
12   Countryside Commission, *Common Knowledge..?*, CCP 281, 1990 (see Ch 5 above, Table 3).
13   See Ch 5 above, pp 64ff.
14   DEFRA, *Common Land Policy Statement 2002*, July 2002, Foreword.
15   Ministerial Statement, February 2001.

16   DEFRA, *Common Land Policy Statement*, p 3, para 11.

17   ibid, p 2, para 5.

18   ibid, p 2, para 6.

19   See G D Gadsden, *The Law of Commons*, Sweet & Maxwell, 1988, Ch 3 [3.25].

20   The government's proposal also means that the hundreds (or, perhaps, thousands) of small, 'commons-like' areas described in Chapter 1 above may now be subject to deregistration.

21   *re Box Hill* is discussed in Chapter 4 above.

22   The *Hazeley Heath* case is discussed in Chapter 5 above.

23   See Ch 2 above, pp 19-23.

24   See Open Spaces Society Website (National News section) at: www.oss.org.uk

25   cf C&RoW Act, Pt II, Sect 63.

26   DEFRA, *Common Land Policy Statement*, Foreword.

27   ibid, p 3, para 9.

28   ibid, p 1, para 3.

29   ibid, p 20, para 83.

30   ibid, p 21, para 90.

31   ibid, p 22, para 92.

32   ibid, p 20, para 83.

33   On the history of the Dartmoor Commons see W G Hoskins and L Dudley-Stamp, *The Common Lands of England and Wales*, Collins, 1963, Ch 18.

34   The preceding discussion of the government's proposals for 'agricultural use and management' draws on Papers (3 & 4) presented to the Stakeholder Working Group. Copies of all of these Papers are available at: www.defra.gov.uk/wildlife-countryside/issues/common/legislation/stekeholder.htm (as at Jan 2003).

35   Garrett Hardin, 'The Tragedy of the Commons', Science, vol 162, 1243–48, 1968.

36   DETR, *Access to the Open Countryside in England and Wales. A Consultation Paper,* Feb 1998.

37   *Hansard* (HC), 1999, Vol 327, No 49, col 27 (8/3/99).

38   ibid, col 21.

39   Countryside Commission, *Rights of Way in the 21st Century*, (98/22), June 1998.

40   Countryside Agency, *Preparation of Rights of Way Improvement Plans: Guidance to Local Authorities*, [NCAF 7/4], Sept 2000.

41   More recently it was announced (DEFRA news release 486/02, Nov 28 2002) that, from 2005, RoW Improvement Plans (RWIPs) would be incorporated as 'a distinct strand' in the Local Transport Plans (LTPs) that are now the basis of local authority bids for central funding. This would seem to imply a statutory basis for the future funding of RWIP implementation. Any improvements for access/ROWs, however, would continue to depend on the discretion of individual local authorities (i) in drawing up their LTPs and (ii) in the subsequent allocation of any funds received. The only LTP funding that is 'earmarked' is that for 'major schemes' costing over £5m (see DETR news release 775, Dec 14 2000, Note 7).

42   DEFRA, *Rights of Way Improvement Plans: statutory guidance to local highway authorities in England,* Nov 2002.

43   See Ch 7.

44   Ironically, it would seem that if the new right of access is to be exercised, this may depend in large part on the purchase of linking paths from farmers and landowners through the kind of incentive scheme referred to here. The access 'market', that is, would simply see a shift of focus from open country itself (existing Access Agreements) to the enclosed land separating the rights of way network from the

newly-defined 'access land'.

45   DETR/MAFF, *Rural England. A Discussion Document*, Feb 1999.

46   ibid, Sect 3.4.

47   ibid, Sect 3.8.

48   The crisis over foot and mouth disease was seen by many as a watershed – in particular for MAFF, which was absorbed immediately after the General Election of June 2001 (along with parts of the former DETR) into the Department for Environment, Food and Rural Affairs (DEFRA). The government was also committed by its election manifesto to a major policy review to be carried out by an independent Commission on Farming and Food (which reported in January 2002). But if it is accepted that policies for farming must change, and if, as a result of the foot and mouth crisis, the importance of countryside access for the rural tourism industry has also been more widely recognised, it is clear (e.g. from the reaction to the 'early' reopening of footpaths) that the attitudes of local authorities and of the farming and landowning lobby have changed very little.

49   *Hansard*, op cit, col 26.

50   ibid.

51   DETR, *Access to the Open Countryside in England and Wales*.

52   DETR, *The Government's Framework for Action: Access to the Countryside in England3and Wales*, Mar 1999.

53   *Hansard*, op cit, col 29.

54   The right, for example, will cease if it '…annoys…any person engaged in a lawful activity on the land' (C&ROW Act, Schedule 2, 1(s)).

55   On the judicial interpretation of the right to roam *(jus spatiandi)*, see Ch 6 above, pp 84-5.

56   *Hansard*, op cit, col 24.

57   The definition of 'the land' implied here is that referred to in Chapter 1, as including not only the land surface, with the areas above and beneath it and any buildings, but also the natural vegetation it produces and the wild creatures that live in and upon it.

9

Conclusion

The 'modern' (capitalist) understanding of property is that it is an absolute good to be bought, sold and traded as the owner so desires. This also implies that owners have absolute rights over their land and property, not only to buy and sell at will, but to restrict access and use. What the 'feudal' tradition has bequeathed to us, in the midst of its reactionary rag-bag of ideas and notions, is the sense of conditionality, that there are shared property interests in any piece of land (use values as well as exchange values), so that public interests are prior and paramount, and have rights over private ones.

Robin Callander, *The System of Land Tenure in Scotland.*[1]

Reprise

If common land is important because of its geographical extent and because of the variety of its natural and cultural characteristics it is also important for what it represents. Repeated attempts have been made to secure its protection and a recognition of its special status. But they have ultimately failed. The view that has prevailed is that the commons are, first and foremost, private land. If they are 'special' in any sense, it is because of (what is usually perceived to be) the anachronistic form of their use as an economic resource:

> ...the use of land in common is probably a unique example, so far as this country is concerned, of a shared use of a natural resource where there is neither a direct legal linkage between the participators nor any public element in the use.[2]

As was suggested in Chapter 1, to accept this legalistic view – which in this case, at least, recognises the uniqueness of common land – is to ignore both the historical significance of the commons and their continuing importance as a paradigm of legitimate public interest claims. Common land is unique, not as a curious example of private property rights, but because it is an embodiment of shared interests in the land whose historical origins lie in a communality of use. The commons debate of the mid-nineteenth century produced a discourse of *public* rights based on a reinterpretation and re-expression of these communal rights of the locality. It is a discourse that has retained its radical implications, both as the original source of present public interest claims and as an alternative view of the nature of property rights in the land. The concerns it defines have continued to determine the stated objectives of public policy. They have had little influence, however, on the form that policy has taken or on the institutions or the mechanisms through which it has been implemented.

The latter have been determined by an archaic notion of exclusive private property rights that originated in the seventeenth-century overthrow of feudalism by the landowning class; a notion that excludes the possibility of any community of ownership, or of any recognition of those natural characteristics of the land that cannot be said to be 'owned' by anyone. As the quotation above from Callander may suggest, the Scottish case, whilst distinct, has many parallels; though what is referred to here as the feudal tradition may be more truly conceived of as the tradition of common ownership associated with the clans. Its importance for the current land reform debate in Scotland is the existence of 'a legacy of treating the land and relationships pertaining to it as essentially social and communal rather than individual and absolute'.[3] The commonties of Scotland were lost in the clearances, but they left an abiding sense of the legitimacy of common ownership claims that has re-emerged, in the context of devolution, as an expression of democratic identity. It has many affinities with the case of the commons of England and Wales.

It is, however, 'the "modern" (capitalist) understanding of property' (with all of its archaic connotations) that has determined the present government's programme of reform. Whilst its stated ends are public ends, the form of the proposals, the limits set for them and the means of their implementation incorporate a determining influence that is the opposite of this. The proposals include important provisions. But the underlying principles by which they were originally defined as part of a radical agenda of reform have either been discarded or thoroughly compromised.

Thus, the so-called right of access to registered common land and open country will, in fact, comprise no more than a permitted use that is to be strictly rationed – a 'commodity' whose supply has been justified by cost-benefit analyses as spurious as the surveys produced by its opponents to prove an absence of public 'demand'. Though it is not, it has been represented by both its proponents and its opponents as a substantial reform. In contrast, the provisions for SSSIs in the C&RoW Act are much stronger – though it is hard to see how anything less could have been justified, given the notoriety of the previous arrangement, whereby one arm of the government was buying back as-of-right subsidies paid by another for environmentally damaging activities. Perhaps as a result of this, the reforms have provoked little opposition. However, they are clearly an anomaly in a policy context that is still largely defined in this way – by the existence, the growing importance and the projected extension of schemes for the purchase of environmental 'goods' (i.e. positive rather than negative actions) from their private 'owners'. Nearly 50% of the English commons, for example, are 'either wholly or partially designated as Sites of Special Scientific Interest'.[4] This is not to say that they have been protected in the past, nor that their protection is any more likely under the 'voluntary approach' that is now proposed for them in DEFRA's *Common Land Policy Statement*. The inadequacy of agri-environmental schemes in this case has already been demonstrated. But exactly the same considerations apply to the new SSSI provisions in the absence of statutory management bodies. The government has ignored this fact. Yet it has repeatedly asserted its intention to 'ensure that the special features of [common] land are protected for future generations to enjoy'.[5]

It is not that the government's reforms, or their packaging together, might be improved by a further dose of pragmatism, or a little more effort in 'joining them up'. It would not, in any case, be possible to 'join up' a congeries of half-formed contingencies that are incompatible with each other and with the policy context into which they are to be placed. What is wrong with the reforms is not to do with their detail but with the lack of any principled commitment, and a consequent lack of any coherent political or ideological framework for change. For the government's declared ends to be achieved would require a radical shift of policy. The opportunity for this, and its necessity, are evident in the scale of projected changes in the CAP. Yet there is nothing in the present reforms or proposals for reform that suggests any fundamental reassessment of this kind. If no such reappraisal is attempted, however, the effects of any changes in legislation or policy will inevitably be determined by the same forces and interests that have determined them in the past.

The fact is that this has already happened, or that it is written into the reforms in the way they are to be implemented. In the absence of any principled intent, it is the principles of market economics and private property rights that have prevailed – whilst any further 'joining up' that may be required must presumably be left to the fabled 'hidden hand' of the market. The present government has ignored the alternatives to this because it no longer believes in them. But this does not mean that the concerns they represent will go away. It is simply not possible to define the public goods that are involved in the way that is proposed. They are not 'commodities', any more than they are 'products'. No one has 'created' them. They are a fundamental given. The preservation of which lies not in their 'fixing' or 'freezing' or 'pickling in aspic' – though this is the way that any serious attempt to define the need for reform is invariably represented – but in securing the possibility of their occurrence, now and for the future. Nor can the importance of this be measured by cost-benefit analysis, or in terms of supply and demand. Simply because what is measured in this case, if anything is measured at all, is not the qualities or the entities that are valued, but the extent to which they have been discounted in the past, and the lack of access to them that has been determined by those who claim their exclusive ownership. Yet these, and calculations like them, are the only criteria of value the present government possesses, because they are the only ones that are available to a mainstream discourse it has allowed to determine the boundaries of change.

Land rights: *A Right to Roam*

Land, like the sea, the air, and outer space, was not created by man but by God or Nature, according to one's belief. True, the kaleidoscope of light and shade, form and colour which makes up a landscape is the result of a dialogue spanning millennia between Nature and the activities of man. But humanity cannot create a single blade of grass, let alone a spider or a woodland ecosystem. The land was not made by man, and it is central to the lives of all living things on the planet, human and non-human, living and as yet unborn. Land is the source of the food we eat, the minerals from which we build shelters and tools and fuel machines, the timber from which we manufacture buildings, tools, newspapers, and the plants and animals from which we derive medicines and clothing. It is the source of the space we occupy, and part of the collective identity of tribes, peoples, and nations. Such a resource cannot simply be treated as private property.

Marion Shoard, *A Right to Roam*.[6]

A Right to Roam is a refreshing – and sometimes a surprising – book, both for the clarity of its argument, and for the passion and honesty of its commitment. It gives the lie to the kinds of notion described above because it takes as its starting-point the living and elemental values that lie at the root of a reawakened public interest in the countryside and the environment, and works through their implications for a democratic society. The argument of the book draws on a shared human experience of the natural environment, which is also seen to be firmly rooted in history and in a recognition of the continuing relevance of history to the concerns of the present. In this light, exclusive rights of ownership are seen for what they are: the rejection of a common heritage, whose only claim to legitimacy lies in an historical theft of land rights that belong to us all. The right to roam, on the other hand, is conceived of as an expression of shared values and common interests, and because of this public rights of access are seen to be a pivotal issue. Their definition in a modern context as a right of citizenship, must necessarily be general, or universal. A 'partial' right, such as that proposed in the C&RoW Act, is not a right at all in this sense, but concedes the case it is intended to deny:

> The kind of right of access to the countryside which makes sense is a general right constrained where this is required for reasons which society can accept, not by crude differentiation between categories of landscape… rights…if [they] are to be convincing…need to be universal in their application, at least in principle. We did not provide women with a partial right to vote. We do exclude Peers and the mentally ill from this right, but these are specifically justified exceptions to a rule which is fundamentally general.[7]

Rights of this kind – citizenship rights – are, in a logical sense, indivisible (though this is not true, of course, of commodities). A universal right would apply to all land. It would entail the abolition of the concept of trespass, so that 'a general prohibition against being present in the countryside would be replaced by a general right to be present'.[8] The presumption would then be in favour of access – so that, though the right would obviously be qualified by considerations of equal importance such as the need for privacy, it would be recognised *as of right* and not as a concession or a grant on the part of its private 'owners'. There might still exist differing views as to its scope which would need to be provided for in some way, but any resulting exceptions or exemptions would also need to be supported by reasons that were generally recognised to be good reasons. They need not, however, involve the kind of complex administrative machinery necessitated by a partial right of the kind that is defined by the C&RoW Act.

The practical difficulties presented by Part I of the C&RoW Act are examined below. But a 'partial' right also raises, in addition to the matter of its philosophical definition, questions of legal principle. A right of this kind may be seen to be unfair (or 'inequitable'). First, because it applies to some landowners and not to others – the former are deprived of their 'property rights' whilst the latter are not. There might, then, be grounds for compensation of a kind that is ruled out by the Act itself. But there is a further point. In the form that is proposed, the right may also be seen to fail in its stated end of providing opportunities for access to the public as a whole because it is directed at areas of land that are remote from the greater part of the population. As a matter of public policy, it might therefore be seen to have adverse effects in terms of its 'opportunity cost'. In the final analysis, this may imply a net loss to the public in terms of its 'costs and benefits' (i.e. it might be considered to be *detrimental* to the public interest). If these points were admitted to be true, the right would be open to challenge, not only on the grounds of its inequity, but also as a 'human rights' violation. According to Article 1 of the First Protocol to the European Convention on Human Rights:

> No-one shall be deprived of his possessions except in the public interest and subject to the conditions provided for by law and by the general principles of international law. The preceding provisions shall not, however, in any way impair the right of the State to enforce such laws as it deems necessary to control the use of property in accordance with the general interest or to secure the payment of taxes or other contributions or penalties.[9]

The question would turn, then, on whether or not the right was 'in' or 'in accordance with' the general interest – and a challenge of this kind has been repeatedly threatened by, for example, the Country Land and Business Association (CLA). Is there, perhaps, a case for compensation of the kind that is rejected by the Act? And would the public benefits conferred by the right be sufficient to balance the taking of 'private property' in a way that would satisfy the Human Rights Convention? As Shoard suggests, in an ingenious reversal of the argument, neither of these points would be valid in the case of a *universal* right. But she also argues in a similar way on the practical difficulties of implementation.

An idea of the administrative complexities involved in the implementation of the proposed right of access will be evident from Table 6, which shows the functions of public bodies under the Act.[10] A first phase will involve the production of maps that are to show all open country and registered common land. The mapping itself is to be divided into three stages (related to the production of Draft, Provisional and Conclusive maps) applied in a 'rolling programme' to each of eight regions of the country.[11] Consultations on the Draft maps – as to the areas which should and should not be shown as open country and registered common land – will be open to representations by any interested parties, including members of the public. The resulting Provisional maps will then be subject to appeal on the part of private interests opposed to the inclusion of particular areas of land, whilst the Conclusive maps will show the final record but will be subject to review every ten years.

The Act gives a right of access for walkers to areas designated as 'access land'. Access land is defined as land that is shown on a Conclusive map as open country or registered common land,[12] but does not include 'excepted land' or land subject

Table 6. Functions of public bodies under Part I of the Countryside & Rights of Way Act (England)

Ch I (4–11) Ch II (33)	mapping & review guidance to other 'relevant authorities'	Countryside Agency	'appropriate countryside body'
Ch II (21–33)	closures & restrictions	Countryside Agency National Parks Forestry Commission Secretary of State (non bye-lawed MOD land)	'the relevant authority'
Ch II	closures & restrictions (advice)	English Nature English Heritage (Defence Estates Agency)	'relevant advisory bodies'
Ch II (29–30)	(appeals) (reference)	by private interests to: by advisory bodies to:	'the appropriate minister' (Secretary of State)
Ch I (20) Schedule 4(4)	codes of conduct model bye-laws	Countryside Agency	'appropriate countryside body'
Pt V (94–5)	local access forums	National Parks Highways Authorities	'access authorities'
Ch I (17–19)	bye-laws notices on site wardens	National Parks Highways Authorities (District Councils)	'access authorities' (District Councils may only appoint wardens)
Ch III (34–39)	means of access obstructions & works	National Parks Highways Authorities	'access authorities'
Ch IV (40–41)	powers of entry	Countryside Agency National Parks Highways Authorities Forestry Commission	'appropriate countryside body' 'the relevant authority' 'access authorities'
Pt II (58)	link paths to access land (including access 'islands')	Countryside Agency on application to:	Secretary of State

to Section 15(1). The latter covers those cases where a public right of area access already exists – largely common land, but also land at present under Access Agreements or Orders, which will continue to apply but will be not be renewed. 'Excepted land' is defined in Schedule 1. It includes, for example, dwellings and other buildings with their curtilage, quarries, works, and areas under cultivation. In addition to these excluded areas, general restrictions are imposed, in Schedule 2, on the activities and the behaviour of 'persons exercising [the] right of access'. Bye-laws may also be put in place by the 'access authorities' (National Parks and local Highways Authorities). Offences against the bye-laws, the exceptions or the restrictions (including the 'local' closures and restrictions described below) may result in the loss of the right of access, for 72 hours, over land in the same owner-ship. Those against the bye-laws may lead to prosecution. But this might also follow, where exclusions or restrictions are ignored, if the offences defined by the Criminal Justice Act ('aggravated trespass', 'trespassory assembly') are seen to be applicable. The government seems to have dropped its promise to review the effects of the CJA[13] in this respect. Under Section 42 of the C&RoW Act, regu-lations may exclude the right of access as a consideration in defining what is 'a public place'. (The offence of 'trespassory assembly' can only be committed '…by 20 or more people…in a place where the public have no, or a limited right, to be…'). Whilst Schedule 5 (Pt II)(17) amends the CJA, in relation to RoWs, to include the restricted byways created by the present Act.

Part I (Ch II) of the Act describes provisions for local closures and restrictions. In England, they will be administered by the Countryside Agency and the National Parks ('the relevant authorities'), though in the case of woodland dedi-cated under Section 16, the Forestry Commission may also elect to act in this capacity. Under these arrangements, landowners (including occupiers and those with sporting rights) will be allowed a total of 28 'discretionary' days for which they may notify closures or restrictions without being required to specify a reason. They may also apply to the relevant authorities (who may take into consideration the use of the discretionary right) for additional exclusions to cover land manage-ment, fire risk or operations on the land that may be of danger to the public. In the case of fire risk or danger, the relevant authority may itself impose closures or restrictions; and may allow them for land management purposes where they are seen to be justified, and the 28 discretionary days are already accounted for.

Local closures or restrictions for nature conservation and heritage purposes will also be determined by the relevant authorities. In this case, however, advice is to be given by the 'relevant advisory bodies' (English Nature and English Heritage) who, where they consider that it has not been followed by the relevant authorities, may apply to the Secretary of State for a 'direction'. The latter, mean-while, may impose exclusions for defence or national security purposes on (for example) MOD land that is not subject to bye-laws (MOD land that is bye-lawed is 'excepted' under Schedule 1). Closures or restrictions for all of these purposes (conservation, heritage, defence/national security) may be enforced at any time. They may be for an indefinite or an 'extended' period, or for a recurrent term over a number of years. In contrast, applications by private interests will be decided annually,[14] whilst the 28 'discretionary' days must not include public holidays, or more than four weekend days, at specified times, in any one year.[15]

The stated aim is that, in all cases, the least restrictive option should be chosen – so that, for example, where it was feasible, linear access with defined entry points would be encouraged (as a limited 'restriction') in the place of complete closure. Owners are also to be encouraged to pre-register discrete 'parcels' of land to facilitate closure notifications. The 28 day allowance, for example, might be applied to each of these separately – so that, though the number of closures may be increased (since they will apply to each parcel of land, rather than the whole area in a single ownership), the areas affected at any one time would be likely to be smaller. Pre-registration will also be used to facilitate short-notice closures in strictly defined circumstances. Otherwise, full details of the areas affected by a notification would need to be supplied in each case.

Some of the complexity of the Act will be evident from this summary – which, as an examination of Table 6 will show, includes by no means all of the rules and procedures related to the right of access. The most telling of Shoard's criticisms, however, are directed at the initial phase of mapping and at the definitions adopted for the different kinds of open country (mountain, moor, heath or down – with coastal land a possibility at some point in the future). In the case of registered common land, official maps already exist,[16] but the required mapping of open country will necessarily be fraught with difficulties. This is particularly evident in the case of heath and down, the greater part of which has been subject to intensive agricultural improvement. The areas that remain are small and fragmented, and present obvious difficulties for the mapping process. The adoption of land cover as the major criterion also means that the areas mapped will be subject to natural changes in vegetation, or to changes in land use, over the ten-year review period. Similar problems are claimed by Shoard to apply to mountain and moor, though this is not entirely true. In the case of moorland, for example, the right will apply to more extensive areas (with a lower boundary/area ratio) where the boundary between open country and enclosed land will often be quite obvious.[17] If, however, Harvey's contention is true (see Chapter 5 above) the greater part of the uplands of Wales, for example, is already 'improved'.[18] Given the exclusion of 'improved' and 'semi-improved' grassland from the definition of open country, it may well be that problems related to land use and changes in land use are as great in the uplands as the lowlands.

As Shoard points out, the arbitrary nature of the criteria adopted is evident from the C&RoW Act itself which, remarkably, fails to offer any actual definition of them. Given that open country is whatever 'appears to the appropriate countryside body to consist wholly or predominantly of mountain, moor, heath or down', and given the definition of 'access land' as 'land which is shown on a map' as belonging to these categories, the open country to which the public is to have a right of access is, in effect, 'whatever the officials of the Countryside Agency and the Countryside Council for Wales say it is'.[19] But this raises the further question of how this information is to be communicated to members of the public. It is not only that the types of land involved (including common land) may, in many cases, be difficult to distinguish on the ground. In the light of the definition above (which includes the further (Section 4) discretion of mapping the boundaries of open country to conform with recognisable features of the landscape), the possession of a map will be essential to walkers. But in itself this will be inadequate. A commercial map (such as an OS map) might well show excepted land, or land subject to permanent or extended closures. But – even in the case of a map incorporating information recently downloaded from the Internet – it may be more difficult to indicate short-term or 'recurring' closures, particularly those that are to apply to limited 'parcels' of land. How the range of possible 'restrictions' is to be indicated is another question, which is probably unanswerable.

A number of solutions to these problems have been suggested in addition to maps – including the Internet, guide books, the local media, information centres, on-site notices, and advice from rangers. All of them imply a burden of effort or expenditure that is, to say the least, inappropriate. But if the effort, on either side, of communication and understanding is successful, so that it is possible to distinguish what is and what is not access land, the arbitrariness of the definition will be only the more evident. Just as the farmer, or landowner, may consider it a legitimate act to take land out of the definition of open country by changes in land use, the walker may find it difficult to understand why one area is included and another is not:

> Inevitably, people allowed to walk on some spaces will want to walk on other similar spaces even when they know they are not supposed to. What about stretches of land enclosed by stone walls or wire fences whose vegetation is actually more interesting than neighbouring unfenced moorland...[or] a meadow...not necessarily in mid-Wales but say on the outskirts of Bath? What happens when a stretch of rough grass and bracken is being slowly invaded by scrub and birch trees? When is this 'woodland' and thus exempt from the right to roam and at what stage is it moorland and legally accessible?[20]...How are walkers to understand why they can walk in

woods that happen to have been embraced by the mappers but not woods which have not? What goes for woods will presumably go for streams, meadows, private roads and tracks and much else.[21]

A Right to Roam, then, brings telling arguments against both the principles and practice of the mapping process. But it is equally critical of the proposed regime of closures and restrictions. In a further ingenious reversal of the argument, similar to that applied in the case of the legal objections that are brought against the right, Shoard adopts many of the practical criticisms brought against the Act by the apologists of private property rights. Again, she concludes, not that the right to roam should be rejected, but that the partial right should be rejected in favour of a universal right. Thus, she fully supports the kinds of criticism (examined at length in Chapter 6 above) brought to bear by the Moorland Association:

> ...surprising though it may seem, the legitimate case for excluding walkers from upland areas is often stronger than in lowland areas – so much so that whether a right of access is partial or universal it is likely to require exemptions for much upland country for a significant amount of the time...Not just farmers and landowners but conservationists would want walkers barred from both heather and grass moorland during spring and early summer, since this is the season for the many often scarce species of wild birds which happen to nest on moors...All in all it could well be argued that if a right of access were to be limited to one kind of countryside only, then moor and mountain would be among the least suitable of types of countryside to choose.[22]

Now this is all very well. But not only does it advance fiction as truth, it also seems to re-admit the notion of access as inherently in conflict with land and conservation management – and this is more than simply for the sake of the argument. Shoard is quite prepared to allow that 'exclusions to any...general right of access would have to be considerable'.[23] But it is at this point that the argument begins to break down. A good deal of empirical evidence is brought, related to countries where a general or a universal right already exists, to support the case for its adoption in this country. The implication is that, on the basis of the evidence from these countries – which is shown to be broadly comparable – there would be few problems for a universal right in the case of England and Wales. A universal right would effectively 'bypass the philosophical, legal and practical difficulties'[24] presented by a partial right. This is certainly true, in practical terms, of the initial mapping process, where the need for a complex administrative machinery would be removed; though if exclusions and restrictions would have to be 'considerable', the same is not true in this case. But there is a more important point. If potential conflicts do exist on the scale that is admitted (why should this be so, if they do not exist in the other countries described, and these *are* broadly comparable to this country?); and if, as the case presented against moorland access seems to suggest, this may also be taken to be an admission of the mainstream idea of access as *inherently* in conflict with land and conservation management; the proper conclusion would seem to be that there are no legitimate grounds for the adoption of either a partial or a universal right of access.

Land rights: the case of Scotland

The idea of access that has emerged from the Scottish land reform debate is similar in many ways to the universal right proposed by Shoard. It is more clearly stated as a land right, which is perhaps to be expected. But it also illustrates, in its passage from conception to draft legislation, the kinds of objection raised above against Shoard's position – that even a universal right may spawn administrative complexities if it is allowed to be defined in terms of the mainstream conception of access as disruptive and destructive. Shoard's view, perhaps, reflects a willingness to pursue a course of compromise, in relation at least to practical questions, if not on matters of principle. But it also reflects the pervasive ideological influence of the mainstream view of access, and the extent of the political power that lies behind it – not least because the argument in *A Right to Roam* is for the kind of isolated (and consequently anomalous) measure defined by the C&RoW Act. The book builds its case on a concept of land rights that is much wider in its implications (citing, for example, the views of Winstanley and the Diggers and those of Henry George). But if a right to roam is to carry this kind of weight, it implies a good deal more than a limited freedom to wander about in a countryside laid waste by otherwise exclusive private property rights; or, for that matter, in an urban landscape increasingly walled off as ('excepted') private space.

In the Scottish context, the question of access must be seen as part of a comprehensive overhaul of the whole system of land law. The land reforms proposed by the new Scottish Parliament included the abolition of the feudal system (which still applied in Scottish law); reforms in crofting law and the law of agricultural tenure; the introduction of a community right to buy (with related measures for crofting communities); the recognition of public and community interests through local representative bodies, and in codes of practice related to the stewardship of the land (affecting all forms of ownership – public, private and trust); and the creation for the first time of National Parks. Even in official circles, the reforms have been represented as an attempt to 'redefine' the relationship between the people and the land. The proposed legislation for a general right of access, then, should be seen in this light. Two points, however, need to be noted.

Firstly, many reformers see the legislation for access as the confirmation of a right that already exists. This traditional right is seen to apply, for those taking access on foot, not only to the Highlands or to uncultivated land, but to all 'land', including coastal areas (and possibly inland waters). The proposed legislation is also to apply to all land (on, over and under the surface), including land covered by water. It is to be for both passage and informal recreation, and it is to include access not only for walkers but also for cyclists, horse-riders, canoeists and others. The second point to note is that the proposals for reform have encountered opposition from landowning interests on a scale comparable to that in England and Wales. The Scottish Landowners' Federation, for example, had previously recognised the traditional right:

> There is no law of trespass in Scotland...If people choose to picnic on a lawn in front of a house, the owner can do no more than point out the private nature of his property and of his entitlement to its exclusive use and enjoyment. He cannot prosecute for trespass. Force cannot be used to remove his uninvited guests, although if they persist in coming and picnicking regularly, an interdict against them could be obtained.[25]

Since the 1960s, however (the statement above is from 1961), an increasing number of landowners – with the backing of what Alan Blackshaw has referred to as 'the new official views'[26] – have openly expressed their opposition to access; though it is also clear that, as in England and Wales, what is involved is a general opposition to public land rights of any kind. The hope for the present reforms was that, in the absence of the House of Lords, the new Scottish Parliament might force through changes defined by a radical, democratic agenda. Although this is how the measures have been 'spun', it is not what has happened. Most of the proposals for land reform listed above have been hi-jacked by private interests which have either determined the drafting of the legislation, or have procured the excision of more radical measures.

The proposals for access reform[27] were produced by the Access Forum[28] on behalf of Scottish Natural Heritage, which had been appointed to carry out the task by the then Secretary of State for Scotland. The intention of the Forum was that a simple Bill should confirm and extend the (existing) public right of access, whilst 'any details related to responsible access should be dealt with under the [Scottish Outdoor Access] Code rather than on the face of the Bill'. The Code 'would be subject to review and could be readily updated or amended', and was 'to be accompanied by an extensive education programme...to promote responsible behaviour'. The right, then, was to depend upon responsible behaviour and 'voluntary restraint' on the part of members of the public, and on a mutual recognition of common interests in the land.[29] Whilst the Code would have 'evidential status' in court, and although existing legal restrictions would still apply, no new machinery of regulation and enforcement was to be introduced. As a result, the resources available could be devoted to the projected programme of education and to the development of (linear) access provision in lowland areas (where, at present, there exist few rights of way, or paths open to the public).

The fundamental difference from the case of England and Wales is clear. The right itself is seen to define a legal framework for access reform and improvement. There is, for example, no question of the general right of access having adverse effects (in terms of its 'opportunity cost') for the paths network. On the contrary, the existing system, whereby local authorities are obliged to expend time and resources in court action or in seeking costly agreements or concessions from private landowners, would be completely overturned. Owners wishing to encourage the use of linear routes must now actively seek the co-operation and assistance of the local authorities who would in turn be required to develop and maintain a strategic network of 'core' paths. The so-called 'voluntary principle' would therefore be reversed, because – and this point cannot be over-emphasised – the policy context would now be defined by the recognition of a coherent framework of public rights. Any exceptions, exclusions or restrictions, and any rules governing them, must therefore be decided, and expressed, in this context.

This, then, is (or was) the distinctively Scottish case. The consensus arrived at by the Forum, however, was (as in the case of the Common Land Forum) more apparent than real. This was immediately evident with the publication of the Draft Land Reform (Scotland) Bill in February 2001. The National Farmers' Union for Scotland (NFUS) walked out of the Forum, and an opposing coalition – including the NFUS, the Scottish Landowners' Federation, representatives of shooting, hunting and fishing interests, and the RSPB – was established.[30] But, clearly, the Draft Bill was equally unacceptable to access campaigners. In the form proposed, it would 'significantly undermine the existing basis on which the public take access to land and water and could easily reduce opportunities for enjoying the outdoors'.[31] Many of the provisions for 'responsible behaviour' had been transferred from the Code into the Bill. So that:

> area exclusions (e.g. for crops and recreational land) have crept into the Bill which will result in a complex set of definitions, registers and possibly maps being required to implement it. Together with the introduction of both a new criminal offence and a power for landowners to suspend access rights, this goes against one of the stated intentions of the legislation (p 14)

to 'avoid such uncertainty and to provide people with confidence to go out and enjoy the countryside'.[32]

Local authorities were to be given broadly defined powers to designate exempt ('excepted') areas, to suspend access rights, to impose bye-laws and other management restrictions, and to enforce exclusion orders on persistent offenders against these or against the Code. Since the right was weakened in this way, the projected role of the local authorities in opening up access and developing path networks was also considerably undermined (it would still be they, and not landowners, who would be seeking improvements in the paths network) – a general point underlined by the fact that the Draft Bill gave the local authorities powers rather than duties. In short, the legal framework defined by the original proposals of the Forum was replaced in the Draft Bill by a set of provisions not dissimilar to those in the C&RoW Act. These might also require, it seemed, the same kind of complex machinery of mapping and regulation, draining resources away from the intended improvements in linear and area access and feeding them into the enforcement of exclusions and restrictions. The outcome, for the supposedly 'universal' right, would be much the same as that implied in the case presented by Shoard, and was, in the end, little different in principle from the 'partial' right recently legislated for in England and Wales – though, in Scotland, it would undermine a right that was claimed already to exist.

The Bill in its final form was laid before the Scottish Parliament on November 27th, 2001. The access proposals had attracted a petition of 15,000 names. And the Draft Bill was itself the subject of 3,500 representations, over 80% of which (2914) related solely to the access provisions in Part 1 (cf the 2000 responses to the access consultation in England and Wales). Perhaps as a result of this, many of the measures objected to by the access lobby (landowner powers of suspension, local authority emergency suspension powers, criminal offence, exclusion orders) had been removed, whilst provisions for the creation of a 'core paths' network were strengthened substantially. However, the areas generally excepted from the new right were extended by the definition of 'grass...grown for hay or silage' as a crop, and local authorities retained broad powers to 'exempt particular land and exclude particular conduct from access rights'. Consequently, the revised Bill was still perceived to be 'a tartan version of the Westminster Bill' – defining an approach that differed fundamentally from the original proposals of SNH and the Access Forum. In particular, the question crucial to those proposals, of the relationship between the existing ('customary') right of access for walkers and any new statutory right, remained unresolved.

As Blackshaw had pointed out,[33] it was for this reason that the Scottish Law Commission had itself determined, in April 2001, that it 'would...not support the enactment of the provisions contained in the Land Reform (Scotland) Bill as they stand'.[34] The Bill as it now stood would constitute a recipe for confusion and conflict. Because it would not 'diminish or displace' existing rights of access, the customary right would continue. Whilst the statutory right might possibly provide new opportunities for a range of recreationists, including cyclists and horse-riders, the accompanying regime of exclusions and restrictions would detract from the existing rights of walkers. Where this was the case, the latter might simply opt to exercise their customary rights – though there would, of course, be no guarantee that these would be recognised by landowners or by the authorities. These and related issues were considered at length during the first two stages of the Bill by the Justice 2 Committee. And in the face of opposition from the Scottish Executive, the Committee proposed a number of amendments that would in some part reinstate the original intentions of the Access Forum. The final fate of the Bill will depend on the confirmation of these amendments by the Scottish Parliament, but it is clear that opposition to its progress from the landowning interest poses a continuing threat.[35]

In the work of Shoard, and in the case of Scottish land reform, the right to roam is conceived of as a fundamental expression of land rights belonging to the people. In the case of Scotland, it is more clearly defined as part of a comprehensive programme of reform whose stated aims include a redefinition of the relationship between the people and the land, an empowerment of local communities, and a radical shift in the concentration of landownership in a country where 'half of the [private] land is owned by 343 landowners with estates of 7500 acres [30 sq kms] and larger'.[36] In fact, these aims were evident in neither the legislation that has already been passed (e.g. related to the reform of the feudal system) nor the Draft Land Reform Bill. The Scottish access reforms may still fail, at least for the moment, if the amendments to the Bill are not upheld and then implemented in the spirit of the Access Forum's original proposals. But this only underlines the need in England and Wales for a programme of change based upon a rethinking of rights in the land, and expressed in a framework of law which incorporates a recognition of legitimate public interest claims. It also reinforces a point that has been repeatedly stressed in the present book: that the law and policy of the countryside and rural areas is necessarily, and essentially, political. There are no 'impartial' or 'pragmatic' solutions.

Ownership and belonging

Common rights are rights of taking. But they are also rights of belonging. Historically, as the basis of a subsistence (or 'thrift') economy, they defined a direct relationship between the people and the land, involving communal interests that were recognised in law to be of equal importance to those of the 'owner'.

The Inclosures replaced this conception of communal rights with one of absolute ownership. Not only was the land physically enclosed, it was re-defined ('inclosed') as an absolute possession. The owner could do as he would with it, it 'belonged' to him, because the land had ceased to be a place where anyone else belonged. The idea of absolute rights is familiar enough, but its application in this instance has far-reaching implications. If all land is private land, to be anywhere (and not the owner) is to be there on sufferance. In a nutshell, the only right that remains is the right to be somewhere else. But there may be nowhere else, since the claim to belong to, or come from, a place would be a nonsense unless the place (literally) belonged to you.

The nonsense lies, in fact, in the notion of 'exclusive' rights of this kind, a notion that is characteristically applied in respect of the countryside and rural land. But the claim in this case is much more than a spatial one. It is to everything that is implied in law by 'the land', including its natural attributes – the earth itself, the natural growth of its vegetation, and the wild creatures that live in and upon it. An entitlement to the temporary use or management of these might make some sense, depending on the nature of the use and its effects, and on a recognition that other people should have a say in what these are. This is just what is claimed in the representation of private owners as the 'stewards' of the countryside. But the metaphor is flawed. The word retains a double meaning, reflecting its origins in the private, family concerns of the landed aristocracy. And whilst public duties are implied, it is these private 'others' who are intended, and who are recognised as the legal beneficiaries. No public *rights* are defined, nor is there any implication of a duty to *the environment* – the (family) steward's concerns are first and foremost for the *economic* well-being of his heirs. So that if 'stewardship' is defined (as in the case of agri-environment schemes) as a commodity which the owner of the land has a right to sell to the public, it can have no such meaning in law. The right of sale itself implies a right of disposal that is incompatible with the stated intentions of such schemes, or indeed with any conception of public rights in the land.

There are other ways of defining the public interest that are not permeated and corrupted by an archaic notion of private property rights. The alternative model suggested in this book is that of common land. The discourse related to the commons offers an altogether different starting point for reform which incorporates a coherent definition of the public interest that is also grounded democratically. The right of access is a fundamental element of this definition. It places people in a landscape which belongs to them because they are a part of it. They have a right, in short, to be in a place by virtue of its valued (natural, spatial, historical and cultural) characteristics – as a member of a society which affords recognition to these characteristics, both as a shared possession and a shared experience. It is in this sense, and on this basis, that 'the land' should be protected and preserved, and the nature and forms of its management delimited. Defined in this way, the right to roam – grounded, as it should be, in a recognition of the shared ownership of the land, and in an agreement on what can and cannot be owned – embodies a coherent conception of the relationship between the different elements of 'the public interest': access, preservation, protection, conservation management and land management for all but the most intensive agriculture. And it is at *this* point, and *within* this defining framework, that any limitations on the right of access ought to be considered, agreed, and expressed as rules. There is little room here, then, for any separate body of countryside 'stewards' (be they private 'owners' or conservationists) whose role is to protect the public against itself by abstracting public rights of access from the arena of conservation.

NOTES

1   Robin Callander, *The System of Land Tenure in Scotland*, WWF Scotland, 1997. Quoted in David McCrone, 'Land, Democracy and Culture in Scotland', the 4th John McEwen Memorial Lecture, Perth, Oct 1997.

2   G D Gadsden, *The Law of Commons*, Sweet & Maxwell, 1988, Ch I, p 1, [1.01].

3   McCrone, op cit.

4   DEFRA Website, Wildlife & Countryside/Countryside Issues/Common Land, Town And Village Greens/Facts and Figures: www.defra.gov.uk/wildlife-countryside/issues/common/index.htm (as at Jan 2003).

5   DETR, *Greater Protection and Better Management of Common Land in England and Wales*, Feb 2000, Foreword.

6   Marion Shoard, *A Right to Roam*, Oxford University Press, 1999, Ch 7, p 258.

7   ibid, pp 286–7.

8   Marion Shoard, 'Off the Track: Problems Looming for the Right to Roam', Countryside Recreation, Vol 8, No 2, Summer 2000, p 2.

9   Quoted in: Andy Wightman, *Who Owns Scotland*, Canongate, 1997, p 201.

10   Separate provisions are made for Wales, where the functions of the National Assembly and the Countryside Council for Wales correspond to those of the Secretary of State and the Countryside Agency.

11   The process commenced in Spring/Summer 2001 in the Lower North West and the South East regions. It is estimated that it will take about four years to cover the whole country.

12   'Access land' will also include land that is dedicated under Section 16, and mountain or registered common that lies for the time being outwith the areas that have been mapped (suggesting the possibility of a fast-track provision for the latter). Part I may, in addition, be extended by order, at some time in the future, to apply to 'coastal land'.

13   Marion Shoard, *A Right to Roam*, p 15 (note). The Labour Party promised in 1995 to review the law on 'aggravated trespass' as it might apply to '…innocent people enjoying the countryside'.

14   Although Section 27(3) clearly implies that longer-term exclusions will also be possible for applications under Section 24, for land management reasons, and

under Section 25 (cf note 15 below).

15   Local restrictions on night access may also be imposed, but the special restrictions on dogs are perhaps the most comprehensive. Dogs must be kept on a lead between March 1 and July 31, and at all times in the vicinity of livestock. They may be excluded permanently, at the discretion of the owner, from moorland managed for grouse shooting, and for six weeks each year, in the interests of lambing, from enclosures of less than 15 hectares (i.e. 500 x 300 metres).

16   Though the extent to which land registered as common is recognised as such by farmers and landowners raises further questions. See Ch 5 above, pp 64-6.

17   The example cited by Shoard, of the Section 3 Map held by the Snowdonia National Park, is atypical. See Land Use Consultants, *Maps of Moor or Heath*, Countryside Commission, 1985, which describes the original mapping, under Section 43 of the Wildlife and Countryside Act, on which the present maps are based.

18   Graham Harvey, *The Killing of the Countryside*, Jonathan Cape, 1997, pp 80ff.

19   Shoard, 'Off the Track', pp 2–6.

20   Shoard, *A Right to Roam*, p 291.

21   Shoard, 'Off the Track', p 3.

22   Shoard, *A Right to Roam*, pp 289–90.

23   ibid, p 309.

24   ibid, p 298.

25   Scottish Landowners Federation, 1961. Quoted in Ian McCall, 'Outdoor access threatened by Land Reform Bill'. The quotations accompanying much of the following analysis are taken from this article. Ian McCall is the Campaign and Policy Co-ordinator for the Ramblers' Association Scotland. The article is available, under the link for Scotland, at www.ramblers.org.uk. The Scottish RA's *Briefing Paper* on the Draft Land Reform Bill is also available at the Caledonia website referred to in note 36 below.

26   Alan Blackshaw, 'Research Note: Historical Perspectives on the Existing Freedoms of Responsible Access and the Scottish Executive's Exclusion and Trespass Proposals', Scottish Environment LINK Research Project, June 2001. Available at: www.mountaineering-scotland.org.uk/access/lrs_bill.html (as at Jan 2003). The opposition of landowners to public access was strengthened with the passing of the 1967 Countryside (Scotland) Act by the adoption of what Alan Blackshaw refers to as 'the new official views'. The Countryside Commission for Scotland (CCS), created by the 1967 Act, took the position that the law in England and Scotland was, to all intents and purposes, the same. As in England, simple trespass was a civil offence, and 'reasonable' physical force might be used to eject a trespasser who refused a request to leave. This position was also maintained by the successor body to CCS, Scottish Natural Heritage (SNH); though, as Blackshaw clearly demonstrates, it had been adopted in 1967 without any legal justification, and 'without reference to the Scottish Law Officers'. As a result of the LINK research project, SNH modified its position substantially, producing in 1995 '[an] unpublished Report...confirming that "Members of the public taking access with implied consent are licensees, not trespassers"...The Access Forum recommendations and the SNH advice to the Scottish Executive during the preparation of the present Draft Bill were on this more moderate basis'.

27   The detailed proposals of the Access Forum are available on the SNH Website at www.snh.org.uk.

28   The Scottish Access Forum was established in 1994, and produced the *Concordat*

for access to Scotland's hills and mountains in 1996. Its membership incorporated the range of public, private and voluntary interests concerned with upland access. A number of other bodies, representing lowland interests, were added to the Forum that considered the present proposals for reform and for a general Access Code.

29   As with the earlier *Concordat*, whose fourth principle acknowledged '...a common interest in the natural beauty and special qualities of Scotland's hills, and...the need to work together for their protection and enhancement'.

30   'Land rights breakthrough', *The Scotsman*, 23 Feb 2001.

31   McCall, op cit.

32   ibid.

33   See note 26 above.

34   Scottish Law Commission, *Discussion Paper on the Law of the Foreshore and Seabed*, 2001, [DP No 113], Para 4.41.

35   The Bill completed its passage through the Scottish Parliament on 23rd January, 2003, going then to receive the royal assent. A public consultation will follow on the final form of the Code, with the Act probably coming into force sometime in the first part of 2004. Excellent coverage of the progress of the Bill, the Act and the Code is to be found at: www.mountaineering-scotland.org.uk/access/lrs_bill.html

36   Andy Wightman, 'Land Reform: Politics, Power and the Public Interest', The 1999 John McEwan Memorial Lecture. Available at the website of the Caledonia Centre for Social Development: www.caledonia.org.uk. A great deal of helpful material on the Scottish land reform debate is available at this site.

Appendix

Commons of the Northern Uplands

Key to columns

Column A gives the CL number with a letter suffix indicating the original county register

Column B gives the name of the land as listed in the commons register

Column C gives the area in square kilometres (sk)

Column D gives the ownership status

Column E gives the legal status with reference to registration, access, management, etc.

See also Note on page 164

CUMBRIA (THE LAKE DISTRICT)

A B	C	D	E
Skiddaw Group			
CL 46 (C) Uldale Fells	13.81 sk	LDSPB	Access common
CL 20 (C) Caldbeck Common	37.27 sk	LDSPB/McCosh of Dalemain	Access common (most pt)
CL 60 (C) Carrock/Mungrisdale Fells	4.40 sk	McCosh of Dalemain	
CL 293 (C) Mungrisdale Common	12.35 sk	Howard of Greystoke	
CL 66 (C) Saddleback	10.83 sk	Earl of Lonsdale	
CL 400 (C) Little Calva	2.63 sk	Mr & Mrs WM Waugh	
CL 252 (C) Skiddaw Common	2.65 sk	Public Trustee	
CL 64 (C) Bassenthwaite & Skiddaw Commons	4.12 sk	Public Trustee	
North East Fells			
CL 65 (C) Threlkeld Common	4.46 sk	Earl of Lonsdale	
CL 67 (C) Matterdale Common	10.54 sk	National Trust (orig Howard)	Access common (reg under 1876 Act)
CL 1 (C) Watermillock Common	3.45 sk	National Trust	Access common
CL 123 (C) St John's Common	15.39 sk	NW Water	Access common
CL 101 (W) Glenridding Common	10.88 sk	Sharman, Marshall (orig Howard)	Urban common
CL 57 (W) Grisedale Forest	8.03 sk	McCosh of Dalemain	Urban common
CL 160 (W) Deepdale Common	7.32 sk	AC Brown, Deepdale Hall	Urban common
CL 413 (C) Whelpside, Armboth & Bleaberry Fells	20.54 sk	NW Water	Access common

Eastern Fells

CL 1 (W)	**Patterdale Common**	**3.85 sk**	**McCosh of Dalemain**	Urban common
CL 157 (W)	**Pts of foreshore Lake Ullswater**	**4.37 sk**		Urban common
CL 2 (W)	Martindale Common (West)	10.60 sk	McCosh of Dalemain	
CL 3 (W)	Martindale Common (East)	6.32 sk	McCosh of Dalemain	
CL 58 (W)	Barton Fell	6.93 sk		
CL 87 (W)	Askham Fell	2.26 sk		
CL 113 (W)	Helton Fell	5.38 sk		
CL 85 (W)	**Bampton Common**	**27.88 sk**	**NW Water (small pts Earl of Lonsdale)**	Access common
CL 86 (W)	**Mardale Common**	**13.54 sk**	**NW Water**	Access common
CL 56 (W)	**Ralfland Forest/Rosgill Moor**	**15.53 sk**	**NW Water (small pts Earl of Lonsdale)**	Access common
CL 67 (W)	Kentmere Dale Head Common	7.76 sk	Pt Commissioners of Kendal Reservoirs	(NW Water?)
CL 117 (W)	*Fawcett Forest*	*(4.0 sk)*	*CH Bagot, Levens Hall*	*Void*
CL 146 (W)	*Whin Fell (Lushington Allotment)*	*(1.63 sk)*		*Deregistered Oct 1993 (unity of seisin)*

Central Fells

CL 78 (W)	**Grasmere Common**	**20.53 sk**	**Earl of Lonsdale (leased to NT)**	Urban common
CL 79 (W)	**Loughrigg Common**	**3.79 sk**	**Earl of Lonsdale (leased to NT)**	Urban common
CL 75 (W)	**Great Langdale Common**	**15.30 sk**	**Earl of Lonsdale (leased to NT)**	Urban common
CL 77 (W)	**Baysbrown Common**	**1.28 sk**	**Unclaimed (2 x rts held by NT)**	Urban common (Sect 9)
CL 76 (W)	**Little Langdale Common**	**3.64 sk**	**Earl of Lonsdale (leased to NT)**	Urban common
CL 167 (C)	**Langstrath & Coombe Fells**	**16.02 sk**	**National Trust**	Access common
CL 58 (C)	**Eskdale Common**	**30.72 sk**	**National Trust (orig Egremont)**	Access common

South (Coniston/Furness)

CL 29 (L)	Coniston, Dunnerdale, Seathwaite Fells; Torver High Common	45.53 sk	Muncaster Estate/National Trust/ Crown Estate Commissioners	Access common (pt)
CL 57 (L)	**Torver Low common**	**1.93 sk**	**Crown Estate Commissioners**	**Access common (Sect 193)**
CL 155 (L)	**Blawith Common**	**4.54 sk**	**LDSPB (leased fr Boughton Estate)**	**Access common (small pt Sect 9)**
CL 55 (L)	Woodland Fell	9.21 sk	Holker Estate Trust	
CL 39/40 (L)	Lowick Low/High Commons	3.79 sk	(2/3 x private owners)	
CL 52 (L)	Kirkby Moor	7.04 sk	Holker Estate Trust	
CL 189 (L)	Bethecar Moor	5.51 sk	Public Trustee (ex small pts)	Regulated Pasture

Western Fells

CL 11 (C)	**Brackenthwaite Fell**	**42.57 sk**	**National Trust (orig Egremont?)**	**Access common**
CL 394 (C)	**Derwent Fells or Common**	**3.83 sk**	**National Trust (orig Egremont?)**	**Access common**
CL 255 (C)	Scawdale Fell	2.89 sk	National Trust (pt)	Access common (pt)
CL 74 (C)	**Brackenthwaite Common**	**1.94 sk**	**National Trust**	**Access common**
CL 110 (C)	**Kinniside Common**	**21.0 sk**	**National Trust (orig Egremont)**	**Access common**
CL 490 (C)	**Stockdale Moor**	**10.10 sk**	**National Trust (orig Egremont)**	**Access common**
CL 59 (C)	**Nether Wasdale Common**	**20.21 sk**	**National Trust (orig Egremont)**	**Access common**

South West Fells

CL 330 (C)	*Muncaster Fell*	*(3.62 sk)*	*Ravenglass & Eskdale Rlwy Company*	*Void (orig Muncaster Estate)*
CL 69 (C)	Birker Fell	13.63 sk	Muncaster Estate	
CL 68 (C)	Birkby Fell	5.60 sk	Muncaster Estate	
CL 73 (C)	Waberthwaite Fell	2.58 sk	Muncaster Estate	
CL 72 (C)	Corney Fell	5.43 sk	Muncaster Estate	
CL 71 (C)	Ulpha Fell	13.15 sk	Earl of Lonsdale	
CL 45 (C)	**Thwaites Fell**	**6.62 sk**	**Earl of Lonsdale (leased to NT)**	**Access common**
CL 8 (C)	Bootle Fell	2.85 sk	Earl of Lonsdale	
CL 112 (C)	Black Combe & White Combe	17.42 sk	Land Register (1994) (orig Lonsdale)	

THE NORTH PENNINES (ALLENDALE, HEXHAM AND WEARDALE)

Northumberland

CL 122 (N)	Garleigh Crags	(1.75 sk)	Reg RA. Cancelled
CL 93 (N)	Morpeth Common	(2.0 sk)	Cancelled 25/2/72
CL 1 (N)	Allendale Common	73.96 sk	Trustees Allendale Settled Estate (Ridley)
CL 2 (N)	Hexhamshire Common	19.14 sk	Trustees Allendale Settled Estate (Ridley)

Weardale (North)

CL 76 (D)	Edmundbyers Common	7.12 sk	Durham CC/Water Comp/Syndicate 'A'
CL 75 (D)	Muggleswick Common	22.92 sk	Water Company/Syndicate 'A'
CL 72 (D)	Muggleswick Park	2.99 sk	Muggleswick Parish Council/Syndicate
CL 66 (D)	Waskerley Park	7.69 sk	Lambton Settled Estates
CL 58 (D)	West Lintzgarth Common	1.68 sk	
CL 59 (D)	Northgate Fell	1.69 sk	
CL 22 (D)	Stanhope Common	31.02 sk	Syndicate (incl Viscount Ridley)
CL 65 (D)	Wolsingham Park Moor	8.27 sk	EA Featherstone-Fenwick
CL 48 (D)	Sand Edge Common	2.16 sk	
CL 4 (D)	Cornsay & Headleyhope Common	2.31 sk	

Weardale (West)

CL 60 (D)	Puddingthorne Moor	1.72 sk	MAFF (Forestry Commission?)
CL 61 (D)	Killhope Moor	5.0 sk	MAFF (Forestry Commission?)
CL 74 (D)	Wellhope Moor	5.75 sk	DM Watson, Wellhope Farm
CL 25 (D)	Burnhope Moor	16.70 sk	Public Trustee — Regulated Pasture
CL 7 (D)	Ireshope Moor	4.13 sk	Public Trustee — Regulated Pasture
CL 21 (D)	Harthope Moor	2.64 sk	Public Trustee — Regulated Pasture
CL 41 (D)	Chapel Fell	1.74 sk	Public Trustee — Regulated Pasture

Weardale (South)

CL 50 (D)	Westernhope Moor	10.68 sk	Syndicate	
CL 38 (D)	Bollihope Moor	29.87 sk	Raago Ltd (Mahktoum)	
CL 40 (D)	Pikestone & Knitsley Fells	15.0 sk	Raago Ltd (Mahktoum)	
CL 9 (D)	Hamsterley Common	7.89 sk	Raago Ltd (Mahktoum)	
CL 6 (D)	Egglestone Common	19.50 sk		
CL 8 (D)	Cockfield Fell	2.38 sk	Public Trustee	Regulated Pasture

THE NORTH PENNINES (TEESDALE AND THE PENNINE SCARP)

Durham (formerly North Riding of Yorkshire)

CL 81 (D)	West Common, Herdship & Backside Fells	(18.0 sk)	Raby Estate	Reg RA. Withdrawn July 1973
CL 343 (NR)	Crossthwaite Common	(2.10 sk)	Strathmore Estate	Reg RA. Withdrawn June 1973
CL 323 (NR)	Mickle Fell & Cronkley Fell	(80.0 sk)	Strathmore Estate	Reg RA. Withdrawn June 1973
CL 324 (NR)	Holwick Fell	(9.0 sk)	Strathmore Estate	Reg RA. Withdrawn June 1973
CL 344 (NR)	Mickleton Moor	(5.0 sk)	Strathmore Estate	Reg RA. Withdrawn June 1973
CL 325 (NR)	Hunderthwaite Moor	(8.0 sk)	Strathmore Estate (?)	Reg RA. Withdrawn June 1973
CL 75 (NR)	Cotherstone Regulated Pasture	20.13 sk	Public Trustee	Regulated Pasture (1866 award)
CL 285 (NR)	Lartington High Moor	(6.0 sk)	Addison, Barnard Castle	Reg RA. Withdrawn June 1973
CL 1 (NR)	Bowes Moor	46.38 sk	Lords in Trust of the Manor of Bowes	Managed under Courts Leet & Baron
CL 27 (NR)	Barningham High Moor	5.58 sk	Barningham Estate Trustees (Milbank)	

East Cumbria (Pennine Scarp)

CL 124 (C)	Melmerby Fell	9.35 sk	AS Agar, Melmerby Hall
CL 125 (C)	Ousby Fell	14.50 sk	Catlin Estates Ltd, Chelmsford
CL 126 (C)	Skirwith Fell	8.80 sk	(Execs) MG Hughes la Fleming
CL 127 (C)	Kirkland Fell	4.39 sk	NERC/Corland Minerals

CL	Name	Stint	Owner	Notes
CL 323 (C)	Blencarn Fell	2.80 sk	Several private owners	
CL 5 (W)	Milburn Forest and Red Carle	20.40 sk	NERC	Moorhouse Nature Reserve
CL 80 (W)	Knock Fell	8.50 sk	NERC	Moorhouse Nature Reserve
CL 81 (W)	Dufton Fell	46.17 sk	NERC/Corland Minerals/One private	Moorhouse Nature Reserve
CL 26 (W)	Murton Fell	13.48 sk	MOD	Warcop Principal Training Centre
CL 27 (W)	Hilton Fell	14.40 sk	MOD	Warcop Principal Training Centre
CL 122 (W)	Burton Fell	14.18 sk	MOD	Warcop Principal Training Centre

SHAP, MALLERSTANG AND THE HOWGILLS

Shap and the Eden Valley Fells

CL	Name	Stint	Owner	Notes
CL 41 (W)	Roundthwaite Common	3.83 sk		
CL 100 (W)	Bretherdale Common	2.03 sk		
CL 108 (W)	Bretherdale Bank	2.04 sk		
CL 9 (W)	Birkbeck Fells Common	7.39 sk	Earl of Lonsdale	
CL 11 (W)	Hardendale Fell	1.94 sk		
CL 10 (W)	Crosby Ravenworth Fell	22.42 sk	Earl of Lonsdale	
CL 33 (W)	Ravenstonedale Moor	2.43 sk		
CL 96 (W)	Tarn Moor	1.79 sk	Public Trustee	
CL 105 (W)	Asby Common (Little Asby Scar)	4.64 sk	Watson Sayer Property Company	
CL 4 (W)	Crosby Garrett Regulated Pasture	6.21 sk	Public Trustee	Regulated (1882) under 1876 Act
CL 37 (W)	'Flass' & pt of Ash Fell	2.35 sk		
CL 40 (W)	Greenrigg	10.34 sk		
CL 44 (W)	Wharton Fell	2.89 sk		

Mallerstang and Stainmore

CL 94 (W)	Mallerstang Common (West)	9.36 sk		
CL 93 (W)	Mallerstang Common (N & E)	16.72 sk		
CL 103 (W)	Nateby Common	2.85 sk		
CL 95 (W)	Hartley Fell	4.61 sk		
CL 21 (W)	Winton & Kaber Fell Reg Pasture	22.0 sk	Syndicate 'B'	Regulated (1911) under 1876 Act. Rights held in gross (Stinted Pasture)
CL 18 (W)	East Stainmore Reg Pasture (S)	10.43 sk	Syndicate 'B'	Regulated (1879) under 1876 Act. Rights held in gross (Stinted Pasture)
CL 17 (W)	East Stainmore Reg Pasture (N)	15.08 sk	Syndicate	Regulated (1879) under 1876 Act. Rights held in gross (Stinted Pasture)

Howgill Fells and SE Cumbria

CL 45 (W)	Tebay Fell	4.92 sk	Earl of Lonsdale	
CL 42 (W)	Langdale Fell	19.28 sk	Earl of Lonsdale	
CL 39 (W)	Ravenstonedale Common	25.12 sk	Syndicate	
CL 26 (WR)	Brant Fell	27.35 sk	J Gibson, Blackburn	
CL 29 (WR)	Bluecaster (Baugh) Fell	30.58 sk	J Gibson, Blackburn	
CL 28 (WR)	Frostrow Fell	3.44 sk	Miss HMT Frankland	
CL 110 (W)	Middleton Fell	14.60 sk	Mr Harrison Beck	
CL 55 (W)	Barbon Low Fell	2.67 sk	Baron Shuttleworth (?)	
CL 164 (W)	Barbon High Fell	(4.0 sk)	Baron Shuttleworth	Void
CL 23 (L)	Ireby Fell	1.47 sk	Unclaimed	
CL 71 (L)	Fenwick Allotment	(1.75 sk)	Baron Shuttleworth	Void
CL 72 (L)	High Leck Fell	(6.75 sk)	(Execs) S Nuttall	Void

THE YORKSHIRE DALES

Swaledale

CL 149 (NR)	Birkdale Moor	27.39 sk	Gunnerside Estate	Mr Miller	
CL 150 (NR)	Ravenseat Common	(6.0 sk)	Gunnerside Estate	Mr Miller	Deregistered Sept 1981
CL 151 (NR)	West Stonedale Out Pasture	12.48 sk	Gunnerside Estate	Mr Miller	
CL 153 (NR)	East Stonedale Moor	(7.34 sk)	Gunnerside Estate	Mr Miller	Deregistered April 1984
CL 154 (NR)	Gunnerside Moor	4.43 sk	Gunnerside Estate	Mr Miller	
CL 155 (NR)	Gunnerside Pasture	3.69 sk	Gunnerside Estate	Mr Miller	
CL 29 (NR)	Muker Common & Ivelet Moor	10.33 sk	Gunnerside Estate	Mr Miller	
CL 152 (NR)	Angram Common & Ashgill Side	12.79 sk	Gunnerside Estate	Mr Miller	
CL 265 (NR)	Keld Side	(0.60 sk)	Gunnerside Estate	Mr Miller	Deregistered March 1981
CL 156 (NR)	Thwaite Common	5.63 sk	Gunnerside Estate	Mr Miller	
CL 157 (NR)	Oxnop Common	2.88 sk	Gunnerside Estate	Mr Miller	
CL 158 (NR)	Satron Moor	2.85 sk	Gunnerside Estate	Mr Miller	
CL 97 (NR)	Whitaside Moor	6.25 sk	Grinton Estate	The Earl Peel	
CL 147 (NR)	Grinton & Harkerside Moors	4.87 sk	Grinton Estate	The Earl Peel	
CL 42 (NR)	Melbecks High & Low Moors	18.78 sk	L Brown, Gunnerside		
CL 43 (NR)	Arkengarthdale Moor	58.59 sk	Earl of Arundel/Dale Ltd (orig Sopwith)		
CL 11 (NR)	Reeth High & Low Moors	10.72 sk	Major HM Martineau		
CL 292 (NR)	Hurst Moor	(7.0 sk)	TEB Sopwith		0.45 sk (peat moss) finally registered.
CL 347 (NR)	Marrick Moor	2.25 sk	HWPE Earl-Drax, Wareham, Dorset		
CL 142 (NR)	Holgate Moor & Pasture	6.01 sk			

Wensleydale

CL 38 (NR)	White Birks Common	2.03 sk	Mr Miller (Simonstone Estate)	
CL 17 (NR)	Abbotside/Stags Fell Commons	38.97 sk	Askrigg Parish Council	Stags Fell reg under 1876 Act
CL 32 (NR)	Askrigg Common	6.77 sk	Askrigg Parish Council	
CL 91 (NR)	Woodhall Greets	1.03 sk	Askrigg Parish Council	

Ref	Name	Value	Owner / Comment	Notes
CL 33 (NR)	Melmerby Moor	3.26 sk	RS Ferrand, Stockbridge, Hants	
CL 52 (NR)	Middleham High & Low Moors	1.72 sk	Middleham Parish Council	
CL 72 (NR)	Tongue Moss Peat grounds	1.04 sk		
CL 145 (NR)	Whether Fell & Ten End	0.91 sk	Lord Trustees of the Manor of Bainbridge	
CL 39 (NR)	Marsett Bardale Common	2.61 sk	Public Trustee	Regulated Pasture

Bishopdale and Coverdale

Ref	Name	Value	Owner / Comment	Notes
CL 220 (NR)	Bishopdale Gavel	1.90 sk	Land Register	
CL 41 (NR)	Bishopdale Edge	1.99 sk	Public Trustee	Regulated Pasture
CL 40 (NR)	Wasset Fell	1.90 sk	Public Trustee	Regulated Pasture
CL 44 (NR)	Walden Moor	12.15 sk	RH Chapman-Robinson, Leyburn	
CL 337 (NR)	Fleensop Moor	(2.0 sk)		Reg RA. Withdrawn
CL 78 (NR)	Braidley Moor & Cow Side	7.7 sk	Cow Side land register; rest Sect 9	
CL 297 (NR)	Woodale Moor	(1.30 sk)		Reg RA. Withdrawn June 1973
CL 296 (NR)	Woodale Bents	(1.0 sk)		Reg RA. Withdrawn June 1973
CL 328 (NR)	Arkleside Moor	(2.20 sk)		Reg RA. Withdrawn July 1973
CL 295 (NR)	Hindlethwaite Moor	(2.30 sk)	Captain Parlour	Reg RA. Withdrawn July 1973
CL 37 (NR)	Swineside Moor	1.01 sk		
CL 105 (NR)	West Scrafton Moor	3.74 sk		
CL 305 (NR)	East Scrafton Moor	(3.30 sk)		Reg RA. Withdrawn June 1973
CL 338 (NR)	Feather Shaw	(1.40 sk)		Reg RA. Void May 1977
CL 20 (NR)	Caldbergh Moor	5.83 sk	RCH Harrison-Topham	

Ribblesdale and the Three Peaks Area

Ref	Name	Value	Owner / Comment	Notes
CL 501 (WR)	Whernside Great Pasture	7.40 sk	Land Register	
CL 272 (WR)	Scales Moor	4.14 sk	ER Hartley & FBH Jackson	
CL 368 (WR)	Winterscales Pasture	2.67 sk		
CL 473 (WR)	Blea Moor/Little Dale Pasture	7.50 sk	Dr AJ Farrer, Ingleborough Estate	

CL No.	Name	Area	Owner	Notes
CL 194 (WR)	Blea Moor	4.37 sk	Dr AJ Farrer, Ingleborough Estate	
CL 103 (WR)	Camm End (Cam Fell)	6.89 sk	Dr AJ Farrer, Ingleborough Estate	
CL 102 (WR)	Crutchin Gill Rigg	1.50 sk	Dr AJ Farrer, Ingleborough Estate	
CL 134 (WR)	Ingleborough Common	7.42 sk	Sir RA Hornby, Viscount Edham, EH Martin (Lords of the Manor of Ingleton)	
CL 208 (WR)	Clapham Bents, Newby Moss, Simon Fell	7.42 sk	Dr AJ Farrer, Ingleborough Estate	
CL 339 (WR)	The Allotment, Ingleborough	1.64 sk	Dr AJ Farrer, Ingleborough Estate	
CL 115 (WR)	Fell Close	1.45 sk		
CL 85 (WR)	Long Scar	2.83 sk	Dr AJ Farrer, Ingleborough Estate	
CL 113 (WR)	Sulber	1.20 sk	Dr AJ Farrer, Ingleborough Estate	Ingleborough NNR.
CL 86 (WR)	Moughton & Long Scars	3.46 sk	Dr AJ Farrer, Ingleborough Estate	
CL 137 (WR)	Newby Moor	2.94 sk	Dr AJ Farrer, Ingleborough Estate	
CL 157 (WR)	*Little Moor Head*	*(1.51 sk)*	*National Trust*	*Reg RA. Withdrawn Dec 1971*
CL 255 (WR)	*Black Hill & Out Side*	*(1.25 sk)*		*Reg RA. Withdrawn Dec 1971*
CL 421 (WR)	Highside Moor	2.37 sk	N Thwaite & M Capstick, Hellifield	

North Bowland

CL No.	Name	Area	Owner	Notes
CL 136 (WR)	Burn Moor (Bentham)	5.49 sk	Hornby Estate	
CL 211 (WR)	Burn Moor (Clapham)	9.49 sk	Dr AJ Farrer, Ingleborough Estate	
CL 209 (WR)	Clapham Common	5.30 sk	Dr AJ Farrer, Ingleborough Estate	
CL 275 (WR)	Austick Common	2.73 sk	Dr AJ Farrer, Ingleborough Estate	
CL 104 (WR)	Lawkland Fell	2.55 sk	Lt Col GWH Field, Austick	
CL 114 (WR)	Giggleswick Common	0.89 sk	Duke of Devonshire	
CL 195 (WR)	Rathmell Common	1.61 sk	GCH Taylor, Pendleton	

Langstrothdale

CL No.	Name	Area	Owner	Notes
CL 515 (WR)	Horsehead Moor	4.05 sk		
CL 174 (WR)	Yockenthwaite Moor	3.53 sk	Unclaimed	
CL 412 (WR)	Scarr House Moor	2.19 sk		

Wharfedale

Ref	Name	sk	Owner	Status
CL 33 (WR)	Whernside	(4.41 sk)	(Obj) Gaitholders of Great Whernside	Void Dec 1984
CL 186 (WR)	Conistone Moor & Bycliffe	(11.59 sk)	Executor Trustee Ltd/Midland Bank	Void Jan 1982
CL 77 (WR)	Grassington Moor	8.28 sk	Section 9 (National Park)	
CL 76 (WR)	Grass Wood	1.93 sk	MAFF	
CL 344 (WR)	Hebden Moor	(0.40 sk)		Void
CL 140 (WR)	Hetton Common	0.35 sk	Parish Trustees of Hetton	Modified. 1.30 sk excluded
CL 409 (WR)	Calton Moor	1.67 sk	Morphet/Henderson	
CL 30 (WR)	Threshfield Moor	2.39 sk	Fenwick, Seeple & Co, Eshton, Skipton	
CL 34 (WR)	Cracoe In Fell	1.86 sk	Duke of Devonshire	
CL 109 (WR)	Cracoe Out Fell	0.90 sk		
CL 158 (WR)	Rylstone Out Fell	2.81 sk	Duke of Buccleuch/Duchess of Devonshire	
CL 213 (WR)	Burnsall & Thorpe Fell	5.43 sk	Trustees of Chatsworth Estate	
CL 417 (WR)	Barden Moor	7.27 sk	Trustees of Chatsworth Estate	Regulated (1881) under 1876 Act
CL 243 (WR)	Embsay Moor	7.63 sk	(Most pt) Duke of Devonshire	Regulated (1881) under 1876 Act
CL 553 (WR)	Hazlewood Moor	7.27 sk	Trustees of Chatsworth Estate	
CL 234 (WR)	Beamsley Moor	3.30 sk	Trustees of Chatsworth Estate	
CL 46 (WR)	Langbar Moor	2.70 sk	Syndicate 'C' (Barrett, Irwin, Mason)	
CL 48 (WR)	Middleton Moor Enclosure	2.24 sk	Syndicate 'C'	
CL 481 (WR)	Kex Gill (Blubberhouses) Moor	11.56 sk	Leeds MBC (Yorks Water?)	
CL 504 (WR)	Denton Moor	(3.75 sk)	Syndicate	Reg RA. Withdrawn July 1973
CL 519 (WR)	Askwith Moor	(4.0 sk)		Reg RA. Withdrawn July 1973

Nidderdale/Washburn

Ref	Name	sk	Owner	Status
CL 526 (WR)	Lodge Moor	(7.0 sk)	Bradford MBC (Yorks Water?)	Reg RA. Withdrawn May 1973
CL 488 (WR)	Riggs Pasture	(11.0 sk)		Reg RA. Withdrawn July 1973
CL 118 (WR)	Stean Moor	13.33 sk	Baron Vestey, Stowell Park, Glos	
CL 165 (WR)	Ramsgill Bents/Raygill House Moor	8.72 sk	JAC Briggs, Catterick	

CL number	Name	(sk)	Owner / Register	Notes
CL 166 (WR)	Ramsgill Bents	1.30 sk	JAC Briggs, Catterick	
CL 357 (WR)	Gouthwaite Moor	9.89 sk	Land Register	
CL 547 (WR)	Pockstones Moor	(4.0 sk)	Leeds MBC (Yorks Water?)	Reg RA. Withdrawn
CL 524 (WR)	Fountains Earth Moor	(2.25 sk)	(Execs) E Haigh, Harrogate	Reg RA. Withdrawn July 1973
CL 438 (WR)	Pateley Moor	1.18 sk	GS Bostock, Tixall, Shropshire	
CL 117 (WR)	**Brimham Moor**	**1.50 sk**	**National Trust**	**Access common**

Masham/Burn Valley/Dallowgill

CL number	Name	(sk)	Owner / Register	Notes
CL 232 (NR)	Colsterdale Moor	(13.0 sk)	Countess Swinton of Swinton	Reg RA. Void July 1975
CL 233 (NR)	Pott Moor	(14.0 sk)	Countess Swinton of Swinton	Reg RA. Void
CL 234 (NR)	Iton Moor	(10.50 sk)	Countess Swinton of Swinton	Reg RA. Void April 1976
CL 335 (NR)	Nutwith Common	(?? sk)	MAFF/Countess Swinton of Swinton	Reg RA. Withdrawn July 1973
CL 168 (NR)	Grewelthorpe Moor	2.14 sk	Countess Swinton of Swinton	
CL 73 (NR)	Kirkby Malzeard Moor	3.77 sk	GS Bostock, Tixall	
CL 212 (NR)	Carlesmoor & K Malzeard Moors	3.04 sk	GS Bostock, Tixall	
CL 476 (NR)	Dallowgill Moor	14.40 sk	GS Bostock, Tixall	Rights void Jan 1981
CL 452 (NR)	Land in the Parishes of Laverton & Kirkby Malzeard	(10.0 sk)	Leeds MBC (Yorks Water?)	Void Jan 1981
CL 612 (NR)	Dallowgill Moor (pt)	(1.40 sk)	GS Bostock, Tixall	Void Jan 1981
CL 609 (NR)	Eavestone Moor	(2.30 sk)	GS Bostock, Tixall	Void Jan 1981

THE NORTH YORK MOORS

Cleveland Hills

CL 85 (NR)	Scarth Wood Moor & Near Moor	1.98 sk	National Trust	
CL 320 (NR)	Whorlton Moor	(10.0 sk)	Viscount Ingleby	Reg RA. Void 1977
CL 258 (NR)	Osmotherley Moor	(4.0 sk)		Reg RA. Void 1977
CL 370 (NR)	Thimbleby Moor	(1.20 sk)	Sir RL Borwick, Bart, Bedale	Reg RA. Void 1977
CL 322 (NR)	Arden Great Moor	(8.77 sk)	Viscountess Pollington	Reg RA. Void 1977
CL 321 (NR)	Snilesworth Moor	(15.0 sk)	Viscount Ingleby	Reg RA. Void 1977

North York Moors (North of Main Watershed)

CL 58 (NR)	Carlton Bank	1.29 sk	Lord Ingleby	
CL 15 (NR)	Cold Moor	2.81 sk	Land Register	
CL 340 (NR)	Greeenhow Moor	(10.0 sk)	Forestry Commission	Reg RA. Withdrawn June 1973
CL 282 (NR)	Baysdale Moor	(14.0 sk)	Feversham Estate (?)	Reg RA. Withdrawn June 1973
CL 192 (NR)	Great Ayton Moor	2.13 sk	FW Fry, CN Wilson	
CL 287 (NR)	Gisborough Moor	7.50 sk		
CL 213 (NR)	Tidkinhow Moor	0.70 sk		
CL 372 (NR)	Stanghow Moor	(2.50 sk)		Void
CL 286 (NR)	Kildale Moor (pt)	(1.80 sk)	Forestry Commission/RM Turton	Reg RA. Withdrawn July 1971
CL 190 (NR)	Commondale Moor	(8.0 sk)	Lord Gisborough	Void Sept 1973
CL 382 (NR)	Kildale & Warren Moors	(1.50 sk)	RM Turton	Reg RA. Withdrawn Oct 1971
CL 8 (NR)	Westerdale Moor	17.24 sk	Savile, Wood, Watson	
CL 63 (NR)	Glaisdale, Danby High, Lealholm, and Danby Low Moors	49.94 sk	Viscount Down	Managed under Courts Leet & Baron
CL 326/7(NR)	Roxby High/Low Moors	(3.55 sk)	RM Turton	Reg RA. Void Sept 1975
CL 288 (NR)	Newton Mulgrave Moor	(3.75 sk)	RM Turton	Reg RA. Void Aug 1975
CL 137 (NR)	Ugthorpe Moor	2.05 sk	Marquis of Normanby (?)	

CL 81 (NR)	Egton High Moor	22.49 sk	Forestry Commission	
CL 4 (NR)	Goathland Moor	31.18 sk	Duchy of Lancaster (HM the Queen)	
CL 109 (NR)	Sleights Moor	6.21 sk	RJ Manners-Rastall, Whitby	
CL 289 (NR)	Sneaton Moor	(8.0 sk)	Forestry Commission	*Reg RA. Withdrawn*
CL 76 (NR)	Fylingdales Moor	28.70 sk	M Strickland, Burton Hill House, Whitwell	

North York Moors (South of Main Watershed)

CL 168 (NR)	Bilsdale West Moor	3.09 sk	Land Register (orig Savile, Pollington & Mexborough)	Modified. N pt of moor excluded
CL 53 (NR)	Urra & Bilsdale East Moors	19.22 sk	Feversham Estate	
CL 241(NR)	Laskill Pasture	2.33 sk		
CL 281 (NR)	Bransdale Moor	(16.0 sk)	Feversham Estate	*Reg RA. Withdrawn June 1977*
CL 284 (NR)	Skiplam Moor	(3.50 sk)	Feversham Estate	*Reg RA. Withdrawn June 1973*
CL 270 (NR)	Farndale West & Harland Moors	(11.0 sk)	Feversham Estate	*Reg RA. Withdrawn June 1973*
CL 279 (NR)	Farndale East Moor	(13.0 sk)	Feversham Estate	*Reg RA. Withdrawn July 1973*
CL 169 (NR)	Farndale East	(2.0 sk)	Feversham Estate	*Void*
CL 162 (NR)	Spaunton Moor	33.0 sk	GW Darley, Hutton-le-Hall	Managed under Courts Leet & Baron
CL 47 (NR)	Rosedale East Side	1.19 sk	Milburn Estates, Newcastle	
CL 280 (NR)	Rosedale East Moor	(5.80 sk)	*Milburn Estates, Newcastle*	*Reg RA. Withdrawn June 1973*
CL 283 (NR)	Hartoft Moor	(10.0 sk)	*Forestry Commission/Milburn Estates*	*Reg RA. Withdrawn July 1973*
CL 49 (NR)	**Levisham Moor**	**7.16 sk**	**N Yorks CC**	**Access common**
CL 330 (NR)	Lockton High Moor ('Saltergate')	3.75 sk	Forestry Commission/F Grant, Lincs	Reg RA. (6.0 sk excluded3)
CL 331 (NR)	Lockton Low Moor	1.0 sk	F Grant, Lincs	Reg RA. (6.4 sk excluded)
CL 332 (NR)	Allerton High Moor	(12.5 sk)	*Forestry Commission/MOD*	*Reg RA. Withdrawn July 1973*
CL 240 (NR)	Ebberston High Moor	(2.30 sk)	*Forestry Commission*	*Reg RA. Withdrawn*
CL 390 (NR)	Land at Ebberston	(1.40 sk)	*MAFF/Forestry Commission*	*Void*
CL 271 (NR)	Snainton Moor	(1.80 sk)	*Forestry Commission*	*Reg RA. Withdrawn*

LANCASHIRE (FOREST OF BOWLAND)

CL No.	Name	Area	Owner	Status
CL 90 (L)	Hare Appletree Fell	1.85 sk	Trustees of Westminster Estate	
CL 123 (L)	Black, Blanch & Haylot Fells	11.27 sk	Trustees of Westminster Estate	
CL 76 (L)	Whit Moor	1.66 sk	Hornby Estate	
CL 18 (L)	Goodber Common	4.64 sk	Unclaimed (Sect 9)	
CL 88 (L)	*Lythe Fell*	*(8.0 sk)*	*Regulated Pasture*	*Void*
CL 182 (L)	Burn Fell and Dunsop Fell	2.25 sk	Lord Clitheroe	
CL 176 (L)	Newton Fell	1.71 sk	Lord Clitheroe	
CL 293 (L)	Low Fell	0.475 sk	Lord Clitheroe	
CL 248 (L)	Newton Fell	0.525 sk	Lord Clitheroe	
CL 66 (L)	Easington Fell	2.50 sk	G Crane	
CL 65 (L)	Harrop Fell	0.86 sk	Unclaimed (Sect 9)	

LANCASHIRE (PENDLE AND BOULSWORTH)

CL No.	Name	Area	Owner	Status
CL 204 (L)	*Meerley Moor*	*(1.0 sk)*	*Huntroyde Estate (Starkie)*	*Cancelled*
CL 217 (L)	*Pendle Hill*	*(5.35 sk)*	*Lord Clitheroe/NW Water/others*	*Cancelled*
CL 44 (L)	Worston Moor	0.67 sk	Lord Clitheroe	*Pt modified*
CL 83 (L)	Pendleton Moor	2.08 sk	Lord Clitheroe/NW Water	
CL 79 (L)	Spence Moor	0.54 sk	Lord Clitheroe/NW Water	
CL 95 (L)	Barley Moor	2.51 sk	Lord Clitheroe	
CL 183 (L)	*Boulsworth Hill*	*(6.50 sk)*	*Bannister Estate /NW Water*	*Modified/all void excepting 0.84 sk*
CL 261 (L)	*Trawden Moor*	*(2.20 sk)*	*Bannister Estate*	*Modified/all void excepting 0.68 sk*
CL 134 (L)	*Trawden Moor*	*(4.75 sk)*	*Bannister Estate*	*Void (urban common)*
CL 258 (L)	*Combe Hill*	*(4.0 sk)*	*Bannister Estate*	*Void (urban common)*
CL 15 (NR)	Ickornshaw Hill	3.13 sk	Pt Sect 9/pt syndicate (?)	*Modified*
CL 11 (NR)	Stott Hill Moor	2.02 sk	Syndicate	*Modified*

THE YORKSHIRE AND LANCASHIRE PENNINES

CL 207 (WR)	**Ilkley Moor**	**Ilkley MBC/ Yorks Water/ Syndicate**	**Urban common**
CL 503 (WR)	*Bingley Moor*	*Syndicate 'D'*	*Reg RA. Withdrawn*
CL 510 (WR)	*Hawksworth Moor*	*Syndicate 'D'*	*Reg RA. Withdrawn July 1973*
CL 347 (WR)	**Baildon Moor**	**City of Bradford/Yorks Water (small pt)**	**Urban common**
CL 119 (WR)	**Hallas Rough Park**	**Land Register**	**Urban common**
CL 605 (WR)	*Stansfield Moor*	*NW Water*	*All but 18.4 ha ('the Hoppet') void*
CL 397 (WR)	*Hoar Side Moor and Park*	*Yorks Water/Savile Estate*	*Modified (rural common (Hepton RD))*
CL 139 (WR)	*Heptonstall Town Moor*	*Yorks Water/Savile Estate*	*Rural common (Hepton RD)*
CL 497 (WR)	*Black Moor and Flask*	*Yorks Water/Savile Estate*	*Void August 1982*
CL 42 (WR)	*Stanbury Moor*	*Yorks Water*	*All but 0.57 ha void June 1973*
CL 655 (WR)	*Widdop Moor and Wadsworth Moor*	*Yorks Water/Savile Estate*	*Cancelled Nov 1972*
CL 606 (WR)	*Hamlet Hill*	*Yorks Water/Savile Estate*	*Reg RA. Withdrawn May 1973*
CL 600 (WR)	**Oakworth or Keighley Moor**	**Unclaimed**	**Urban common**
CL 2 (WR)	**Haworth Moor**	**Yorks Water**	**Urban common**
CL 498 (WR)	**Oxenhope & Midgeley Moors**	**1 x private owner/Syndicate 'E'**	**Urban common (Pts void Mar 1986)**
CL 297 (WR)	*Dimmin Dale*	*1 x private owner/Syndicate 'E'*	*Rural common (Hepton RD)*
CL 72 (WR)	**Todmorden Moor**	**(Execs) JP Dearden, New Zealand**	**Urban common**
CL 472 (WR)	**Inchfield Moor**	**(Execs) JP Dearden, New Zealand**	**Urban common (1.30 sk void Dec 1981)**
CL 407 (WR)	**Inchfield Pasture**	**Yorks Water/Public Trustee**	**Urban common**
CL 13 (L)	**Darwen Moor**	**Blackburn & Darwen Council**	**Urban common**
CL 156 (L)	**Darwen Moor**	**NW Water/1 x Private**	**Urban common (3.30 sk void)**
CL 153 (L)	*Hoddlesdon Moss*	*A Carus & Sons Ltd*	*Cancelled Mar 1973*
CL 139 (L)	*Jackson Height & Pike Lowe*	*NW Water*	*Void July 1981*
CL 82 (L)	**Haslingden Moor**		**Urban common**
CL 205 (L)	*Hambledon Common*		*Rural common*
CL 215 (L)	*Long Grain Moor*	*NW Water*	*Void Jan 1982*

(Stock rate column, between name and owner)

	Stock rate
CL 207 (WR)	10.85 sk
CL 503 (WR)	*(4.40 sk)*
CL 510 (WR)	*(2.40 sk)*
CL 347 (WR)	2.79 sk
CL 119 (WR)	1.15 sk
CL 605 (WR)	*(3.0 sk)*
CL 397 (WR)	1.76 sk
CL 139 (WR)	6.69 sk
CL 497 (WR)	*(5.50 sk)*
CL 42 (WR)	*(4.15 sk)*
CL 655 (WR)	*(18.50 sk)*
CL 606 (WR)	*(0.90 sk)*
CL 600 (WR)	3.10 sk
CL 2 (WR)	4.08 sk
CL 498 (WR)	27.64 sk
CL 297 (WR)	*1.62 sk*
CL 72 (WR)	3.04 sk
CL 472 (WR)	0.70 sk
CL 407 (WR)	1.93 sk
CL 13 (L)	1.11 sk
CL 156 (L)	1.26 sk
CL 153 (L)	*(2.0 sk)*
CL 139 (L)	*(0.65 sk)*
CL 82 (L)	2.28 sk
CL 205 (L)	1.21 sk
CL 215 (L)	*(1.40 sk)*

CL 42 (L)	Holcombe Moor	4.60 sk	National Trust	Urban common
CL 93 (L)	Holcombe Moor	(1.50 sk)	MOD	Void Sept 1982
CL 177 (L)	Harden Moor	1.15 sk	Unclaimed	Urban common
CL 175 (L)	Scout Moor & Turf Moor	2.58 sk	NW Water	Urban common
CL 162 (L)	Knowl Moor	3.96 sk		Urban common
CL 163 (L)	Rooley (or Shore) Moor	3.14 sk		Urban common
CL 213 (L)	Brandwood Higher End Moor	1.04 sk	Unclaimed	Urban common
CL 257 (L)	Whitworth Lower End & Jackson Moors	(1.20 sk)	NW Water	Reg RA. Void April 1981
CL 278 (L)	Cold Clough (Cow Clough Pasture)	(0.70 sk)	NW Water	Void Sept 1978
CL 165 (L)	Whitworth (Trough) Common	1.92 sk		Urban common
CL 166 (L)	Wardle Common	1.73 sk		Urban common
CL 168 (L)	Shore Moor	1.70 sk		Urban common
CL 172 (L)	Ramsden & White Slack Common	1.24 sk	(Execs) JP Dearden, New Zealand	Urban common (1.0 sk void Feb 1983)
CL 673 (WR)	Walsden Common	2.40 sk	(Execs) JP Dearden, New Zealand	Urban common
CL 121 (WR)	Langfield Moor (Todmorden)	6.05 sk	Trustees of the Freeholders of Langfield	Urban common (Regulated Pasture)
CL 24 (WR)	Withins Moor/Sunderland Pasture	(2.89 sk)	Wakefield & Dist Water Board/For Comm	Cancelled Sept 1971 (Upper Cragg Vale)
CL 653 (WR)	Witheral Moor	(1.20 sk)	Wakefield & Dist Water Board/For Comm	Cancelled Mar 1973 (Upper Cragg Vale)
CL 654 (WR)	Blakes Moor, Turley Holes & Higher House Moor	(4.25 sk)	Wakefield & Dist Water Board/For Comm	Cancelled Mar 1973 (Upper Cragg Vale)
CL 674 (WR)	Blackstone Edge Common	6.63 sk	(Execs) JP Dearden, New Zealand	Urban common
CL 675 (WR)	Butterworth (Bleakdale) Common	8.40 sk	(Execs) JP Dearden, New Zealand	Urban common
CL 669 (WR)	Denshaw Moor	1.50 sk		Urban common (modified)
CL 427 (WR)	Rishworth Moor	16.0sk	Yorks Water	Urban common
CL 310 (WR)	Castleshaw & Denshaw Moors	1.30 sk	Unclaimed	Urban common
CL 494 (WR)	Castleshaw Moor Delph	1.28 sk	Unclaimed	Urban common
CL 39 (WR)	Marsden Moor	12.17 sk	National Trust	Urban common
CL 40 (WR)	Holme Moor	0.93 sk	National Trust	Urban common
CL 41 (WR)	Binn Moor	0.82 sk	National Trust	Urban common
CL 37 (WR)	Wessenden Moor	9.66 sk	Pt National Trust/pt unclaimed	Urban common
CL 386 (WR)	Thorne Moors	12.84 sk	Pt Land Register/pt unclaimed	South Yorks (rural common)

THE CUMBRIAN COAST

CL 26 (C)	Skinburness/Calvo Marshes	6.42 sk	Public Trustee
CL 27 (C)	Walton Moss	2.30 sk	
CL 70 (C)	Burgh Marsh	4.70 sk	Trustees of Burgh Marsh
CL 313 (C)	Wedholme Flow	6.83 sk	Land registration final (8/72). All rights cancelled at hearing, with land allotted as shares (8/82)
CL 324 (C)	Drigg Common	2.48 sk	

THE LANCASHIRE COAST

CL 273 (L)	Salt Marsh (Silverdale & Warton)	(3.70 sk)	Void Oct 1982
CL 154 (L)	Silverdale Marsh	(2.40 sk)	Void Oct 1982
CL 264 (L)	Salt Marsh	1.68 sk	
CL 160 (L)	Warton Salt Marsh	5.53 sk	
CL 45 (L)	Salt Marshes	4.19 sk	
CL 283 (L)	Salt Marsh	(4.0 sk)	Cancelled Nov 1972
CL 193 (L)	Colloway & Overton Marshes	2.87 sk	Duchy of Lancaster
CL 119 (L)	Pilling Marsh	(2.50 sk)	Void Feb 1977
CL 203 (L)	The Salt Marsh (N Moels)	(21.0 sk)	English Nature (Ribble Estuary NNR). The registrations for both CL 232 and CL 203 were declared void in Feb 1979 under Decisions by Consent. The land was purchased in the same year by the Dept of the Environment for £1.75 million to prevent its development for agriculture.
CL 232 (L)	Hesketh Bank Marsh	(6.50 sk)	

Note on listings

(i) The listings cover Northern England. All of the larger areas of registered common land – broadly, those over 1.5 square kilometres in extent – are included. These are almost invariably upland commons, though several coastal commons of Lancashire and Cumbria are also shown.

(ii) Each common is identified by the 'CL' number under which it is referenced in the commons register. The letter suffix indicates the original county register – (N) Northumberland; (C) Cumberland; (W) Westmorland; (D) Durham; (NR) Yorks, North Riding; (WR) Yorks, West Riding; (L) Lancashire. A number of registrations were reallocated under the local government changes that took place in 1974. Some have also moved as a result of the more recent creation of 'unitary' local authorities.

(iii) Commons are arranged in geographical groups. The groups and the listings within them run, by and large, from north to south and from west to east. CL units shown in **bold type** are areas to which the public already has a right of access. The 'urban' commons amongst these will qualify as Section 15 land under the Countryside and Rights of Way Act (i.e. the new right of access will not apply). The CL units shown in *italics* were provisionally registered as common under the 1965 Act but failed to be finally registered as such. Their extent is indicated in brackets, thus: *(sk)*. Of these, registrations that were cancelled did not reach a hearing. Those that did were declared void by a commissioner or were modified so that (e.g.) only a small area of land was finally registered. All, or most, of the land that failed to be registered will qualify as 'open country' under the C&RoW Act. The areas involved may also be candidates for 're-registration' if the proposal in DEFRA's *Common Land Policy Statement 2002* is incorporated in any new legislation.

(iv) The information included in the listings is based on the entries in the commons registers, though it has been added to and updated from other sources where these were available. Details of the registration process are to be found in Chapter 4, together with a number of case studies.

References

AICHISON, J W, HUGHES, E J, and MASTERS, S, 1984, *The Common Lands of England and Wales: Report to the Common Land Forum* (Countryside Commission).

ALLABY, Michael, 1983, *The Changing Uplands* [CCP 153] (Countryside Commission).

BLACKSHAW, Alan, June 2001, 'Research Note: Historical Perspectives on the Existing Freedoms of Responsible Access and the Scottish Executive's Exclusion and Trespass Proposals' (Scottish Environment LINK Research Project). Available at: www.mountaineering-scotland.org.uk/access/lrs_bill.html

BONYHADY, Tim, 1987, *The Law of the Countryside: the Rights of the Public* (Professional Books).

CALLANDER, Robin, 1997, *The System of Land Tenure in Scotland* (WWF Scotland). Quoted in McCrone, David, 1997, 'Land, Democracy and Culture in Scotland', the 4th John McEwen Memorial Lecture, Perth.

CENTRE FOR LEISURE RESEARCH, 1986, *Access to the Countryside for Recreation and Sport* [CCP 217] (Countryside Commission).

CLAYDEN, Paul, 1992, *Our Common Land* (Open Spaces Society).

COMMON LAND FORUM, 1986, *Common Land Forum Report* (Countryside Commission).

COUNTRYSIDE AND COMMUNITY RESEARCH UNIT, 1998, *Good Practice Guide on Managing the Use of Common Land* (DETR).

COUNTRYSIDE COMMISSION, *The Commons Registration Act 1965: Decisions of the Commons Commissioners*.

COUNTRYSIDE COMMISSION, 1989, *Common Knowledge..?* [CCP 281].

COUNTRYSIDE COMMISSION, June 1998, *Rights of Way in the 21st Century* [98/22].

CURRY, Nigel, 1994, *Countryside Recreation, Access and Land-Use Planning* (E & FN Spon).

DEFRA, July 2002, *Common Land Policy Statement 2002*.

DEFRA, Nov 2002, *Rights of Way Improvement Plans: statutory guidance to local highway authorities in England*.

DEFRA website, Wildlife & Countryside/Countryside Issues/Common Land, Town And Village Greens: www.defra.gov.uk/wildlife-countryside/issues/common/index.htm (as at January 2003).

DENMAN, D R, ROBERTS, R A, and SMITH, H J F, 1967, *Commons and Village Greens* (Leonard Hill).

DETR, Feb 1998, *Access to the Open Countryside in England and Wales. A Consultation Paper.*

DETR, Mar 1999, *The Government's Framework for Action: Access to the Countryside in England & Wales.*

DETR, Feb 2000, *Greater Protection and Better Management of Common Land in England and Wales.*

DETR/MAFF, Feb 1999, *Rural England. A Discussion Document.*

DOWER, Michael, 1966, *Fourth Wave* (London: Civic Trust).

LORD EVERSLEY, (J G Shaw-Lefevre), 1910, *Commons, Forests and Footpaths* (Cassell).

GADSDEN, G D, 1988, *The Law of Commons* (Sweet & Maxwell).

GREEN, Kate, 1997, *Land Law* (3rd ed) (Macmillan).

HANSARD (HC), 1999, Vol 327, No 49.

HARDIN, Garrett, 1968, 'The Tragedy of the Commons', Science, Vol 162, 1243–48.

HARRIS, Brian and RYAN, Gerard, 1966, *The Law Relating to Common Land* (Sweet & Maxwell).

HARVEY, Graham, 1997, *The Killing of the Countryside* (Jonathan Cape).

HEWITSON, A, 1969, *Northward* (SR Publishers).

HILL, Howard, 1980, *Freedom to Roam* (Moorland Publishing Company).

HOSKINS, W G, and DUDLEY-STAMP, L, 1963, *The Common Lands of England and Wales* (Collins).

ITE/NERC, 1989, *Heather in England and Wales* (HMSO).

LANCASHIRE COUNTY COUNCIL, June 1998, Response to the DETR's *Consultation Paper on Access to the Open Countryside of England and Wales.*

LANCASHIRE RECORD OFFICE, Ref DDQ (Garnett of Quernmore).

LAND USE CONSULTANTS, 1985, *Management Schemes for Commons* (Countryside Commission).

LAND USE CONSULTANTS, 1985, *Maps of Moor and Heath* (Countryside Commission).

LDSPB, 1990, *Lake District National Park Commons Project.*

MacEWEN, Ann & Malcolm, 1982, *National Parks: conservation or cosmetics?* (George Allen & Unwin).

MAFF, 1996, *Your Livestock and Your Landscape: a guide to environmental conditions attached to livestock subsidy schemes.*

McCALL, Ian, 2001, 'Outdoor access threatened by Land Reform Bill'. Article available at Ramblers' Association website: www.ramblers.org.uk

McCRONE, David, Oct 1997, 'Land, Democracy and Culture in Scotland', the 4th John McEwen Memorial Lecture, Perth.

MINISTRY OF LAND AND NATURAL RESOURCES, Nov 1965, *Circular No 2/65.*

MOORLAND ASSOCIATION, 1987, *Comments on the Government's Consultative Proposals for further Legislation on Common Land.*

NATIONAL TRUST, April 2000, Response of the National Trust to *Greater Protection and Better Management of Common Land in England and Wales.*

NORTH PENNINES AONB STEERING GROUP, 1995, *The North Pennines AONB.*

NORTH YORK MOORS NATIONAL PARK COMMITTEE, 1984, *Areas of Moor and Heath.*

NORTH YORKS CC, Sept 1997, *Draft Management Plan: Nidderdale AONB.*

RIDDLE, David, 2001, 'The National Trust and Agriculture – An Overview'. Available at the National Trust's website: www.nationaltrust.org.uk

ROBINSON, J M, 1988, *The English Country Estate* (Century/National Trust).

ROYAL COMMISSION ON COMMON LAND, 1958, *Royal Commission on Common Land 1955–1958: Report*, Cmnd 462, HMSO.

RURAL SURVEYS RESEARCH UNIT, *Biological Survey of Common Land* (DEFRA. Completed 2001. Volumes by counties).

SCOTTISH ACCESS FORUM, *Proposals*. Available at Scottish Natural Heritage website: www.snh.org.uk

SCOTTISH LAW COMMISSION, April 2001, *Discussion Paper on the Law of the Foreshore and Seabed,* [DP No 113].

SHOARD, Marion, 1998, *This Land is Our Land* (2nd ed) (Gaia Books Ltd).

SHOARD, Marion, 1999, *A Right to Roam* (Oxford University Press).

SHOARD, Marion, 2000, 'Off the Track: Problems Looming for the Right to Roam', Countryside Recreation, Summer 2000, Vol 8, No 2 (Countryside Recreation Network).

SINCLAIR, Geoffrey, (ed), 1983, *The Upland Landscapes Study* (Environment Information Services).

SISSONS, Michael (ed), 1997, *A Countryside for All* (Jonathan Cape).

THOMPSON, E P, 1991, *Customs in Common* (Merlin Press).

WALTON, J K, 1996, *Lancashire: a Social History. 1558–1939* (Manchester University Press).

WATKINS, Charles, (ed), 1996, *Rights of Way: Policy, Culture and Management* (Pinter).

WIGHTMAN, Andy, 1997, *Who Owns Scotland* (Canongate).

WIGHTMAN, Andy, 1999, 'Land Reform: Politics, Power and the Public Interest'. The 6th John McEwan Memorial Lecture. Available at the website of the Caledonia Centre for Social Development: www.caledonia.org.uk

WILSON, Olivia J, 1992, 'Landownership and Rural Development in the North Pennines: a Case Study', Journal of Rural Studies, Vol 8, No 2, pp 145–58.

WILSON, Olivia J, 1993, 'Common lands in the Durham Dales', Area, 25.3, pp 237–45.

WILSON, Olivia J, and WILSON, Geoff A, 1997, 'Common Cause or Common Concern?', Area, 29.1, pp 45–58.

Index

Principal entries are shown in **bold**